THE TAO OF

BOB

SPIKE GILLESPIE

Dear Laura,
Thanks for
all the
love &
support
FN

Love,
Spike

Bob grant me the serenity

To accept the things I cannot change

The courage to change the things I can

The wisdom to know the difference

And the power to let that shit go

The Tao of Bob

Copyright © 2018 by Spike Gillespie

Produced & Published by

March Girls Studio

3409 Caldwell Lane

Garfield, TX

Some names of people and places have been changed because I don't want to hear folks bitch and moan about my take on things. Other names have been changed because, even though a part of me would love to out the assholes, I really am trying to walk a different path.

Cover photo by Wyatt McSpadden © 2017

www.WyattMcSpadden.com

Back cover author photo by Carol Buchanan © 2018

www.CarolCards.com

Design by Erin Mayes, EmDash

CONTENTS

INTRODUCTION

HAD BOB ARRIVED JUST A FEW WEEKS SOONER THAN HE DID, IT'S ENTIRELY possible the six-foot rattlesnake that showed up near my door one October night, the one I nearly stepped on with a foolishly unbooted foot, might have survived. Instead, the poor bastard met a different fate, sloppily dispatched with a couple of 9 mm bullets and the business end of a cheap snow shovel, the latter slicing into his belly and revealing a not-yet-digested rat, fur slick with exploded snake guts, body bloated.

Had Bob arrived fifty-three years earlier, been my real father instead of the one I got, perhaps things would have been different for me, too. I might have grown up, if not entirely fearless, then at least self-assured enough to better assess the true dangers of a given situation before reacting wildly. Instead, courtesy of pulling a bad brain chemistry card when genetics were being dealt and another bad card from that external deck known as Childhood Trauma—dished out daily by a mentally ill rage-aholic—I learned to greet all situations with equal trepidation. I was trained early on to catastrophize every life event great and small, giving equal weight to spilt milk and sudden death. Consequently, I have spent decades screaming as loudly at the sound of a balloon popping or a book dropping to the floor, as I might at the sight of a deadly car wreck or a masked intruder in my home.

But things unfold at their own pace. In this sense, there is the argument that Bob arrived right on time. By the time he did, I was a half-century plus into wrestling with restless demons that ongoing therapy, shelves full of self-help books, and nearly twenty years of meditation had failed to adequately tame. There were lulls, yes. Even stretches when I believed great progress had been made, when delicious calm visited now and again, cranking down anxiety's volume from its typical 11+ to a manageable 3 or 4. This *was* real progress. Maybe that's what made the backslides seem so burdensome to reckon with, frustration coursing through me every time the effects of those poorly drawn cards reverberated yet again, catapulting me back seemingly to the beginning of trying to heal, no branches or toeholds within reach as over the edge I went for the umpteenth time, thinking as I tumbled into the darkness toward rock bottom truths below, that I would rather die than try to climb back up one more time.

Bob first appeared as I was poised to take my next plunge. His arrival did not stop me from falling. But his presence provided a voice, far away at first, hollering down to a badly broken me to hold on, he was here to help, and that he would show me the safe way out. Given that he was on the cusp of eighty-eight when he appeared, frail from recent widowhood and the years immediately prior spent caring for an increasingly ill wife, he was moving slower than he had as the young strapping Midwestern farmer he once was. Still, he would help me, he promised. My job, crumpled so far down in the hole, was to keep breathing, reach up, take his hand, make myself try to believe.

I still think about that poor snake every time I pass the spot I encountered him. I go over his passing, and how this might not have occurred given the slightest shifts in attitude and logistics. If only I had taken into consideration he was not coiled or rattling, just stretched out flat, letting his stomach juices break down that long-tailed last supper of his. If only I had used a different entrance, one that was not obstructed by his body, and flipped on the outside light for a better look. If only I had observed him through a window, thought it through, not called out across the darkness to my gun-toting boyfriend and his shovel-wielding brother, the pair of them at least six sheets to the wind after a long day of hard drinking. If only I had given him a little time to slither away, he might still be out there today, across the field from the house, the two of us living, if not in total peace, then at least giving one another necessary space.

Instead I panicked. Though I did not personally kill him, I called for his death. Me, Pontius Pilate, condemning him to an abrupt and brutal ending. My fault entirely.

As unwelcome metaphors go, the rattlesnake at my door serves with excellence. Like everything else that ever scared me, his presence inspired irrationality, blindness to best choices in tense situations, wild reactionary urges, and a surge of adrenaline so great and so immediate as to make logical thought utterly impossible. And what of the rat, the one that never did get fully digested? He serves, too, a half-rotted, stomach-turning mass of wet fur and bloat, like my own never fully digested childhood memories, constant invasive recollections of my father's voice drilling me on a loop from the start: *You are worthless. You are stupid. You are not loved.*

Just as culpability for the premature demise of the rattlesnake falls squarely upon my shoulders, guilt over his cruel death my burden to bear, so too does responsibility for falling into the last hole I fell into. Some would argue—and I would be wrong to protest—I did not fall but rather jumped into that pit of my own accord. As with the biggest holes I've huddled in, this one took the physical form of a man. The same man who, on my orders, shot the snake. By the time Bob arrived, this man and I had already spent more than a year doing the Tumult Tango. We had three breakups and three reunions on our record and mountains of indisputable evidence that being together could not have been a poorer choice. But compulsion is a strong drug and pain a fascinating place. I should have slithered away and hid from him. Instead I parked my heart at the door of his, an easy target, out in the open, my mind, body, and spirit all at the mercy of a merciless man.

And when, at last, it really, truly ended between us, I lay ragged and undone, my entire being torn apart, revealing the rat of ancient trauma, its twisted death mask grin exposed. I was not dead, despite so many times thinking that death might have been the better outcome. Instead, splayed out, I looked at the man with the gun and I hissed again and again, *"Look what you did to me! This is all your fault."*

But it was not his fault. Not entirely. I like to believe it was not entirely mine, either. Still, I understand now, I am the one that put myself in his sights, assumed a prostrate position at his boot-clad feet. I am the one that begged him, in my own fashion, in my refusal to flee. "Pull the trigger," I demanded. Until he did.

Again and again and again.

PART ONE

Connecting Dots

ONE

SOMETIMES I PLAY HISTORICAL CONNECT THE DOTS, a variation of that song about the foot bone being connected to the ankle bone, the leg bone, the knee bone, etc. I look back over time and allow myself to momentarily buy into a notion I otherwise detest, the idea that everything happens for a reason. An example that always comes to mind when engaging in this exercise occurred when, at eighteen and about to graduate very near the top of my high school class, I was accepted to a prestigious university. My father declared attending college to be a stupid idea in general, and definitely not something to be pursued by women. My high school counselor, too busy enmeshing himself in an illicit affair with a student teacher, failed to explain scholarships and financial aid, noting that since my parents did not have the means or interest in helping me get to this fancy institution, that instead I should enroll in the nearby state school and become a teacher.

Thus, I missed the opportunity of attending an esteemed school. I did go to that state college for a semester but, aspiring to get further away from my paternal tormentor, stealthily applied to another college much further away, chosen because a couple of my drinking buddies went there and, more importantly, their brother had once attended, too. As I'd had a huge crush on the guy, the lure of breathing in the air he had once also breathed sealed my decision.

Stumbling through applications for admission and loans and begging my father to let me leave his house (falsely believing him when he told me that, despite my being a legal adult, he got to make all of my choices until I reached 21), I finally secured approval on all fronts and fled my little South Jersey hometown. Completely clueless about the ways of the world, I arrived at the University of South Florida in January 1983, a few days before I turned nineteen, eager, excited, nervous.

At this school, I honed my skills as a high-functioning, binge-drinking alcoholic, a quest first begun in eighth grade when I regularly pinched whisky from my father's stash, spirited this elixir to my room in repurposed vitamin bottles, at once terrified of being caught and grateful that the booze at least momentarily relieved the terror that stealing it ignited. I also tried on different personalities at college, settling on a mix of punk rocker, new waver, feminist, and surfer chick. My fledgling writing efforts found a regular home in the school's daily paper. I made many friends, contracted a host of STDs, went on crazy benders, and, the school being in the Sunshine State, sported a tan year-round.

I have, many times, belittled the education I received as a child living in poverty in a blue-collar town, and later at this mediocre college. However, when playing Historical Connect the Dots, my perspective shifts. Had my father not forbidden my attendance at that fancy institute of higher learning, had I found myself surrounded by kids who'd gotten a better primary education than me, my whole story likely would have turned out quite differently. I might have faded into the background, lost my footing, failed to thrive. Despite all the booze-induced puking and poor choice-making that accompanied me as I attended a party school, I see now I got so much out of that place. Primarily, the opportunity to spread my wings as a writer, which set the pace for a solid journalism career and some incredible writing adventures post-graduation.

From a psychological standpoint, I play the game in an attempt to fashion a revised life narrative full of hope and explanation.

I do this even, and especially, in the face of so many memories that reveal more than a few hopeless moments, and plenty of proof that, no matter how much we mull certain experiences, not everything can be tied up in a neat box labeled *Ah! So That's Why That Happened.*

This rearview mirror connection-seeking, I understand at least intellectually, is a vain attempt to feel some sense control. I recognize my desire is admittedly futile. I know that, even if I can reframe my past, I cannot change the facts about abuse so acute it continues to affect my every waking moment, courtesy of PTSD, the greatest souvenir of my childhood. Ironically though, it is a specific PTSD trait, a tendency toward perseveration, that keeps me examining the fragments, the haunting memories, seeking ways to reorganize terrifying flashbacks into something less nonsensical.

My quest to seize the reins of my own story, to soften the focus of hindsight's lens, is driven by having felt so often out of control growing up. Firstly, because I was entirely controlled by a maniac in my youth, and later, because again and again I recreated that unsafe but all too familiar out-of-control feeling in my booze-driven, reckless pursuits as a young adult.

When I give myself permission to explore the notion that everything really does happen for a reason, I have a pretty good time making positive connections between my faraway very bad past and my immediate present, which is very good (even if sometimes bad brain chemistry days obscure my view). For this, too, I have a wonderful example of one thing leading to another and another until the movie in my mind makes its way from a foreboding opening score to the crescendo of happy outcomes.

I call this example the Tiny T Ranch, a thirty-acre spread just east of Austin, Texas, a place that I often tell visitors simply fell into my lap. But that's just what I say when I'm looking to quickly explain how I gave up living in a interminably hip city after twenty-four years and hightailed it out to the country, where concerns over rattlesnakes are greatly mitigated by the joy felt at not having to deal with constant gridlock traffic and an exploding population.

To explain the longer version of my migration, there is no choice but to go way back to the very beginning, 1964 to be exact, my very first dot, when I arrived on the planet during a Northeastern blizzard, the fourth of what would eventually come to be nine siblings, born to a homemaker mother and a truck-driving father, he prone to frequent bouts of random fury and driven by a personally crafted variation of Catholicism. This crazy devotion to his self-styled religion prompted daily fire and brimstone proclamations that God would punish us kids for any and all infractions—including making a sound at the dinner table—and that we were all surely going to Hell.

According to contemporary experts who study things like Adverse Childhood Experiences, a steady childhood diet of constant berating and violence takes a permanent toll on the adults we terrified children become. This was not a trendy psychological notion in the sixties and seventies though. Even if it had been, I doubt my father would have picked up some parenting magazine, read an article on how love is crucial to proper parenting, and thus traded in his cruelty-based dogma for something kinder, shifting to a place of compassion that would've left us healthier instead of suffering from severe anxiety, as we all do.

Dutchie, my father, was a stubborn man. Change was not in his repertoire. A narcissist in the extreme, he unwaveringly remained steadfast in his belief that he was always right. He held as irrefutable that I was the biggest fuck-up that ever crossed his path. Ultimately, Alzheimer's took his mind and, eventually, his life, with no miraculous apology or request for forgiveness at the end. Just violence and misery from start to finish.

For her part, my mother suffered, I suspect, a severe strain of Stockholm Syndrome, unquestionably tending to Dutchie's every want and need. A unified front was demanded, and regardless of how hard he came down on us kids, he was the one she defended, insisting in classic Orwellian doublespeak that yelling was his way of demonstrating how much he loved us. We followed her anticipatory lead, every last one of us, and, without even understanding what we were doing, became a band of empaths, incredibly intuitive to a one. We trained ourselves to watch for imperceptible signs of irritation, to not rock the boat, to accommodate, to not set him off, all of this in the interest of not having to come in contact with his glare, his outbursts, his belt, of trying to keep the damage of being forced to live under his roof to a minimum.

Do you believe in silver linings? I have to. Silver linings are what kept me from taking my own life all those times, those hundreds of times, his voice—even after his death—rose unbidden in my ears, telling me I did not deserve to live, the world would be better off without me, might as well step off.

So exhausting that voice. So persistent. So crazy-making. But there it was in my youth and here it is still now, whenever darkness again descends. Sometimes all day every day for sweeping stretches of time. Sisyphus had it easy. My boulder? Dutchie's vicious voice, echoing from beyond the grave, a rock so huge I can barely budge it an inch, let alone up the hill. And etched into this rock, carved ineradicably, are helpful hints, detailed instructions to do his bidding: *Pills, Guns, Rope, Razors. Look at all the options!*

Every time I hear that voice spewing those instructions, I shove at the rock with all my might. *No*, I tell it. *No. Shut up.* This is how I push. I breathe. I push again. I call up the silver linings. I push some more.

There are so many silver linings of my father's abuse, ways to convince myself, at least to some extent, that maybe all that cruelty *did* happen for a reason. These silver linings do not come without serious neurotic hitches, but nonetheless they exist.

So desperate for the positive attention he refused me, I grew to become an overachiever, a people pleaser, my heart overflowing with sympathy for underdogs. I learned to radiate high wattage energy that pulls into my orbit both good and evil, but far more of the former. In short, it was my father's rage and hatred and abuse that ultimately brought so much light into my life. Or more accurately, it was my will to defy him. This ranch is the culmination of that defiance.

More dots. Jump now to Fall 1981. I entered my senior year of high school as president of the student council, in the top three percent of my class. This put me in the regular company of a classmate named Patrick, ranked just above me academically, and just below me in student government. We were friends. In June 1982, we all graduated and, half a year later, far away I ran, to that school of sunshine and keg parties and the former breath of a summertime crush.

Thirty-three years passed, and after having seen each other just one other time since we tossed our graduation caps in the air, Patrick and I again crossed paths. I was on a rare trip back to New Jersey, the occasion being my mother's 80th birthday. By then, social media was already as much a part of my daily routines as brushing my teeth and taking a shit. I reconnected virtually with many of my old schoolmates, some of whom I'd known since kindergarten. We enjoyed each other's online company very much, but it stopped there.

Now, knowing I would be posting pictures from my visit to the home planet, and not wanting to seem rude for not making time to see these old peers while I was there, I sent a private note to a small handful. I explained there would be no real-time visits with them, that my trip would be whirlwind and my anxiety off the charts. This was not hyperbole. Anxiety, depression, OCD, and Exaggerated Startle Response are all components of my PTSD. Revisiting my past comes with a torrent of paralyzing triggers. My job, as I saw it, was to get there, sing *Happy Birthday*, and beat a hasty retreat.

Among the recipients of my apologetic correspondence was John Logan, my kindergarten crush, who replied, informing me that he and some of the others were glad to know I was coming north, and they would be hosting a party in my honor whether I liked it or not. They'd see me there, he said, sending a date, address, time. I sucked up my fears and agreed to attend. I stumbled into the party clutching a cake, worried I might drop over dead from my nervousness at the prospect of an evening spent amidst these long-lost friends.

In roughly five minutes though, I was put entirely at ease. This was remarkable, more so as it was achieved without the assistance of booze, my longtime go-to in such situations, but something I gave up many years before. I'm not sure why it surprised me to be treated with such kindness, to be welcomed back like some prodigal daughter. By evening's end I understood that I had hurled the baby out violently with the bathwater of my childhood trauma, resisting seeing all of these wonderful people for decades because the thought of maintaining any connection to my past rattled me with terror.

Patrick was among those in attendance, having made the drive down from North Jersey. He exuded positivity. We caught up. He had retired early, courtesy of a successful stint on Wall Street. He spoke of his great wife, great life, and three great kids, one of whom was contemplating a move to Austin. He was planning to bring her for a visit soon. I told him to look me up when they were town, that I would love to give them a tour. I had, by then, lived in Austin so long, had put my people-pleasing skills to such use, built an incredibly wide circle of friends and acquaintances. I am a connector. Anything they needed, anyone they cared to meet, I assured Patrick I could make it happen.

This is how the Dream of the Ranch began, all of the dots

about to connect, though of course I did not know that yet. Patrick and his daughter visited, then visited again. I took them to my favorite places. During this time my creative energies were being poured into a blog decrying explosive population growth and impossible cost-of-living increases in the city that, when I arrived in 1991, was still an affordable place to live, populated by a joyful, ragtag assembly of hippies, students, musicians and artists. No more. Now cranes towered across the skyline hurling skyscrapers chock full of condominiums toward the heavens. Newcomers arrived in droves daily, the Austin City Limits sign a hipster Holy Grail. Patrick and I discussed all of this.

Somewhere in these conversations, we talked about my job. Life as a journalist, my calling for twenty-three years, had grown financially untenable by 2010, with so much free content on the internet proffered by so many amateur "writers," that publications came to pay little or nothing at all. Frustrated, I committed to transitioning my sideline job performing secular weddings—started in 2006—into my fulltime gig. The career switch worked out astonishingly well, thanks in no small part to my over-achievement streak. By the time Patrick and I rekindled our friendship, my wedding business was thriving, my services in high demand, the pay far better than journalism ever netted.

Other dots connected. Because I was well-known as an officiant, people shared wedding-related information with me. One day I received a notice about a tiny chapel for sale. Perusing photos, I was astounded at the beauty of this 250-square-foot gem, all reclaimed bead board, pressed tin ceiling, and antique stained glass. I visited it in person and was instantly smitten. I proclaimed my desire of ownership to my social media world. My social media world roared its approval. Many promised that if I set up a fundraiser, they would help me buy this little building, the one with an astronomical price tag.

Patrick and I discussed all of this. Then he said something that my ears could not quite comprehend. If I wanted to sell my house and buy the chapel, he and his wife would invest in my business, help me purchase land and build this whole enterprise up. I thanked him so many times over the course of this and ensuing conversations that Patrick finally stopped me one day and very gently explained a few things.

He said while it was fine to keep thanking him if I must, I should remember this was a business deal, that he'd be getting something from it, too. He reminded me that he knew where I came from, that blue-collar sensibility, because he came from the same place. True, he had better financial means and a better college education, but he was no stranger to how growing up where we did, when we did, had fed some false, lingering notions that, if excised, would allow me to fly as high as I wished. Sometimes it felt nearly impossible to not cry during these talks, to have someone so smart and kind and supportive voicing a desire to give me a true leg up. Patrick remained patient.

This was how, four months after my mother's birthday party and my homecoming party, I found myself shopping for property, planning to leave Austin, a place I lived longer than any other, and, as yet unbeknownst to me, readying the way for Bob.

When I am connecting the dots just right, indulging in the notion everything happens just as it is supposed to, even the shittiest stuff, I can, if only momentarily, almost believe that the abundance that soon rained down upon me came not despite the suffering of my childhood, but in large part because of the ways that suffering shaped me.

TWO

RUSH INTO THINGS. SOMETIMES THIS PAYS OFF. OFTEN IT DOES not. Still, during giddy moments of triumph when a split-second decision yields a favored outcome, I tell myself that haste is an excellent choice-making technique, often confusing luck with an ironclad gut instinct. In the summer of 2015, I made two very hasty decisions, one of which paid off in spades, the other of which eventually amplified that ghost voice of my father regularly urging me to kill myself.

The good choice was stumbling across a parcel of land, upon which was situated a 3200 square-foot ranch house and an old five-car garage. A survey of the property revealed a long rectangle a couple of acres across and fifteen acres long. I met with a realtor who showed me around. I barely noticed the stunning disrepair of the place or smelled the stench of the disgusting carpet in the house. Instead I envisioned a brilliant future here, in my mind already manifested. I overlooked an array of junk scattered across the yard: old car parts, broken culverts, the odd boot, giant hunks of busted concrete. What I saw instead was paradise, a perfect place for the chapel, bedrooms aplenty for visitors, a location that would allow me to host overnight retreats, weddings, and concerts, and space in which I could teach writing and meditation classes. The garage, full of horseshit, walls crumbling, was to my eyes a palatial reception hall, soon to be filled with music, dancing, laughter.

"I found a turnkey operation!" I shouted into the phone at Patrick.

He flew down, took a look, and offered his opinion. "It's a teardown," he said evenly.

But Patrick did not veto my request that we put in a bid, which would have been well within his rights, as his financial underwriting greatly outweighed whatever I could bring to the table selling my house in Austin. Ten days of inspections revealed relatively solid house bones and not too many major worrisome spots, unless I considered the need for a full interior demo and renovation a worrisome spot, which optimistically I did not, my lack of construction knowledge an ironic boon toward my naïve belief we could turn the place around in no time on a reasonable budget.

During this stretch, darker things came to light however, rumors of a history unsettling enough to question the energy of the ranch. There was an eviction notice, taped inside the front door, revealing a feud among the adult children of the long-dead folks who built the place. A sister had turned to the law to get her brother to vacate the property, where he had been squatting in squalor. There were large liens against the title, including a couple of delinquent five-figure child support sums. And there were the tales, constant and spooky, served up by neighbors who came by to chat, of much evil that occurred here.

Eventually I pieced together a story of parents who spent a fortune bailing out two bad seed sons who never weren't in the sights of the sheriff. Not surprisingly, drugs were said to have been behind these run-ins with the authorities. Toward that end there was still, according to local legend, a school bus buried somewhere out back that had once been an active meth lab. Reports of how the Brothers Bad augmented the income of their crank dealings by using the land as an informal junkyard were easily supported by the mountains of shit scattered from the front fence line to way out back, where the flotsam and jetsam of discarded country living punctuated a mesquite-choked landscape dotted with rough snout holes dug up nightly by an army of invasive, non-native wild hogs.

Nonetheless, my rose-tinted glasses remained firmly affixed. Despite Patrick's assurance that if our bid wasn't accepted we would find an even better place, I poured every bit of hope and desire I had into acquisition of this rundown place. I wrote a letter to the executor daughter and laid on thick my plans to move a church here, leaving out the bit about how the building would be used secularly. I brushed off the fiscal reality associated with an overhaul. I had to have this ranch.

This attitude was not unlike the one I brought to my relationship with Peter, who showed up just as my conversations with Patrick were getting underway. There was one big difference. Whereas my enthusiasm for the project with Patrick started strong, I had some serious reservations about Peter. Though we'd been Facebook friends for a stretch, sharing in common his best friend Chuck, who was one of my closest friends, too, I didn't really know anything about Peter. Chuck introduced us in person when Peter drove up from Houston for a Fourth of July party. We chatted a little, and then a little more the next day at the tattoo shop where Chuck, an artist, was giving Peter some new ink. During this conversation, Peter revealed details of his incredibly tragic and dramatic childhood and I listened with rapt attention, piteous and harrowing stories always calling to me, a booming Bat-Signal aimed straight at my vulnerable heart.

Peter and I began a series of texts after this, and then, despite how much I loathe the phone, we started speaking regularly, sometimes for hours at a time. When I told Chuck about this flourishing connection, he warned me repeatedly not to get involved with Peter romantically. The sole purpose of his introduction, he said, was just so that maybe I could help Peter lead a cleaner life—namely cut back on self-medicating into oblivion on a regular basis—because I was, at this point, seventeen years into sobriety.

The calls and texts continued and then Peter visited Austin again, where we enjoyed a platonic weekend together, him sleeping in my guest room. He drove me all around the gorgeous Hill Country in his black Mustang. We shared conversation and silence, both of which pleased me. I felt a pull toward him, just a hint of a stirring, intensified when he reached over and scratched a mosquito bite on my back that I couldn't get at, a small gesture but one that in the moment felt oddly intimate. Given the relative ease of conversation, I think I already had an idea where we could be heading, but at least I tried to stop myself.

After he left, I couldn't stop thinking about what seemed like strong a romantic interest on his part—much greater than the pull I felt on that drive—the way he looked at me all weekend, how he sat on the ottoman by my bed Saturday night as I fought off exhaustion, trying a little too hard to impress me with his music collection. I sent a long email voicing my concerns about his seeming intentions, detailing my reluctance. I made it clear that I could be nothing more than a sober buddy for him. I suggested that in return perhaps he could help me feel safer around men, because despite having many men friends, I still get very edgy around the opposite sex, harkening back to the one who spawned and abused me.

This virtual epistle was quickly answered with a phone call in which Peter announced that he very much wanted to be my "next big mistake." It was a funny line. Nervously I laughed as my stomach flipped. I knew in an instant I would accept. Maybe the truth is that I knew this before sending the email stating otherwise, that those words I wrote him were just me trying to convince myself to stay away, to heed Chuck's warnings.

Listening to him lay it on thick, I flipped the switch from *NO* to *YES*. As with every *yes* I have ever committed to, I did so wholeheartedly. Just as I vowed the ranch would be mine and I would make it work, with this second hasty decision, I promised myself this man would be mine and I would make it work with him. Despite Chuck's cautionary advice, I used the fact that he was friends with Peter to convince myself my choice was fine. Chuck was such a good person how could he be friends with anyone who wasn't the same?

I drove to Houston the very next weekend, and though it was Peter's town, not mine, I orchestrated a mini-itinerary to show him my favorite places. After gourmet pizza at Café Brasil, we headed over to see Magritte paintings at the Menil Collection. Then we tossed pennies into the fountain outside the Rothko Chapel, and I made a wish that this would, at long last, be a relationship that lasted. Later at his apartment, I sat on the couch, he on a chair, and we watched TV and chatted, like some modern day version of Victorian courting traditions. Standing on his front step, saying goodbye, I shyly leaned in for a chaste kiss. Already I was falling.

The next weekend Peter came to my place. We tumbled into bed, debated briefly if we were moving too fast. But he was about to embark on a three-week trip and I was scheduled to go away for a week the day after he returned. Who wanted to wait that long? He was assertive and attentive, his stamina impressive. With this, my amnesia kicked in, and I forgot all past lessons I had learned about confusing sex with love. *Look at us go! This is real chemistry!*

I did note that Peter "needed" to smoke weed when he woke up and then throughout the day. That he poured himself many fingers of whisky straight up, topping off his glass regularly like it was free refills at a 7-11 soda fountain. As he indulged in these habits, little alarms went off. I silenced them. At least, I told myself, he had recently quit K2, that scary-ass street drug also known as fake weed, which, because it is undetectable in urine, he had been using, he said, to keep from getting busted at his job during random drug tests. Now that he'd solved that problem—concealing

fake piss capsules in a special pouch pocket in his boxer briefs—
he was back to smoking the real deal. Nothing wrong with weed,
I reasoned. Perfectly organic. And anyway, if he had quit that hard
shit, surely he would make other changes, too, slow down some.
He said as much himself, that he wanted help with this. I needed
to let him go at his own pace, that was all.

One other thing nagged me about committing to Peter, but
the matter seemed vain on some level and so I was afraid at first
to voice it. Then, during a conversation when I decided I must
speak my mind, nearly at the same time he mentioned the very
same concern. We each admitted that we were afraid that if our
attraction didn't last, the one to say so first would gravely hurt
the other, something which we both agreed was nothing we ever
want. With this mutual confession, I exhaled.

"I won't ever leave you worse than I found you," he promised.
I could not believe my great fortune, to have a man say something so thoughtful, to acknowledge in advance that things don't
always work out, to vow that should this fate befall us, we would
be gentle with one another.

The non-stop flirty texts and long phone calls continued when
we were in our respective cities during the week and when we
went away on our solo vacations that first month together. A
bond formed quickly with these constant exchanges, the kissy
face emojis, the terms of endearment. I was his Silver Fox, his
Pretty Lady. He missed me so much he told me nearly every
day we were apart. He couldn't believe I was in his life, he was
obsessed with me, he didn't deserve such love, and it was, he
said, his primary goal to never fuck that up.

Really though, what bonded us fastest was a high-pitched
sound not everyone can hear, a human version of a dog whistle
that only those who have been subjected to extreme trauma can
recognize and cannot resist running toward. Peter's past would
have given Dickens pause, my own hardly sunny childhood pal-

ing by comparison. I listened to his stories, the details horrifying me, and my heart went into Rescue Mode. It was my job to make up to him a lifetime of hellish suffering. With me he would suffer no more. That he had survived, cared for himself from a very early age, and raised a child on his own all pulled me in like Magneto beckoning a paperclip.

Peter was a survivor. So was I. Together we would shelter each other from all future storms. This shelter, this love, would inspire a healthier life. He would live cleaner. I would, at long last, know the love and respect of an equal partner. Peter was on board with all of this. How amazing that we had found each other, that I had overridden my early reservations, that now I had someone with whom to share my life and my ranch dreams. Together we began fantasizing a bright future together.

Patrick and I closed on the ranch the first weekend of October 2015. He called with news of the final sale from his home in New Jersey. I blubbered joyfully in response and Patrick could barely discern my words. Though I had been an integral part of the process, finding the land, overseeing the inspections, writing and rewriting the business plan, composing and revising spreadsheets, I could not wrap my head around the idea that the ranch was really mine.

Unfortunately, the day was not just filled with joyful anticipation of a fresh start, a new life in the country, the thrill of building a successful business. Peter and I were in the throes of our first heated argument, initiated days before, when, after watching him get blasted the previous weekend, I sent a long email, going on about addiction, about how I would not stay if he did not slow down, as he had sworn he would. He did not take this well, accused me of ultimatum, and threatened to break up before shutting down almost entirely, barely responding to my calls and texts, finally suggesting tersely that at least we should discuss things in person. Now he was on his way and worry gripped me.

Peter arrived, and I was a ball of confusion, a mix of ecstasy at the ranch news and unease that he would end things. Despite my insistence that I could not sustain a partnership with an addict, the idea of losing him, after only just starting things six weeks prior, ratcheted my anxiousness to new heights. We opted to hold off the talk and let our naked bodies converse instead. This pheromone fest, followed by an exuberant celebratory dinner, gave me the motivation I needed to resume telling myself time would iron away our problems. *He will get better. He says he wants to. He will. We will live at the ranch together. It will all work out.*

Spoiler alert: Happily Ever After with Peter was not to be. I have in my possession a diary, well over two hundred pages, full book-length, which might be titled *Life with Peter* or, more accurately, *The Rage Journal.* No one but me will ever see it. I have requested that upon my death close friends destroy it. I keep the document though, because to this day I still refer to it, still scroll through, re-read random passages, most of which detail at length one argument or another we had and my attendant feelings of anger and frustration.

I engage in this exercise not as a masochist, but to try to educate my heart. I must learn to keep myself from ever again repeating what I now believe to be the greatest error of my life. To never again whip out a hasty *yes* like I did the day I caved in, relented to his full-court press, said he could be my next big mistake. Sadly that was not a joke at all, just one of infinite warnings he waved before me, him the human Red Flag Factory, and me, perfect complement, a the human Blinder Factory, finding ever-creative ways to shut out all those blatant alerts.

Re-reading the journal, I find passage after passage, often written in all caps: *I MUST GET OUT. HE IS SO BAD FOR ME. HE IS SO MEAN. HE IS AN ADDICT. HE SAID SO MANY TERRIBLE THINGS.* There are also, parenthetically and often in the same breath, observations like: *Even as I type this, I just want to make it work. I love him so much. I do not want to lose him.*

Over the nearly two years I spent with Peter, there were three breakups and reunions prior to the fourth and final ending. Even as I discovered evidence and more evidence still, revealing the shocking extent of his secret other life—which he managed to keep hidden courtesy of us living apart and the masterful deceitfulness exercised by hardcore addicts—I found myself begging him. *Please don't go,* I cried again and again and again, engaging in texts and phone calls that matched in length and frequency, if not tone, those of early courtship. I was possessed by an unstoppable desire to make him stay, driven not by commonsense or what was in my best interest but wild agitation. Unhinged by rejection, pushed to the brink by abandonment, I watched and listened as words poured out of my mouth and fingers, as if composed by a stranger. Being with him was killing me, but I convinced myself that being without him was truly what caused my pain.

The more untenable things got with Peter, the further I delved into psychological explanations, enlisting two different therapists to try to help me recover some semblance of sanity, which had gone totally out the window by the time of our third breakup. This penultimate parting occurred on the cusp of a trip we had long planned to England to meet up with his family there. Though we went our separate ways upon arriving in Heathrow Airport—me to stay with friends instead of the original plan to stay with him—we connected one day at his cousin's flat, again repeating that cycle of hopping into bed and letting our bodies overrule our minds.

The night Peter shot the rattlesnake fell a week after our return, a time during which we continued to sleep together, but had yet to officially negotiate terms of a reunion. Perhaps I should have waited until our rattlesnake adrenaline had settled, but not knowing our status bugged me. I questioned him.

What was his intent regarding us? His response—to take a year off from all relationships to "find himself"—annoyed me. Why hadn't he revealed this before spending a week indicating with his body he was ready to recommit?

Then, the bombshell. I asked if he had he been with anyone else during our time apart. I expected him to laugh in my face or grow angry at such suspicion. Instead, he confessed to having gotten drunk, picked up a stranger, and hooked up with her in a hotel room, insisting he was within his rights to do so as we were broken up at the time. Technically I could not dispute this. My heart though, felt betrayed to no end, sliced to ribbons to discover that he had pushed me away only to leap into bed with someone else a few weeks later. I exploded with rage, stayed up all night, a double dose of Benadryl offering no reprieve at all.

But, thank you childhood programming, rather than exiting for good—the only healthy choice—my mind once again flicked on the neon sign flashing the lie that had followed me through so many bad relationships. *I am not being lovable enough.* I had to prove to him I was The One. I had to prove to myself I could fix everything. I had to show us both I was worthy of his love, that this other woman had been a terrible mistake, and only my love could make his life complete. The next morning, I shifted from yelling to soft crying. I pleaded. I cajoled. *Please take me back.* At last, after first denying regret, he cried, too, and said the one-night stand had been a mistake, later pointing out that at least being with another woman served as catalyst to convince him I was the one he truly loved. Yes, we could try again, he deigned. Yes, we would be monogamous and committed, no other women.

But we never did find a way back to the heady infatuation of our first few weeks. Not even close. We did not find a way to turn the hurt into lessons to heal together. We did not find a way to ease the arguing. Nor did we learn how to extract ourselves from an increasingly ugly dance in a timely fashion. There was no grace when the true end finally came. After he announced he was done for good, no going back this time, bitterness prevailed, weeks of angry exchanges, and then, ultimately, the silence of amputation, phantom pains of his absence throbbing ceaselessly, hours of crying every day, tears that sometimes began even before I awoke.

This is a Very Big Dot. The time I found myself far, far down in the deepest, darkest hole—*Did she jump or was she pushed?*—I've ever dwelled in. As I floundered in that bottomless well of grief and confusion, Peter's voice, insisting that it was in my best interest that he cut me off, bounced off the walls. That might have been the only honest thing he ever spoke to me, but the shock of his rejection and abandonment in the face of my love and dedication was so fierce, my stress so high, I could not recognize the truth in his statement, just as I had not been able to see, for years, all of the lies he fed me.

Bob arrived late October 2016, a couple of weeks after the rattlesnake was blown to bits, a mess of bullet holes and ragged shovel slashes. I was still with Peter then, our third and final reunion fresh, hoping we still had a chance, not seeing I was teetering at the lip of the crevasse, the final, true breakup brewing, me about to free-fall into depths of Hell heretofore unknown to me. The process of landing took many months. Repeatedly I found myself at what I felt surely must be the bottom, only to realize, no, this was a false bottom, a little collapsible shelf, that I was falling yet again, the real bottom much further below.

As Peter receded, Bob stepped forward, coaxing me slowly back to the land of the living. I resisted his efforts at first, refused to believe his insistence, when Peter finally left for good, that I was so much better off without him than I knew. Bob, the personification of resistance being futile, didn't give a shit. He made it clear he would make me understand the truth, no matter how long it took him.

THREE

S WITH MOVING TO THE COUNTRY AND ALLOWING Peter into my life, the decision to invite Bob to stay at the ranch was also hasty. I didn't think twice about it. I barely thought once. My friend Ellen's dad needed a safe spot that would provide him comfort after a couple of grueling years of watching his wife decline, ravaged by dementia, and finally die. He was worn out. He wanted a warm place to live, close to Ellen in Austin and far from the Indiana snow, someplace rural as, being a retired farmer, cities were not to his liking. The Tiny T Ranch easily fit this bill.

Helper. Rescuer. One of Service. Taker of Risks. These traits best reflect my core life desires, and Bob's needs easily satisfied them all. I had a huge house and thirty acres to myself, so why not share it?

I asked no questions about Bob's disposition or quirks in advance of his arrival. Ellen assured me that he was easygoing and that dogs loved him more than steak. *How bad could it be?* I asked myself.

A question I did not take into account at all regarding taking on a nearly ninety-year-old roommate was this: *How good can it get?* If anything, I figured I was doing *him* a favor without stopping to consider he might potentially be doing me a much bigger favor. Which makes the unfolding story of Bob that much more remarkable.

I look back now on our first months together with emotion bordering on disappointment. Not that I made a poor decision. Not at all. But rather that in the beginning there was much to keep me from getting close to Bob. There were my trips to Houston to be with Peter several days most weeks. There were the weekends Peter came to the ranch and I was so focused on trying to please him that I did not see Bob much or even at all. There were the many weddings I had to drive all over the Hill Country to perform, which also took me away from the ranch frequently.

More than these ongoing events and appointments though, something else kept me at a distance. Though my job as an officiant performing weddings in front of crowds and my social media presence make me out to be an extrovert of the highest order, in reality I am an introvert. Times I am not required to be around people, I am more than a little content to be alone, holed up in my room, in the company of my dogs.

Though unfamiliar with all the theories about what causes introversion, personal experience leads me to hypothesize much of the condition lies in nurture, not nature. Growing up in a house with eight siblings, no doors on our rooms, and in a state of constant chaos, taught me that being alone, truly alone, furnishes a level of safety. Letting others in compromises this. While I have no shortage of friends—true, intimate friends— these friends also understand that I am often wont to hide for weeks or months on end.

I told Bob early on that I would be in my room for long stretches, not to avoid him but because this was my nature. He took no issue with this and enjoyed alone time, too. I was also pleased that he was accepting of my increasingly bizarre eating habits. Or, more accurately, my lack of eating. My eating disorder, triggered by Peter's ongoing complaints that my body did not excite him with desire, was in high gear. One fear I had in living with Bob was that he might insist on three big meals per day, to be taken together at the kitchen table. I was having a challenging enough time eating one meal a day. Bob, it turned out, ate like a bird. A very, very small bird. We promised ourselves and

Ellen that we would both try to eat more, to gain some weight. Still, it was a relief knowing I would not have to dedicate time each day to preparing us food and then just pushing it around on my plate while making small talk.

When I reflect on his earliest days at the ranch, I try to imagine how I must have appeared to Bob. Me, always running and running, to Houston, to weddings, to my room. Did he think me standoffish? Feral? Avoidant? Slowly over time though, seemingly in reverse proportion to Peter's intensifying erraticism, irritation, and flat out meanness, I began to rely more on Bob, coming to understand this old man was more than just a roommate.

Possibly he didn't think too much at all about our early dynamic because Bob, from the get go, made himself ridiculously useful. He wrote long lists of projects that needed to be done to improve the land and buildings and set himself to accomplishing these things. Though I insisted that he was not required to work to earn his keep, he always replied the same: "Work keeps me alive."

Primarily Bob mowed. And mowed. And mowed some more. I stopped protesting about the mowing rather quickly. Of all the craziness that went down during the conversion of a meth lab and junkyard into a venue people would pay to rent, mowing invariably presented the greatest ongoing trial, one I hated dealing with. Yes, there were other huge headaches: my first contractor, a narcissistic blowhard, grew increasingly arrogant, and I had to fire him, which did not go well; negotiating terms to buy the Tiny Chapel wore me out, as the builder, too, was a narcissistic blowhard prone to insulting me; moving the chapel once it had finally been purchased was no small nightmare, and it nearly fell off of the truck as it made its way to the ranch; two weeks after the chapel was safely in place, a tornado ripped across the property, taking out twenty-six towering trees and dropping limbs on the two cars Peter and I had acquired just the week before to replace two other cars we lost in a Houston flood. (Unbelievably, the tornado spared the chapel).

But the mowing. The mowing was (and remains) a necessary, constant and never-ending battle, made more exasperating because I evidently purchased a mower possessed by demons. More than one mower. The first never started. The replacement took some time to arrive. One of the post-tornado stumps beckoned, sirenesque, to the blades of the second mower, destroying a major component. Off to the shop that mower went, held prisoner for months.

Bob never stopped working, even with the mower gone. The picture of appearances being deceitful, his frail frame and the difficulty he had walking due to neuropathy brought on by diabetes did not impede his insistence on going outside every day and finding something to do. Sure, he moved slowly, but he never stopped moving. He knew about land management, saw things that needed to be done that I conveniently chose not to see, and got those things done.

A few weeks after he moved in, Bob turned eighty-eight. Ellen and I threw a party for him. This was the first turning point, when I got glimpses of the true enormity of Bob's appreciation for life, his sense of humor, his constant gratitude. Surrounded by an assembly of Ellen's friends and mine, he sat like a king at the fire pit, flames orangey and blue leaping from thick logs hewn from old trees, leaning eagerly into the heat, his shrunken, fat-free body and the effects of his blood pressure medication leaving him forever chilly, even in the house, even with the heater cranked up. He radiated true joy to be in the company of us younger folk, delighted at being the center of our attention. Later, inside, he opened his gifts and blew out his candles like a giddy five-year-old.

There was a clear hierarchy to the things demanding my attention when Bob first moved in. Living with him required the commitment of having a roommate, but still was so easy. Running the business was far more taxing, since, really, I was running multiple businesses, continuing to lead writing workshops and perform off-site weddings constantly, as I pushed to get the ranch where I want it to be. My greatest struggle though, always lay with Peter, our relationship never untroubled for more than a week or so at a time. There were ongoing arguments over his increasing withdrawal of attention and my corollary increasing need for same. The more I complained, the further he pulled away. The more he pulled away, the greater my anxiety became.

The breakup in the fall of 2016, just prior to our England trip and Bob's arrival, pushed me into a severe depression. I am no stranger to depression, which has been fucking with my mind off and on since at least adolescence. For decades, from the ages of fourteen through thirty-five, I poured fuel on the fire of these dark stretches, self-medicating with booze, growing darker still. Sobriety and meditation, both of which I began practicing in 2000, help lengthen remission and shorten the cycles of darkness when they do arise. Still, depression comes, often triggered by external events, like being discarded weeks before a long-planned international vacation.

When that month-long bout subsided, I took comfort believing that, if past interims were any indication, at least I would experience a break from the blackness for another year or so. I was wrong. The next wave crashed into me on Inauguration Day 2017. Refusing to see that this depression, too, was directly related to Peter, I conveniently convinced myself this second major episode hinged on falling victim to the collective dismay gripping the country, that the new regime would find a way to blow up the planet inside of weeks. Unshakeable doom gripped me. Into the pit I went, paralyzed by sadness, hostage to my brain chemistry, withdrawing more and more into my room.

Bob watched as I disintegrated before his eyes. I could hide some of my distress from friends seen only occasionally, but I could not secret my edginess from someone who lived with me. Zombielike I shuffled around, struggling to keep too many balls in the air. Time and again I apologized for my sorry state, my poor attitude, my ongoing inability to eat. Time and again Bob listened, reassured me. Slowly my eyes opened to the true reality before me: This man was no mere roommate. He was a father. A new father. A true father. The kind of father I'd heard other people talk about having, intellectually understanding Good Father was not an oxymoron, but never connecting with the concept.

Until Bob.

As this truth dawned on me, I had a hard time embracing it. Bob understood. He looked at me the way he had surely looked at so many different broken animals encountered in his farmer life, recognized the need for patience, coaxing, constant reassurance, and a necessary passing of time for trust and healing to take place. He applied himself to nurturing me with the same fierce dedication he put toward taming our unruly acres, slowly but surely scrubbing away more than fifty years of the damage and self-doubt sprung from seeds of self-loathing planted in me as a little child, pain that grew like untamable vines choking my heart. Bob was so good with pruning, with knowing where to cut and what to leave alone.

So many nights we sat and played checkers, amazed at how such a seemingly simple game could take so many odd turns. Often, I scrutinized the board, searching for a best possible move, made it, then took my finger off the checker, only to have him execute a triple jump. *I never even saw that!* I'd say. Bob laughed every time.

He also showed me how to make better moves, in checkers and in life. His presence showed me that if you are very lucky, you can, regardless of age and circumstance, find a true guide, a loving soul to drag your tired heart gingerly away from the rut-riddled past where it has insisted forever traipsing, and lead it to higher, safer ground, where the view is glorious and peace prevails.

During my lengthy healing time, when I felt like I was not healing at all— so incremental and backsliding was the process—I wasted the majority of my waking hours contemplating my pain. This pain was compounded by the sense that I was "bad" for not being able to simply move on and be grateful for the undeniable abundance surrounding me. I felt like I was looking at a 3-D picture without those funky red and blue glasses— seeing two outlines, one very bad, one very good, frustrated at my inability to integrate the two and take in a true image of my great fortune. Bob functioned as my glasses, though, and the more we time we spent together, the more things began to align, and a crisper, truer picture of all that I have, this exceptional embarrassment of riches, emerged.

Welcome to The Tao of Bob. What follows are some of my favorite tales of how the steady love and wisdom of an old Indiana farmer healed my broken, middle-aged punk rocker heart.

PART
TWO

The Tao of Bob

RITUALS PART I

I N THE IMMEDIATE AFTERMATH OF PETER'S DECLARATION THAT we are done, really finished for good, there comes what feels like an interminable period of adjustment. Instead of texting or calling him to say good morning, now there is the glaring absence of contact. Or, when I cannot resist begging him some more, driven by compulsion, I send a message or call, which sometimes leads to a heated exchange, but often enough is greeted by stone cold silence or an automated voice sending me directly to voicemail.

Sometimes I try to convince myself that his motive for ghosting me is not what it seems: mean-spirited emphasis that he has discarded me, that he has no interest in helping me through my pain. Instead I strive to believe he is trying to force me to accept, sooner rather than later, what I am sure I will never be able to accept, that he will not come and share a life at the ranch with me, something we have talked about since we first met. In this latter cruel-to-be-kind scenario, I still hurt so much, but grapple to make room for the idea that, if I can follow his lead and maintain silence, too, I might hasten my journey toward putting this all behind me.

Now there are new morning rituals. I come to the surface after welcome unconsciousness—sleep that, even if fitful, delivers six or seven hour stretches of forgetting—once again remembering that this man who was my alleged best friend is no longer a friend at all. I contemplate that we will likely never see each other again, feel violently ill, and begin to cry. Or, slight variation, some mornings I wake up already crying, the tears the thing that wakes me.

I meditate, as I always do. For the first few weeks post-breakup, I meditate for a full hour per sit, three times my standard meditation, another strategy as I seek relief sooner rather than later. The goal is to clear my mind, steady my breathing, get focused, recognize that I am in the moment, and that no matter how frightened and traumatized I feel, the truth is that, really, I am safe, sitting upright, taking in air, releasing it, that there is not, as I could swear there is, a knife in my heart.

The reality of my meditation though, is that without fail now, a looping image fills my mental screen, a little horror movie in which Peter is getting it on with that other woman he confessed to hooking up with during our penultimate breakup. They are in a non-descript hotel room. I have spent more hours in that hotel room with them than they ever spent with each other there.

The agony of watching this mind movie does not revolve around garden variety jealousy. As I told Peter, repeatedly, all the times I cried in anguish, asking him how he could have done such a thing, his choice dredged up in me the ancient trauma of being born into a family where nearly every year came a new sibling, and with each new one even less of a chance of getting the kind of nurturing all children deserve. *Rejected and replaced*, this is the refrain in my mind every time my mother returns from the hospital with another little baby. No time for me.

Rejected and replaced. This is how I feel often, when I revisit the night of the rattlesnake and that conversation in which Peter confessed his tryst. I labored to forgive him when we got back together, thought at times maybe I had, but in truth, even after he is gone for good, I remain haunted by how cavalierly he leapt into bed with another woman. My pain is exacerbated as I reflect over our first year together, when Peter repeatedly fell gravely ill, requiring a number of hospital and doctor visits, some of which occurred during breakup periods. Every time his health failed, and it failed regularly, I cared for him regardless of our status, entailing much rearranging of my schedule, many trips to hospitals, and putting on hold things I needed to do to get the ranch client-ready. These illnesses kept him from lavishing me with the physical affection he once deployed to seduce me, though, apparently, they did not prevent him from fucking someone else.

Times I cared for him, I said repeatedly, to myself and Peter both, all this selfless caretaking was about unconditional love, he owed me nothing. Of course, I was full of shit, in not consciously so. All along as I fed him, waited on him hand and foot, cleaned his house, helped him up when he fell, walked him to the bathroom because he was too weak to walk alone, I harbored great hope that once he healed, he would resume demonstrating the love, adoration, and passion for sex he showed in the early days, all of which continued to diminish the longer we were together.

The movie never ends. That it invades my daily meditation, my supposed time and place for grounding, makes it all the more unbearable. Still, I sit, day after day, refusing to give up a practice I have spent thousands of hours building and maintaining, a daily ritual that has become a part of my true being. Breathe in. See them in bed. Breathe out. See them getting it on. Chant silently the Serenity Prayer, ask some god to help me, this despite being nontheistic. I need the repetition of the words as a focal point to try to counter the repetition of the images burning deeper into my mind every day. I fear that the growing association between my meditation and this looping image might ruin my practice. Still I sit. Still I breathe. Still I beg for serenity, courage, wisdom.

As I breathe in and breathe out, tears stream down my face. Often, I sob audibly, sometimes howling, sometimes doubled over, torso folding over legs folded in half-lotus in front of me. There is no serenity in these hour-long sessions, only crushing sorrow. I persist.

Fortunately, my morning routines also include checking in with Bob. This habit, too, is not entirely new. What is new is the regularity of the check-ins. When Bob first arrived, I still had seven months of Peter Hell left to endure before the ultimate ending. Days spent with him in Houston were days I did not see Bob at all. With no Peter in the picture now, Bob and I see each other every single morning.

Stepping out of my little living pod, formerly a garage, I cross over to what I call the business side of the house. That's where Bob stays anytime we do not have rental guests, in the room known as The Bridal Suite. I find him in the kitchen, drinking his coffee before making a run to feed the horses.

"How are you today?" he asks, even though he knows the answer.

Without fail, I respond the same way for seven weeks straight. "Well you know, it's the morning. I hate mornings. I'm so sad."

Speaking these words, answering his simple question, reactivates my crying, and I sit across from him, unable to gain my composure, my sadness deepening, knowing my pain causes Bob pain, sure that I am letting him down. Ever thoughtful, Bob creates his own ritual in response to mine. Working his way slowly through a bowl of Honey Nut Cheerios, he looks me directly in the eyes. "You'll be alright," he promises.

This sentiment is not some off-hand platitude to shut me up. By now I have memorized much of his life story, the hardships of his childhood, the hardships of his life as a farmer, the hardships of raising five kids, the hardships of being married for sixty-six years to a difficult woman, the hardships of watching her die a slow death. The depths of my grief, the blurry blinding of my ceaseless tears, not even these things can keep me from seeing in Bob's beautiful, well-lined face, that one can withstand, emerge, survive, and thrive. Half-heartedly I will myself to believe that one day, with Bob's help and the passing of time, I can become like him, find peace, joy, contentment and gratitude every single day.

With the breakup still fresh though, that day, if it really is coming, is too far down the path to even glimpse yet. In the first few weeks of The Coffee Crying Exercise, I still want to discuss with Bob the possibility of a reunion with Peter. Day in and day out, even while reviling choices he made that hurt me irreparably, I nonetheless backpedal on his behalf, defend him to my breakfast companion.

"Life dealt him such a shitty hand," I tell Bob. "That's not an excuse for the things he did but..." and then more thoughts which, despite my protestations to the contrary, really are excuses for Peter's inexcusable behavior.

Bob, so wise, has already intuited much about me in our relatively short stretch as roommates. He spent a lifetime around animals, studying them, understanding them, recognizing how to spot unwanted behaviors and gently coax better ones. This knowledge, I'm certain, he applies during my daily breakfast crying jags. He knows that flat-out advising against engaging in foolish thoughts of a reunion will inspire contrarian me to scheme more impossible schemes to bring Peter and all his disrespect back to me. Bob understands the economics of this situation, that Peter has cut off the supply of himself from the demands of me, and how this drives me to want more, my own addiction patterns resurfacing in cravings not for the booze long ago quit, but for a different poison—life with Peter at any cost. Rather than tell me how stupid I am, Bob just keeps going at his Cheerios, listening attentively before serving up his steady refrain.

"You know, I don't dislike Peter," he begins, though I can tell this opening statement is more to calm me than it is a truth. "But I never did hear him say a nice thing to you. And the only time I saw him speak to you was when he wanted food or for you to clean up one of his messes."

Each time he says this, I listen. Sometimes I absorb the message, at least a little. Other times my defense continues. Sometimes Bob, surely vexed, even if the steadiness of his tone does not belie such, cuts to the chase more quickly. "You know hon," he says, "he really did shit on you."

Once in a while, upon hearing me again list the injustices I put up with, he can't resist smiling and, choosing his tone carefully, announces, "Sucker!"

Oddly, though this label irks me slightly, it doesn't anger me. If anyone else tried saying this, I might protest and storm away. But Bob calls it like he sees it, in a manner that does not provoke defense. I *was* a sucker. Over and over and over again. I am still a sucker, clinging, as I do, to reunion fantasies. Bob is not belittling me. He's identifying the problem. He wants me to stop being a sucker. He wants me to know that if I can manage to release any preposterous notion I have that Peter had been anything but awful, if I can figure out how stop defending his indefensible actions, stop wishing aloud he might change his ways and come back, then I will earn the right to stop being called sucker. Until that day comes, Bob will dole out his annoying but true verdict whenever he deems I need to hear it most, times I go on ad nauseam about how Peter just couldn't help himself, he had it so bad as a child and *blah blah blah fucking blah.*

These morning sessions last a half-hour or so, before I beg off, head to my room to cry some more and wonder if the feeling I have, that I am literally dying from heartbreak, is just a feeling or a true harbinger of untimely demise. Bob allows me the space to fall to my knees with grief then, heading off to mow acre after acre and look after the animals, activities that, while physically exerting, replenish his emotional energy, which I selfishly, and with his blessing, drain from him day after day.

So focused am I on my own suffering, I cannot immediately see in these morning meetings the greater impact Bob's steadiness is having on my heart. Yes, he is getting me through the breakup. He is also demonstrating the benefits of consistency, of what it's like to have someone show up again and again and again, to be fed a consistent diet of love and respect, the very things I wished for but did not receive from Peter. While I have plenty of friends who provide the same, there is a difference in Bob's availability because he is more than a friend. He is a new father and he is re-parenting me.

My biological father never showed up. Or, more accurately, he showed up only with hate, criticism, and terror. As a child, the sight of him, the mere thought of him, left me in a state of constant hypervigilance, wasting so much time strategizing how to minimize the wrath of his rage. This took a heavy toll on my mind, body, and spirit, actual physiological changes scientists with their fancy studies and MRIs have quantified. Post Traumatic Stress Syndrome causes brain chemistry changes, corrupting and rutting out neuropathways, which sufferers then get stuck in, just as I find myself repeatedly stuck in that hotel room with Peter and another woman hundreds of times.

Meditation, also now studied closely, is a proven tool in changing neuropathways, in reprogramming one's mind and fostering healing. Bob's ever-calming presence is another tool. His kindness and steady reassurance smooth over some of the ruts. His physical presence and loving words counter the ghost of my father's voice in my head telling me how stupid I am, how I might as well die. I push away my father's urgings to off myself, because I understand, if only vaguely, a better life post-Peter will arrive. But in my truly darkest hours, when thoughts of checking out visit me as regularly as that hotel movie, I remind myself that I have others to whom I am responsible, chief among them my son, Henry, and Bob. Bob tells me I am worthy. He shows me the joy of living. He promises me over and over this joy is coming soon to a mental theatre near me. That if I will hold on to his promise and let go of my past, I will get there.

RITUALS PART II

N 1986, WHEN I WAS 22, I HAD A MISCARRIAGE, A MOST AWFUL experience, physically and emotionally crushing. I declared afterwards I was going to stay in my room until I died, that I would grieve for the rest of my life. My mother told me no, that actually I was going to get dressed and go to work. And so I did. Being at work sort of helped in that I could, at least momentarily, distract myself by waiting on tables in a busy restaurant. It's not that I stopped grieving—the grief went on for well more than a year and even thirty-one years later I can, with little effort, tap into it. Still, in the routine of work, there were moments of, if not forgetting, then focusing elsewhere. Bursts of respite.

Now Bob acts as my daily reminder of the importance of work and routine, of suiting up and showing up to chip away at grief. If he were not here, I might stay in my room, crawl out only to perform weddings, let the ranch go to Hell, wallow in my misery. But he will have none of that. We are accountable to one another. We work together to make this place both our home and a successful business. After a few weeks of letting him tend to the animals by himself, I start to join him on his morning rounds.

Slowly, with the aid of his cane, he makes his way from the table to the front door, using his eyes to direct his feet the days he has no sensation in them or when they burn relentlessly from the neuropathy. Just outside the front door, near the hoe we keep for killing snakes should the need arise, sits his scooter. This he employs to rumble over to his shed behind the reception hall. Inside the shed is his pride and joy: a golf cart. I meet him as he backs the cart out, take my place in the shotgun seat, and off we roll to the feed shed. The horses, Tiny and Queenie, well familiar with our routine, have established one of their own. The sight of the approaching cart elicits the same response every time. They push their big noses under the canopy, eager to get to the pans of horse feed on the seat between us. Bob shoos them, laughing. Sometimes they abide. Often, they do not. Tiny, especially, wants to stay close and walks alongside the cart to the barnyard, flanking Bob, eager for the rattle of the pellets to hit the shiny galvanized tub nailed to the wall of his stall. Feed dispensed, he takes his place and, curiously, lifts a hoof as he eats, making a figure four with his front legs, as if this is some superstitious act he can't not perform, lest something terrible befall him.

Once the horses are fed, we roll back over to the feed closet, beneath which lives our favorite chicken, Nancy. Our other eight hens are dark-feathered—some red, some gray. Daisy is bright white and the others pick on her for being different. No amount of coaxing will convince her to come out, so we meet her on her terms, fill her little water dish and leave a small mound of scratch for her breakfast while we discuss strategies for convincing her to resume life out in the light, to run across the many green acres with her mean sisters.

Next stop is the reception hall, also called the barn, and officially named the Molly Ivins Pavilion in honor of my writing mentor. It never really was a barn, it was a five-car garage, dilapidated and on the brink of collapse when I got the ranch. Nor is it a pavilion. But no one minds the misnomer. Current residents of this space are two ginger barn cats adopted from the local shelter with the idea they might keep snakes away from the house. Mostly they just hide under the old wooden stage I rescued from Habitat for Humanity, its worn boards holding secrets I'll never know of a former life in some small town high school or little church annex. I fill their food dishes and empty their litter box, wondering if they will ever fulfill their duties or if, like all the other animals around here, they will just hang out, no likelihood of being fired for failure to perform assigned duties.

Our motley crew tended to, Bob and I part ways. He heads back to his shed to plan more repairs I am continuously blind to. Or he mounts the rider mower and sets out to tackle the acreage up front around the chapel, and then out back behind the house. Most days he stops for a nap in his golf cart. Summer is an extended affair in Texas, and as long as it is hot outside, this is where he prefers to take siesta, because Bob detests air conditioning, his personal thermostat leaving him perpetually cold.

Inside, I tackle the housekeeping, grumbling sometimes about the never-ending mountains of laundry, the messes left by rental guests. Like nature, I abhor my vacuum. There are also emails to answer, as-yet-undiscovered income streams to dream up, bills to pay, marketing campaigns to launch and tweak. Whatever complaining I do is lighthearted because I am never not aware that these tasks are what allow Bob and me to live in our country paradise. In the wake of Peter's disappearance, I am especially grateful as the busy work, without fail, generates much-needed distraction from my heart and mind, both cluttered with remorse and sadness.

With early evening come more half-hearted attempts to nourish our bodies as we catch each other up on all the work we accomplished and that which still remains. We could work twenty-hours a day, like Bob did when he was a farmer all those years, and still never finish everything that needs to be done. That's fine by us. How we both love working. After our supper, we often follow up with checkers or watching a little TV. Which brings us, at last, to our favorite time of day: sunset.

Back to the golf cart we go, apples in the cup holders for the pushy horses. We choose our route depending on whether or not there is trash to be hauled to the big bins up at the road or if we've remembered (or not) to check the mailbox earlier. Whichever way we go, we take our time, except those evenings when Bob cannot resist flooring the cart and careening toward the gate, amused at my squeals that he please slow down.

Once Tiny and Queenie are satisfied with their evening snack, the eggs gathered, and the chickens cooped, we watch the sunset. The tiny chapel sits at an angle chosen so it will be magically backlit by the sun's daily final rays. We drink in this view, look at our own horses grazing, and then across to the neighbor's place, more horses there, and donkeys, too, that bray goodnight to us.

Always we give thanks. Never is our gratitude without awe. We are amazed at all this natural beauty around us, incredulous that we live together. Discussing this never gets old.

"Can you believe we get to live here?" one of us asks the other.

"No," the other laughs.

"Can you believe we found each other?"

Again: "No."

Again laughter.

"I felt dead for so many years," Bob says. "I'm so happy now."

Even when these twilight exchanges occur during my broken-heart period, when I am nowhere close to happy, I still appreciate all that I have here: this ranch, this sunset, this man beside me. Anomalous duality, to hold such sadness inside while simultaneously inventorying the outward bounty, spilling over all around me. I lean into this gratitude practice, which is becoming a sort of evening meditation. Slowly, I move toward believing that if I keep breathing and keep giving thanks, these acts will become less rote and give way to true change on a cellular level, leading me to a calm I know I have felt before, a calm now so remote as to seem like it was only ever a mirage, a calm Bob keeps reminding me is possible to reach, if I will just keep going forward, stop looking back.

PERSISTENCE

ONE DAY, NOT LONG AFTER THE BREAKUP, I TAKE off for a one-day vacation with my friend Carol. We go to a spa where I have traded teaching for overnight stays. It is a world-class facility, inordinately opulent, every detail tended to, just short of having servants wipe your ass. Carol and I talk and talk and talk. I practice eating. I swim. I sit in the sunshine. All of this helps. Then it is time to go back to the ranch, the place that is both my sanctuary and, for now anyway, a labyrinth of triggers, so many reminders of Peter.

Bob is waiting. Bob is always waiting. I'm bowled over by his patience and tenderness. I'm also something like embarrassed at how needy I am, that I feel like nothing but a burden to him.

"What did you do while I was gone?" I ask him.

"I finished the ramp," he says, referring to the ramp he has built to the entrance of his new shed, where he keeps his tools and parks his golf cart.

I reply that I am both impressed and a bit alarmed that he took on such a big job alone. I wish he'd waited for my help because the project required taking a pick-axe to the packed dirt and moving a huge, mighty heavy piece of plywood, all of this in the brutal heat. I allow myself a moment to visualize what would've happened if he'd fallen or fainted while undertaking this endeavor, with no one around to tend to him. But worrying is now, as worrying is always, futile. Reality is before me. The ramp is done. Bob is fine, smiling, upright, unscathed, triumphant.

"How'd you move that plywood?" I ask.

"Dragged it a few steps. Took a break. Dragged it a few more steps," he says. He's not sarcastic, just explaining the process.

Bob is always tackling projects with the patience of Job. When the lawnmower blades wear out or break upon making contact with a hidden stump, it might take him two days to replace them. His strength has lessened to the point that the trickiest part of the job involves strategizing how best to lower himself to the ground and wiggle under the mower. Then he must maneuver a two-by-four just so, to keep the blades from spinning when he sets himself to loosening very tight bolts and determining the proper leverage required to get the damn things off, before finally figuring out how best to stand up again once new blades are installed. I always offer to call in help. He always declines. He can do it. He wants to do it. He just needs time. I give him time.

Not long after Bob's arrival at the ranch, we acquire Tiny and Queenie. He soon determines they need a better holding area than the back acreage fenced off to corral them during weddings, explaining this section is too full of mesquite and thorny cacti, not enough grass for good grazing. He devises a plan, plotting out a better space for them, employing a collection of short, heavy, concrete discs, each centered with a vertical rebar post, which he dubs *Forever,* because, he notes wryly, "They'll be around forever."

The Forevers came with the property, part and parcel of the makeshift junkyard that preceded my arrival. I have no idea their original purpose. They are only here because the cost of moving them and the attendant disposal fee at a real junkyard is prohibitive. Bob, a fan of repurposing, sees in them not obstacle but opportunity. Over the course of many months, he drags them one-by-one behind the mower, positions them at intervals, strings two parallel lengths of yellow nylon rope from one to the next, then adds a third tier of electric wire, which will emit a mild shock to the horses should they try to breach it, something they immediately learn to not do after one shock.

When Bob starts the Forever Project, I am skeptical. How could a couple of nylon ropes keep two half-ton horses from breaking out into the main yard? Even with the electric fencing, visually the setup looks like it could easily be leapt over or barged through. But the fence proves amazingly efficient, the horses content to graze in this smaller area times they must be contained. Bob, humble, never says he told me so, just takes quiet satisfaction in another project successfully completed.

This is Bob. To look at him, you might conclude he's frail. And on one level he is. But he's also the toughest person I have ever met. Every single day he gets up, gets himself around no matter how badly his legs and feet bother him, tends to the animals, mows the lawn, then comes up with more ideas to better the place. The whole time he says how happy he is. To be here. To be alive.

I observe his persistence, his attitude, his refusal to complain. My bruised and shrunken heart is like a wobbly just-hatched chick, trying to imprint on Tiny T's Resident Rooster, unsure of my own footing, striving to listen to that voice telling me, *Follow him. Follow him. Do what he does. This is what will heal you.*

And so, each day, under his wise tutelage, I grab onto the unwieldy sheet of plywood that is my unstable state of mind and, step by step, I drag it a little closer to what I hope will be more level ground, the place where stability will rule and there will be good use for my feelings, a source of proper purpose versus thorny splinters. Bob demonstrates how, even in a weakened state, if I will just go a little bit at a time and stop for proper rest, I will get where I need to be.

LIGHT

NE THING WE LOVE OUT HERE AT TINY T RANCH is the light. Every moment of every day the light is doing something wonderful. In the mornings, the earliest rays illuminate a lacy blanket of dewdrops, a million prisms sparkling across a field of vivid green grass dotted with tiny wildflowers. Midday, inside the Tiny Chapel, a dove fashioned of sunshine rests on an worn antique pew. Sunsets are spectacular. Sometimes it pours rain and is sunny at the same time, a magic trick of Mother Nature, curiously known as "the devil is beating his wife," which always give me pause, the way it serves as a great metaphor for duality—how it can be stormy and bright at once, that this is how life goes, never mind how much I try to force things into either The Black Box or The White Box.

One evening, Bob and I are sitting outside on the old wooden chairs by the front door, watching the sky as sunset gives way to dusk. We talk, as we so often do, about our great fortune in getting to live here and with each other and of how beautifully peculiar it is that we found each other at all. These talks are like bright sunshine breaking through in streaks through the storm clouds that continue to obscure my heart as that bloodthirsty shark that is breakup grief circles and circles, bites and bites.

Tiny comes sauntering up to Bob for a nose scratch. This massive, twelve-hundred-pound beast, nuzzling a one-hundred-and-twenty-pound man, nine decades into his life. The differences between them are stark. With a single kick or push, Tiny could demolish Bob. Bob shows no fear. He baby talks Tiny, reaches up and gives him a pat. The sky frames them in both darkness and light as day slips into night. This imagery—young horse and old man, sun setting and dusk rising—overtakes me. Bob, has seen so much more darkness than I have. He's got thirty-five years on me.

Sometimes he shares stories of the darkness he's known, mistakes he's made. Mostly though, he focuses on the light. He's reminds me that even in the darkness, some light is out there, and how even in the light there are going to be some shadows—you don't just get one or the other, but rather you find a way to live with them both.

IMPERMANENCE

N 2010, A BURGLAR BROKE INTO MY LITTLE HOUSE IN AUSTIN. I was not home when this happened, but upon arrival surveyed the mess and determined that my three dogs drove the intruder out before he could grab anything. Not that there was anything of financial value to take, as I fill my world with sentiment, not gold. Still, I felt violated and shaken. This led me to the decision that it was time to expand my pack, get another big dog—one that would keep intruders from entering the house at all—as my biggest, fiercest dog had recently died, and the current biggest was getting old and was not intimidating enough.

Upon meeting the new "guard dog," my son, Henry, laughed at me. Dante was a large, friendly Labrador. "Seems like he'd be more likely to carry shit out to the car for burglars than scare them off," he said.

But I was unable to resist adopting Dante, rescuing him from an execution slated for just a day after the day I found him. As I filled out paperwork, a shelter employee volunteered caveats about the big guy, said he was a constant barker, aggressive with cats, and not housebroken. I was also informed that he was around eight. In reality, he rarely made a sound, was fine with the cats, never shit in the house and, according to my vet, was much younger than reported. So pleasant was his demeanor that Henry gave him a slogan: "Just happy to be here." And he was. As if understanding he had been spared death, he smiled and wagged constantly.

A lesson I derived from life with Dante is that, whatever story we come with, there exists the potential for an equal and opposite story to reveal itself. Bob and I cultivate in each other new stories, revised narratives. Just as it is possible Dante really did bark excessively and go after cats in his prior life, Bob and I each truly did experience great tribulations in ours. But as Dante showed only a sunny side once I brought him home, so does Bob. I'm working on this, too, striving to focus on the present, the joy of our ranch life.

A huge challenge Bob and I each faced in our recent past lives came in caring for increasingly ill partners. We process together, commiserating over how overbearing our tasks had been. We concur it's exhausting for the person being cared for, too, the indignation of enduring chronic physical pain compounded by helplessness and the anger this helplessness in turn fosters. Both caregiver and receiver grow extremely cranky, potentially creating relationship fissures too deep to repair. Neither of us can deny how this care-taking changed the course of our life stories. But we also agree on this: The intersection of love and duty demands you take care of your loved ones no matter how rough the road gets, no matter how much they snarl and lash out. You show up. You do the best you can. This is just the way things are done.

Now we take care of each other. I'd like to think that, even without our respective traumas of the past couple of years, we'd be very good at this co-nurturing. But what we each went through in helping our partners, his now dead and mine fled, also gives us a greater appreciation of caring for and being cared for by each other. The words we share most frequently are these: "Do you need anything?" "Thank you." "I love you."

We are changing each other's stories. I note that, despite my grief, the ever-tightening noose of anxiety that restricted me when I was with Peter—his explosiveness, his unpredictability, his constant needs—has loosened considerably as I no longer must steel myself in anticipation of his never-ending, always unwarranted complaints and wildly erratic behavior. I give Bob so much credit for this quieting. There is a growing calm at the center of my storm, knowing that every day we can count on the steadiness of our routines, the rhythm of this infrastructure rendering the security that comes with the reliability of knowing what needs to be done, of doing it.

Some evenings, I bring Dante down to Bob's room, leaving the other two rambunctious dogs in my room. Dante, ever the gentle giant, loves head pats from Bob, wagging his approval and grinning his just-happy-to-be-here grin in gratitude. Observing the two of them together, I see pure happiness. I see mutual appreciation. I see something else, too, a vivid image of impermanence, which seems to be the lesson I have come to this planet to try to learn—that things and people and pets and opportunities arrive and then depart, that there is nothing I can do to prevent this.

I know, and hate knowing, but try to accept knowing, that not too far down the road I will be left to go on without them. When the thought of Bob's departure visits me, I push it away. I imagine feeling so lost, so unable to go on without him. I then use this thought to develop true presence. I lean in on the truth and try to fashion it into something more useful, a reminder to share as much time and love with Bob and Dante as I can, while I have the opportunity to do so.

On my better days, when I achieve shifting from being afraid to being aware, I observe truths about myself. I am an incredibly impatient person. Outwardly I can present as infinitely patient—when teaching, when talking, when listening, when helping others. But inside, so very often my mind is racing to figure out what is next, and what is next after that, and what must I do, and then what must I do after that? This sense of urgency springs from the hypervigilance I developed to try to anticipate and save myself from my father's rage. It is the same sense of urgency that has a positive side, allowing me to get shit done in an astonishingly timely and efficient fashion. I multi-task when I can—tidying the house or doing my hula hoop workout while taking business calls or listening to audiobooks. I stack errands and gigs so tightly in succession that one minor mishap might send the whole itinerary to Hell.

When it comes to Bob Time though, I consciously note any impatience as it arises. Never is this directly connected to him—as in, *Oh I wish he would finish telling this story, so I could get going,* or *Gee, I sure hope we wrap up this game of checkers fast, so I can hide in my room.* I understand my impatience is the tug of my mental To Do List trying to convince me I don't have time to just hang out. I then recognize this as bullshit, that all of it can wait until later, that my most precious resource, my Bob, might only be here another day, another week. The knowledge, this reminder to self, immediately brings the present moment into focus and I settle into enjoying whatever time we have left together.

FOOD

HAVE BEEN EATING DISORDERED FOR DECADES, BUT I'VE ONLY recently come to terms with this truth. Eating disorders are very complicated. Mine, which I trace back to adolescence, when I would subject myself to periods of only ingesting saltine crackers and powdered diet iced tea for weeks on end, can lie dormant for long stretches. When it awakens, most often the problem takes the form of starvation, though sometimes it runs in other direction, and bingeing becomes the demon.

In the spring of 2016, Peter announced one day, "You've really blown up." This on the heels of my request that he stop bringing so many cookies and so much candy home because, while I can be quite disciplined at resisting junk food, when I do start in on a package of Oreos, stopping at just two is impossible. Besides, his diabetes was worsening due to the sugar he sucked down regularly.

Two seconds after the critical words left his mouth—his cruelty magnified when he denied that he was body shaming me, insisted instead that I was "too sensitive" and that I "took things too personally" and furthermore that I needed to "grow a thicker skin"—seeing my face twist, he added, "I guess I just ruined the weekend."

In fact, he ruined so much more than the weekend. I understood, intellectually, that I should, under no circumstances, internalize his cruel remark. I have been immersing myself in feminist doctrine for thirty years and am a bit of an expert on just how fucking distorted the media is when it comes to convincing women that we are all physically unacceptable no matter what lengths we go to. I have seven sisters, all of us at some point subjecting ourselves to too much exercise and not enough food, sometimes temporarily moving us closer to the anorexic ideal heralded by magazines and movies, but ultimately collapsing under the dictates of genetics. We are round-hipped and ample-bottomed and soft-bellied courtesy of our DNA, this revealed by photos of so many female relatives in our extended family. By the time I met Peter, though I still regularly engaged in some self-scrutiny and body-image disappointment, I'd gotten the volume on that voice turned down pretty low and was relatively content with my size.

And yet, despite these efforts and this knowledge, internalize his criticism I did. Slowly at first, I began to shut off my appetite button. I consumed less. I lost a few pounds. I never forgot his comment. Resentment stewed. So, too, determination. I would show him, not out of desire to please him, but out of warped spite, that I could be smaller.

Then came another conversation that summer, one so vicious that, revisiting it, and having to own that I did not run away as far and as fast as I could, but rather ran toward him begging, makes me flinch. Peter launched into a commentary about how when he thought about having sex it wasn't with me, that he wanted a sexy girlfriend he couldn't keep his hands off and I did not meet that desire. A few days later he added that I was "a boner killer."

Looking back, I see his commentary about how my body displeased him long pre-dated judgment about my weight and sex appeal. Just weeks into our relationship, he noted after sex one night that he hadn't seen pubic hair like mine since stealing glances at his mother's copy of *The Joy of Sex* as a child, and would I please get rid of it. He added he would even gladly pay to have this done at a place called The Pretty Kitty, a business name so ridiculous as to seem fictional to my ears.

Shocked, ripped open when he announced that summer day that I was sexually repugnant, I declared us finished. But, not long after, we danced back together, as once again I made excuses for his inexcusable meanness. Another few weeks together, then, and another episode where I rushed him, his failing body—the one with the soft, droopy belly crisscrossed in stretch marks from when he was obese, his feet swollen and toes curled grotesquely from neuropathy, none of which I ever complained about but only ever loved—to an ER in the middle of the night. I got little sleep and received no gratitude for my dedication. The next day he declared that we were finished, that he did not want to touch my body anymore, that he had no interest in hearing my arguments in favor of working things out, that he was the man and so this decision was his alone to make.

This was when my eating disorder kicked into high gear, spurred by a combination of anxiety and knowing I would soon be forced to see him again as we flew on the same plane to England. I planned to show up at the airport and look hotter than he had ever seen me, to fill him with regret at his idiotic choice. I had only a few weeks to achieve this transformation. Fortunately, the early stages of starvation bring amazing results. The pounds fell off easily, this loss abetted by an obsessive daily workout routine to which I subjected myself, involving hours of hula hooping, hundreds of crunches, a little weightlifting, and regular rapid punching of my heavy bag, which had the added benefit of helping me let off some of the steam of my rage at having been shamed and abandoned.

Not eating doesn't just wreak havoc on one's body but takes a huge toll on one's mind. Disorder in full swing, I did not have the ability to start eating again once I dropped what I considered to be the desired amount of weight, felt compelled to keep going. Or, more accurately, I was unable to stop. Many days I ate just a single apple or a pint of ice cream, nothing more.

My body was perpetually hungry, though my mind told my body to shut the fuck up. Of course, my mind wasn't a very reliable pilot at that point, the fog of hunger and a mostly sugar diet inciting a particular strain of insanity that feeds on deprivation. Irony abounded. Everywhere I went people said, "You look so great!" By which they meant, if not intentionally, *Skinny is much better than not skinny*.

I wish such validation had not egged me on but, let me be honest, it did, as did being able to see the outline of my ribs, appearing like some hash marks of triumph placed in the success column of Beauty by Society's Standards Achieved. Still more irony came when Peter, after our foolish reunion in England, complained that now I was too bony, that my shoulder pressing into him hurt. And then, not long after that, bemoaning that in losing weight so fast, I was now unattractively saggy.

When I was in the absolute throes of my eating disorder, I reached a point of trying to understand it better by seeking information. I found an article proposing that some eating disorders are directly related to PTSD, one theory being that when you come from an abusive background, it is damn near impossible to shake seeking the familiarity of pain and shame, and that being eating disordered is a way to be both the abuser and the abused. In that sense, being out of control has a very odd way of feeling in control, or at least not controlled by someone else. I get to dictate, through eating or not eating, how much I will physically suffer. This allows me a perverse sense of agency. The suffering itself recreates a landscape so well-known that I can relax into it even as I am constantly on edge from hunger.

Peter's final departure further killed what little appetite I had, and as still more pounds dropped from my body, even I could no longer deny I was entering a true Danger Zone. I sought help from professionals and friends. It's a bit embarrassing to have to say to someone, "I'm sorry, but I seem unable to eat. Could you bring me food and sit with me and watch me get through a meal?" But needs must, and so ask I did.

Bob is a key helper in this quest to re-learn proper eating as his presence forces upon me a witness. It is way easier to destructively and methodically create a world of pain when no one is around to call you on your bullshit. Plus he, too, needs to eat more. We employ an informal buddy system, day by day working together to get better at taking in healthy sustenance, something that once brought us much joy before we met, but, courtesy of our respective grief, has morphed into a distasteful job, a laborious necessity. He eats with me to ensure I stop hurting myself through deprivation. Likewise, I have an opportunity to help him. If he isn't going to let me get away with skipping fifteen or more meals per week, I am going to make the same demands of him.

Lapses abound. One night, I spot him heading off to his room with a Butterfinger and insist he needs something more nutritious. "Well, what are you having for dinner?" he asks, both joking and not. I admit I have yet another pint of ice cream on the menu, nothing else.

Some days though, we get it right. With summer comes a bounty of beefsteak tomatoes from the garden. Tomato sandwiches don't pack a huge caloric punch, but the sweet fresh-from-the-vine flavor wakes up our taste buds, reminding us of the pleasures of eating. These simple meals lead to more meals. Good weeks we might manage nearly every day to mindfully stop midday for a bite, expanding our options to include fried eggs, laid that morning by our chickens, or cheese sandwiches punctuated with bread and butter pickles. Sometimes we go crazy and I, having oddly lost my once excellent cooking skills, will make us half-burnt grilled cheese sandwiches, heavy on the butter and paired with store-bought tomato soup. Sitting together, making more time for conversation, reinforces better habits. As does joking when either of us slips up and unnecessarily drops another pound or three.

Nowadays, we still don't eat quite as much as we could or should. But the refrigerator always holds an array of decent choices—pound upon pound of Bob's favorite red grapes bunched up beside the half-gallon bottles of Pace picante, for which, since his move to Texas, he has developed a strong affinity. Hardly a day passes that we don't sit down and have a bite together, food always tasting better thanks to the sharing.

DELIGHTFUL

ANY YEARS AGO, I CREATED A MOTTO TO live by: *Be Delightful.* You don't even need to read studies, though they exist, about the boomerang effect of bringing joy to others. Try it yourself and get immediate results. This can be as simple as smiling at a stranger, who almost always will smile back, which elevates good brain chemistry for both of you. Mostly though, it's just fun to be delightful. This is one reason why I, introvert, nevertheless engage strangers in conversation. I really want to know how my grocery store cashier is doing. I really want a passerby to know her dress looks cute. I really take joy in retrieving a dropped toy from the ground, handing it back to the carriage-bound toddler that tossed it, along with a few gurgling sounds and a goofy face as I do.

Bob is the picture of *Be Delightful* every day. He is super consistent. He laughs a lot. He makes me laugh a lot. Listening to stories of the challenges he faced in his long life, especially the last couple of years before moving to the ranch, I understand that he once reached a point of not being able to be delightful for some time. His delightfulness had not entirely left him, but rather went dark when pushed up against long days in a nursing home watching his wife slowly slip away.

Ranch life brings back the delight. I need look no further than his giddy demeanor to verify this, but further evidence exists. I am in the habit of following Bob around with my phone, snapping pictures of him on the lawnmower, with the horses, eating the occasional hearty meal, playing checkers. There is a Benjamin Button quality to this collection, and his increasingly healthy glow is due to more than just the Texas sun. Running the ranch breathes new life into him. He didn't look a day over eighty when he arrived. Now he appears closer to seventy. "I feel more alive than I did when I was twenty-one," he tells me, often.

He cannot resist being silly. One day, when I am hosting a summer writing camp for kids in the barn, the door swings open unexpectedly. In saunters Bob, face masked by a bandana like some movie bandito. Wielding a Nerf gun, he swaggers over to my pleasantly confused charges, teenagers clearly not accustomed to having an old prankster in their midst. "Stick 'em up!" says Bob, and laughs and laughs, prompting the same in the kids.

More delightfulness shows up as a truly hilarious side effect of discovering a great way to ease the Bob's neuropathy symptoms, to alleviate the severity of the burning in his legs and feet, by introducing him to the wonders of THC. Marijuana has changed drastically over the past couple of decades, with different strains providing different nuanced effects. With legalization occurring across a growing number of states, so is acceptance that this is not a mere recreational drug, but a plant with plenty of medicinal benefits.

Alcohol having been my preferred poison, I never was a big fan of weed, mostly because when I did experiment with it years ago, each time I invariably confirmed this truth: I am a lousy stoner. I get stupid, slurry, sleepy, tongue-tied. During my time with Peter, though, I took to smoking a little. At first, I resisted when he offered me hits off the joints he smoked throughout the day. My refusal was in large part due to my aforementioned lightweight reaction to the stuff. Also, having quit drinking in my thirties, I wondered if getting high might count as some black mark against my sobriety. Eventually, I loosened up and partook, came to enjoy how it slowed me down. Did I rationalize using marijuana to have a shared interest with Peter or was I simply pursuing a non-addictive means of relaxation? Quite possibly both. Slowly my resistance built and I made up my mind that having a few evening tokes was not a bad thing at all.

Though initially discreet around Bob, I ascertain fairly quickly he has no opposition to my usage. When I mention pot, he does not recoil, lecture, or even seem to care. Instead, he expresses curiosity, and recounts a workday in his youth, when he and some friends drank some of his homemade cherry wine during lunch. Over-fermentation or some other alchemical reaction caused hallucinations. "I kept trying to pull my hand off like a glove," he says, grinning and reenacting that day, holding up his arm, pretending to peel off his palm and fingers.

Armed with the knowledge that at some point in his life he enjoyed mind-altering activities—even if it was just once, inadvertent, and a half-century prior—I half-jokingly leave a joint out on the table for him one day. It disappears. Eventually he reveals he smoked it. And liked it.

His admission leads me to some conversations with a friend who uses THC to control severe chronic pain, an alternative to the opioids big pharma is so fond of getting people hooked on. My friend assures me that Bob, too, will notice positive results if he starts using some form of marijuana regularly. Bob says he's game and so we begin experimenting to figure out the best delivery system for him.

Toking weed does not serve him well, given the COPD he developed after smoking cigarettes for decades, a habit he started at age eight and likes to say he "quit cold turkey during open heart surgery." Edibles are a little too dicey, with the potential for an unpredictably strong hit that could last hours and be accompanied by an uncomfortable sort of paralysis, with a top note of paranoia. An oil pen is relatively to his liking, but still not easy enough on the lungs. Ultimately, we go with capsules, coming up with just the right dosage to ease some of his discomfort without making him too loopy.

A little leery to embark on this adventure when the rubber actually hits the road and I present him with the first batch, he agrees to try when I, gesturing to our supply, say I'll gladly take one for the team. Observing me send a pot pill down the hatch, emboldened he follows suit. Within a half-hour we are both insisting the pills have very little effect. "This Mary Jane ain't doing nothing," Bob says, although a video of our maiden voyage—which thankfully does not exist—might inspire a different opinion in anyone viewing it, as we sit and giggle and giggle, losing our place in the conversation repeatedly, neither of us at first making the connection between our pot pill party and my sudden need to dash off to the kitchen to procure the crunchiest, saltiest snacks I can forage to sate appetites that have sprung up from nowhere.

We're hardly Cheech and Chong, but we do enjoy our happy hours, getting a little evening buzz on, and watching a TV station Bob stumbled on, which seemingly only plays movies featuring either Elvis Presley or Diana Ross. He sits in his La-Z-Boy, leaning back as the burn in his legs and feet quiets. I sit on his bed a couple of feet away, knitting very, very slowly, aware that my altered state makes me more mistake-prone.

Sometimes, we switch channels and indulge in some *Walker Texas Ranger*. Before Bob moved in, though I'd heard of the show, I'd not ever seen it. Nor had I seen Chuck Norris perform in any other capacity. Bob loves Chucky Baby, as he sometimes calls him, loves educating me on Mr. Macho. Walker reruns play back-to-back on Friday nights and we often while away hours watching, buzzed, with Bob providing side-splitting running commentary.

"Chucky looks like he has bad breath," he says one night. He loves how a band of fifteen villains with assault rifles can come charging at Walker who, wielding only a handgun and mad martial arts skills, subdues all of them in mere moments. "Did you ever notice how he kicks the shit out of bad guys all the time and never loses his hat?" he asks.

One night I ask, "Hey Bob, did the credits just say Chuck Norris sings the theme song?" He grins. "If you can call that singing."

My favorite narration comes during an episode with a plot ridiculous even by *Walker* standards, and if you've not ever seen the show, you must take my word that it is never not over the top. This time though, the writers have outdone themselves. Bob, familiar with the episode—I suspect he's seen it at least two hundred times before—perks up during a hyper-dramatic scene and lets loose a spoiler. "No wonder nobody can find Sasquatch," he says. "Chucky already killed him. Now the bear's eating him."

Confused at first, thinking this bit about Sasquatch is a Bob fabrication created to amuse me, I very nearly pee my pants moments later to discover, no, not a joke. Sasquatch really does make a cameo.

The more we watch together, the more hooked on Chucky Baby I become. Add another one to the Father Firsts list then: joyful viewing time together. The only memory I have of watching a movie with my own father was one Christmas Eve as he, prone on the couch, yelled at me about how poorly I was placing tinsel on the tree as *The Bells of St. Mary's* played on the big fake wood console in the corner. In my healing journey, it never would have dawned on me that such a basic thing as TV nights might help my heart. Bob, clever life professor, shows me otherwise.

One night, when we opt for playing stoned checkers over stoned watching *Mahogany* for the twelfth time, or *Walker* for the thousandth, something seems off. Either we have again forgotten to eat, or I have managed to pull from our hidden stash not one but two "supplements" that hold a heavier THC dose than that to which we have grown accustomed. Whatever resistance we have built up is no match for the sudden confusion that engulfs us.

In mere moments we transform from relatively cognizant human beings to space aliens obliterated out of our minds, our once familiar surroundings suddenly having morphed into a strange new planet. We sit across from each other, perched sideways on the edge of his bed, me at the headboard, he at the foot, staring in shared stupor at the checkerboard resting between us, admiring the beautiful pattern of squares. We have forgotten entirely how the game works, looking at the black and white disks for clues, unsure whose turn it is. Comfortably numb is an understatement. We try to speak. We cannot. Nor can we stop giggling.

An urgent need to sleep washes over me. I tell Bob I have to go, but not before I help him to his feet, so he can go to the bathroom, take out his teeth and don his pajamas. I want to monitor him until he is safely beneath the covers because it's all fun and games until a near-ninety-year-old falls on his skinny stoned butt and breaks a hip.

Bob continues to laugh uproariously. "Help me!" he says stretching his arms out. As soon as I grasp his wrists and gently tug him forward, he purposefully transforms himself into rubber and melts backwards toward the mattress, disallowing me to gain purchase. He laughs louder. I can't pull him to his feet. Or rather, he won't let me. Like a little child that never wearies of Peek-a-Boo, again he says, "Help me!" Again he turns to rubber when I try, his laughter now maniacal.

These buzzy times, I take in the picture of us chilling out, cracking each other up. I joke that we should rename the place Pippi Longstocking Ranch, the way we indulge ourselves when the workday is done, acting like children who've been left alone to our own devices, ecstatic that no one is the boss of us, deriving added satisfaction from breaking rules leftover from our past lives: *You shouldn't smoke weed! You shouldn't watch too much TV! You should be using this time productively!*

Bob's antics infuse me with still more healing and, as I heal, I resume being delightful to others, something I had mostly lost the ability to do as back-to-back Peter-fueled depressions and breakup trauma consumed me. No more scowling in the grocery store or ignoring toy-hurling, babbling babies, as I came to do in my despondency. I wake up a little more each day to small joys all around me. Bob watches me emerge with pleasure. He never frames it as such, but sometimes I think my broken heart is the biggest restoration project he has ever undertaken. He seems just fine with that, stripping away my layers of sadness, self-doubt, and self-criticism, leading me slowly, delightfully, back to my happy pre-Peter self.

FUCK IT

F ALL THE LESSONS BOB SHARES WITH ME, maybe the greatest comes with his determination to convince me to be done with the past. One day we are out running errands and I am crying yet again over Peter, messy unceasing tears blurring my vision to the point that probably I should pull over. This crying is accompanied by a repetitive apology to Bob, how sorry I am that he has to see me like this every day, how sorry I am that I can't seem to move past negativity, how sorry I am for not being able to see that being discarded by an abusive drug addict is not exactly a bad thing.

Bob reaches across from his co-pilot seat, pats my leg and says, "You're the strongest woman I know." This, of course, only opens the faucet wider and I cry harder still. But he isn't done yet.

He goes on to say the way he sees my grief is that I am fighting two big battles—ancient childhood trauma and breakup pain, which we both know are tightly intertwined, Peter's oppressive cruelty so closely mirroring my father's constant abuse. Bob urges me to try to just let it all go. "That's past now," he says, a message he often repeats, sometimes emphasizes by hilariously misquoting the Lion King. "Makuna Hatata!" he tells me.

On this day, we are driving to Lowe's to pick up still more supplies for the ranch, our beloved bottomless money pit, our source of never-ending projects. That I am crying every day, thoroughly drained and exhausted, makes no difference. Business doesn't stop even when my heart seems to.

By the time we pull into the parking lot, my Inconsolability Gauge is pushing past ten. I dislike crying in public. I don't really like crying in private. Making a spectacle like this ironically incites more crying still, as I am aware and something like ashamed that my inability to get a grip might well make the strangers around me uncomfortable. They, out just to make a simple purchase, but forced to awkwardly witness a middle-aged woman stumbling through the aisles, unable to control herself.

In the vestibule of the hardware store, we stop so Bob can grab an electric scooter to zip around beside me. I continue to cry. I continue to apologize for crying. "I'm so sorry," I say, leading to a continuation of our call-and-response routine, my apologies repeatedly greeted with Bob's reassurance: "You don't need to be sorry, hon."

I let him in on the secondary source of my weeping. "This is the first time in my life I've been able to hand my broken heart to a parent and have it handled tenderly," I reveal to him.

Now Bob gets a little misty. We hold our places for a few moments, him seated in the scooter moist-eyed, me standing beside him eyes brimming, him reaching for my hand. *Reassurance, reassurance, reassurance.* The thing I craved and was only ever denied by my own father. The thing I craved from Peter and a string of other avoidant men before him, all of them refusing to be present, instead playing the go-away-come-back game, withholding love to maintain the upper hand. Even now, with Peter maintaining mostly radio silence peppered only by the occasional angry phone call or text message, my warped and clouded mind continues to hold out hope that, all evidence of the previous two years to the contrary, he might suddenly reappear, become truly present, and make amends for his awful behavior by showing me with astonishing regularity true, dedicated love.

For someone who claims to aspire to live a Buddhism-inspired life, I admit I suck at the practices of letting go, non-attachment, and accepting impermanence. Maybe that's what draws me to Buddhism—how, on the surface, its philosophy comprises a short list of rather simple tenets. But, of course, these key components are not simple at all. Bob, the living Buddha, nudges me toward at least giving the ideas a go.

When he tells me, as it were, to put the past in my behind, Bob doesn't mean one shouldn't examine one's personal history. He means you can only chew on an old bone for so long before you finally must admit the meat is long gone, and that bone won't magically grow more meat upon which to chew. That striving for solutions to some of life's most infuriating puzzles isn't necessarily going to bear answers, it's just going to make you crazy with grief. Like the proverbial people in Hell craving ice water, I get so stuck wishing to understand things I will never be able to understand. And so, says Bob, *Let it go, Let it go, Let it go.*

I doubt I'll ever achieve fully letting go of the things that haunt me. But having a live-in coach sure helps. With Bob by my side, I am forced to see things from which, alone, I avert my eyes.

One night we attend a fancy cocktail party at the LBJ Library on the campus of the University of Texas. Walking across the immense plaza toward the door, we spot a bunch of students looking preposterous as they partake in one of those exercise boot camps. They are flailing, running hard a few yards to nowhere and back, exerting themselves to exhaustion. The temperature is roughly two hundred degrees. "What's the point?" I ask Bob. He laughs. He has no idea.

Later I tell him those sweaty jumpy kids strike me as a good representation of my mind, running around crazy, pushing and pushing toward some impossible goal that can never be attained. Bob is like their trainer, only instead of pushing me to whip myself into a state of collapse, his job is to teach my mind the importance of resting, rejuvenating, refreshing. Just as the boot camp coach does not coddle his charges, Bob is also capable of cutting to the chase, giving a direct instruction when he can see I'm hitting the wall, not in the headspace to listen to longer and more eloquent advice. These times, he sets aside his common tactic—a loving lecture reminding me that I am strong, beautiful, and worthy of love. Instead, he looks at me crying, knows my heart still is struggling to let go of trying to understand how it was so tricked, to just accept it was tricked, to move on. These moments, Bob speaks but a mere two words.

"Fuck it." he says.

Though I can't do his bidding and just snap out of it, his directness in these moments invites a little laughter, a sort of weight lifting as he trains me to develop strength and stamina for a future he promises me is coming soon, one in which happiness will easily supplant this ocean of tears. *Fuck it*, his words echo in my mind. *Fuck it, fuck it, fuck it.*

SNAKES

T'S BEEN THE SUMMER OF SNAKES, REAL AND METAPHORICAL, actual slithery reptiles in the yard and boa constrictor thoughts squeezing my mind and heart so tight that the pain feels impossible to reckon with some days. I am trying to figure things out from both kinds of snakes. As usual, Bob takes the lead in teaching me.

The real snakes start showing up in early June, just days after Peter leaves me for good. These are not the first snakes I have encountered at the ranch. There was that poor six-foot rattler Peter and his brother obliterated with bullets and shovel blade. Before that, there was another big snake, discovered one night as I set out to lock the chicken coop, whereupon I spotted the thing stretched across the top of the nesting boxes, six chickens perching upon him as if he were a convenient branch put there for that purpose.

Because that coop snake was my first close encounter, the Shit Your Pants adrenaline rush that accompanied seeing him was quite high on the Loose Sphincter Richter Scale. I stood, immobilized, hoping not to spontaneously evacuate my bowels. Then again, though the rest of my body remained paralyzed, given my devotion to social media, my thumb managed to summon enough motion to allow me to take a picture of this freakish tableau, which I immediately posted on Facebook. Even dozens of comments assuring me I was dealing with a non-venomous, quite helpful rat snake did little to allay my hysteria. Not understanding that six chickens versus one snake was a fight with odds heavily favored toward feathers over scales, my superpower of catastrophizing kicked in as I imagined a scene in which that slithery thing would constrict each of my girls, one by one, before unhinging his jaw and swallowing the lot of them whole. Finally, I took the advice of a friend who counseled, "Just go to bed. He'll be gone in the morning."

I forced my frozen legs to move again, abandoned my sentinel's post, wished the hens well, and retreated to my room. Sure enough, the next morning the snake was gone, the girls fine, and I never saw that big black thing again. I did, however, encounter another snake a few days later, watched helplessly as with lightning speed it zipped across the threshold of my door, into my room, and behind my upright piano. I screamed. Then, using this latest adrenaline rush, I pulled the piano away from the wall and, yes, took another snake picture to post on Facebook.

I scrutinized this snake. The snake scrutinized me. In my eyes, it coiled. In my eyes, it was also a good couple of feet long. In the eyes of my neighbor Jesse—whom I called, shrieking, and who showed up a few minutes later, plucked the critter from the corner and held it up between thumb and forefinger—what I really had on my hands was a tiny garter snake. Jesse did his best to not make fun of me, nodding his head when I explained I thought it might be a baby rattler and that I'd heard baby snakes are more dangerous, not having control over their venom the way adult snakes do.

The post-breakup snakes seem different. The first comes into view one evening as I am lugging groceries into the house. I spot him ironically sprawled across the welcome mat, have my usual snake rush—tight stomach, gastrointestinal mayhem, and a weird, confusing combination of simultaneous fight/flight/freeze. I yell. Maybe I poke a stick at him. I can't even remember, such is the memory-marring effect that stumbling across snakes has on my mind. He moves a ways away, off to a shadowy corner. I go inside, drop the groceries on the counter, track down Bob and alert him of our unwelcome visitor just outside the door. Then I grab a bag of Snake-A-Way, a product I'm nearly certain does not act as a genuine deterrent, but rather promotes a slight bit of psychological relief in that it provides an opportunity for action.

Bob is in favor of killing the snake but I suggest we just sprinkle some of the foul-smelling granules around the door and hope for the best. I empty the entire bag, watch the snake retreat, then set out to retrieve the remaining groceries. These I carry inside, turning around to close the door only to discover that our little buddy has returned and is now in the living room. "BOB," I shout. "SNAKE!! *IN. THE. HOUSE!!!*"

Bob, excited and moving a little less slowly than usual, makes it across the kitchen and into the living room in record time. I stand hollering, pointing in the general direction of the snake. "Looky there!" he says, sounding overjoyed. "A sidewinder!"

Sidewinder? I think. Then it hits me. *That means rattlesnake!*

That I manage, yet again, to not actually shit my pants in this moment does, to my mind, count as a miracle worthy of Vatican recognition. How I do succeed, in my panic and excitement, to grab the rake just outside the front door remains a mystery. But suddenly here I stand, wielding the rake, screaming like a banshee.

"We should kill it!" Bob says.

"I don't want to kill it," I protest, all the lessons of all the Buddhist books I've ever read and memories of all the meditation retreats I've ever attended deluging me in an instant. This latest snake might want to kill me, but he is a sentient being and, excepting only mosquitoes—well, okay, and that six-foot rattler I condemned to death, and about which I still carry guilt—I prefer to leave alive all sentient beings, even cockroaches.

"Flip the rug!" cries Bob. I have no clue what his strategy is. I simply obey.

With the little rag rug flipped, the snake disappears beneath it. More screaming on my part, more laughter on Bob's. The snake reappears. I thrash the rake wildly, finally ensnaring him in the tines, hurling him out into the night. This flinging motion is so violent that I wonder if, perhaps, as he is flying through the air, the snake wishes I had just let Bob behead him.

As I tremble and hyperventilate, Bob bursts into such a fit of laughter at my City Girl in the Country naiveté, I worry he might damage internal organs. I grab his hand and pull it to my chest. "Feel my heart!" I demand.

"Damn! It's hammerin'!" he notes, then laughs more, harder still. This laughter goes on for days. We'll be out feeding the horses or sitting down for coffee and, upon making eye contact, he loses control and I know it is because he is remembering my Crazy Snake Rake Dance. I laugh, too.

There are more snake sightings that week, always at the front door. While the actual number of encounters is minimal—two or three—the terror they stir in me is on par with confronting a plague of biblical proportions. I begin wearing my snake boots— the ones that left me feeling a bit Eva Gaborish when I purchased them shortly after moving to the ranch—during all waking hours. Hypervigilance, already my constant state, ratchets up.

Before long, another snake slithers into the house. This one, too, appears to be a sidewinder, though with my paranoia-colored glasses on, even stray bits of yarn popping out of my knitting bag seem to wriggle in S-formation.

"BOB!" I holler. "SNAKE!! *IN. THE. HOUSE!!!!*"

Again, he comes charging into the living room. I point to the overstuffed leather chair. "IT'S UNDER THERE!"

"We're killing this one," he announces.

Cautiously, I push the chair across the floor revealing this latest unwelcome visitor, no more than a foot-and-a-half long, thick only as a kindergartener's starter pencil, backed into a corner. Bob heeds the Call of Death clearly blaring in his ears. Undaunted by the snake's swift bobbing and weaving, he moves in for the kill, landing a judicious blow with the rubber tip of his aluminum cane, finishing the thing off before it can even assume a striking position.

Bob reaches down, pinches the lifeless reptile by the tail, holds it up triumphantly. "Let's feed it to the chickens," he says, pragmatic as ever, like he's just made deviled eggs for a church picnic, not clobbered a rattler to death in the house. The chickens are thrilled at this protein-packed treat, laid gift-like at their feet.

I won't go so far as to say these repeated snake encounters pave the way to full country-life acclimation. I don't suppose I'll ever achieve a state of total non-reactivity upon coming across them. Still, there is a notable shift in my attitude, which I observe when, just a couple of days after the second snake appeared in the living room, I swing the front door open one morning and spot our latest scaly visitor relaxing on the doorstep like some patient, limbless Avon Lady. I stand, coffee in hand. He sneers at me. I glare at him. I do not shriek. I do not holler for Bob to get the shotgun. The bowel-rumbling is negligible. I shut the door, march back into the kitchen in my snake boots, and resume caffeinating as if nothing has happened. Later, I open the door. The snake is gone.

We cannot always keep snakes at bay. A price you pay for country living is learning to make peace with, or at least be mindful of, a variety of critters that, when cornered, are prone toward aggression: snakes, coyotes, feral pigs, scorpions. There are measures to be taken to reduce risk. Snake prevention includes new weather stripping around the entrances and a search around the house foundation for cracks and holes we might fill in to eliminate hiding places. Sharp-bladed garden tools now stand at all doors, should decapitation prove necessary in a truly life-threatening situation. And, as a very last resort, I also have snake shot on hand for my sixteen-gauge, double-barreled shotgun as well as my snub-nosed .22 revolver. And then there are these boots of mine, full leg armor, the perfect accessory for whatever I happen to be wearing—pajamas, work clothes, a dress.

Whether I am fending off a true snake or a mind snake, Bob responds very calmly. This repetitive, steady response teaches me by example how to quiet down the internal hollering that has been my soundtrack for decades. Quieting my mind has the rippling effect of teaching me to quiet my banging heart and quivering bowels in the presence of snakes. I have gone from yelling at the top of my lungs whenever I see one now to stopping, breathing, observing, and making a decision what to do. Which, as I learned, can often be as simple as closing the door and waiting for danger to recede.

Observe but don't react. This has been the challenge of a lifetime for me, a world class reactor. I apply myself diligently—through therapy, silent retreats, and a twenty-year meditation practice—to try to understand what non-reaction is, how it works, how to attain it. Still I react. I react all the time. I react loudly. I react irrationally. I react not just to the actual threat of a rattlesnake in our midst, but to imagined threats when the mind snakes take over. Living with Bob is like wearing heavy boots when it comes to these metaphorical snakes trying to devour me. He is my secret weapon, showing by example how to observe, breathe, and only then choose the proper course of action. Sometimes the snake lives. Sometimes the snake dies. But always, as I am oh-so-slowly learning, the best way to deal with snakes of any sort is to take Bob's approach, quit the hollering and flailing, and make a better plan.

TINY

THE FIRST TIME I VISITED THE RANCH TO SEE IF IT was worth buying, I found a lone occupant on the property, a mighty Palomino horse, skittish to understate the matter, grazing off in the distance. I immediately dubbed him Tiny. During pre-bid inspections, for ten long days I met with various contractors: plumber, electrician, foundation engineer, septic installer. During this time, Tiny allowed me to approach him now and again, but always ran off quickly. His left eye seemed to be gone, leading to speculation that he'd lost it to a cactus or mesquite thorn. I have always been afraid of horses, but Tiny's beauty drew me in as did his underdog status. Surely, he was lonely out here all by himself. Who would just abandon him with no food or water, save for a shallow pond that had been sucked dry to mere muck by years of drought?

When we did put in a bid, I held out hope that Tiny would convey with the property and become part of the dream, that I might nurse him back to health and that together we would surmount our fear of each other. This was not to be. The so-called owner of the horse, a relative of the ranch's owners, perhaps falsely believing I had money to burn, put a steep price on Tiny's head, communicating his verbal ransom note through the realtor.

On the one hand, I felt pulled to pony up the dough. Tiny did bestow a nice visual touch upon the place. More importantly, I dreamed of trying to make up to him whatever he suffered out here on his own. I could have given in to my impulsive tendencies and squeezed the money from somewhere. But I had my reservations, too, and so instead let commonsense prevail when an acquaintance with horse knowledge pointed out that Tiny might have other medical issues in addition to his eye injury, and that my lack of horse experience presented a real problem. I refused the seller, lamenting when the horse was taken away shortly before I moved in.

This turned out not to be the end of the Tiny Tale however. He didn't go very far at all, finding a new home among the horses living next door. I still got to see him every day, albeit through a fence.

Not a year after Tiny's departure, the neighbor calls to say he is moving. If I want the horse, he is mine for the taking, as is another, Queenie. This time I let impulsivity rule, my enthusiastic *yes* fortified by my neighbor's promise that horse care really is no trouble at all.

The hand-off happens a few days before Bob turns eighty-eight, his second birthday at the ranch. This I use as an opportunity to be delightful, informing him that the horses are his birthday gift. My neighbor walks them over on leads, and as this little parade comes down the long driveway, Bob lights up, aptly enough like an octogenarian's birthday cake. It might as well be his eighth birthday. He approaches our newest bridled family members with an unbridled joy so palpable that any worries I have regarding my horse ignorance vanish in an instant. Never mind that Queenie is, according to our neighbor, thirty-six, about the equivalent of ten thousand years for a horse. (Later, our vet will guess she's closer to twenty, but we nonetheless hold tightly the myth that we have on our hands the Equine Methuselah.) Never mind that Tiny's eye socket is oozing. At least Bob has horse knowledge. We will figure out what to do next together. In this moment, we just celebrate.

For a few weeks, we extend our Pippi Longstocking lifestyle to the horses. Just as Bob and I do whatever we wish, so we spoil them with sugar cubes and apples nearly every day. This leads to the horses training us, though I do not understand what is happening at first. Allowed out of their enclosed pasture to wander the front acreage whenever we do not have rental guests, Tiny and Queenie take to hanging out by the front door often, having quickly picked up that my response, upon finding them waiting, is to reward them with sweets.

Eventually, a young farrier informs us that these pasture pets, as he calls the horses since we never ride them, are going to succumb to diabetes if we don't knock it off with the sugar routine. He also explains that Tiny's injured eye needs immediate medical attention, that it is an open wound that could prove deadly. I take his admonitions seriously and put away the sugar cubes, unintentionally setting the course for some very expensive personal lessons.

The country vet visits a week later and, without hesitation, announces Tiny has eye cancer. So, Tiny hasn't lost an eye to a sharp thorn after all. This news dismays me. The cancer has been in him for more than a year, may have spread, and might imminently kill him. The vet, more optimistic, explains that he can do surgery to remove what is left of the eye, and hopefully all the cancer cells with it. For this to happen first we must convince Tiny to allow himself to be haltered so that he can be held and anesthetized. Though Tiny made his return to the ranch on a lead and is not unfamiliar with being haltered, since we have let him wander around freely for months, he now has no interest in being restrained. I set out to find a trainer to help us.

During this quest, before I find a true horse whisperer who will help me understand the magnitude of my ignorance, I open the front door one afternoon and find Tiny standing at the threshold, still holding out hope that the sugar cube ritual might resume should he persist. What some might see as bad boundary setting on my part, I find to be hilarious. *LOOK! A HORSE AT THE DOOR! HAHAHAHAHA!*

Whereas once I was scared of Tiny, by now I have grown more comfortable around him, thanks to Bob teaching me how to approach the horses, feed them, respect them. Now I can, with growing confidence, reach up to scratch Tiny's giant nose, pat his huge head, and sometimes even move in to hug his neck. In his developing familiarity with me, Tiny has become quite receptive to these gestures. Occasionally he startles, as do I, but our friendship moves along at a steady clip. So, I am in no way prepared when, on this day, as I go from nose pat to neck caress, Tiny, with no warning, clamps down on my collarbone. I do not just feel the crunch, I hear it.

Even after he releases me from his bear-trap grip and pulls back, and I retreat inside and slam the door between us, I can still feel those teeth against my bones. So exquisite is the pain of the colossal jaws of an animal ten times my size seizing my shoulder, I literally go into shock. Like a little child fallen on the playground, seeking consolation from any nearby adult, I wander in a daze down the long hall to find Bob in his room readying for a nap.

"Tiny bit me," I announce, pulling back my t-shirt collar to reveal an already ferocious dark purple bruise in the outline of Tiny's upper teeth. "I don't think it's broken," I say, more hopeful than convinced, the excruciating pain ripping through me still, second only to the pain I bore during a seventeen-hour, drug-free childbirth.

Bob brings his Midwestern sensibility to this moment. He consoles me without escalating my alarm. We concur no bones seem to be broken. He says there's tissue damage and it's going to hurt for a while. Neither one of us is interested in a trip to the hospital. I urge him to nap. Returning to the living room, I sit on the couch and try to think. *Maybe it is fractured? Maybe I do need to go to the emergency room? The skin doesn't seem to be broken, but surely, I should wash it thoroughly just in case? And ice. I need to ice it.*

After contemplating these options, instead of pursuing any of them, I stand up and begin pacing around the house. I resume dusting, which I had begun earlier, and this act further verifies that I am in shock, since I have dusted about six times total in fifty years, and if I were in my right mind, would seize this very reasonable excuse to just let the dusting go. I observe that some part of me wants to shoot Tiny and then further observe this is a crazy desire, fed by anger incited by pain, and that of course I do not really want to hurt this horse I have grown to love.

I post a picture of the angry, swollen, red and purple bite mark on Facebook, prompting a torrent of unsolicited advice, consolation, and disbelief. Many comment that I should have punched Tiny in the face to show him who is boss. Besides the fact that I don't believe in being violent with animals to "teach them a lesson" (my earlier fleeting thought of putting a bullet in his head notwithstanding), I will say that, at least for me, when you are standing face-to-face with a force that could effortlessly kill you, the flight response kicks in quickly. Fighting back in the moment never even crossed my mind.

One friend who sees my post, a country neighbor, insists I allow her to come by to make sure there are no broken bones. I resist this offer once, twice, three times, maybe four. Finally, though, her persistence wears me down and I allow her to come by to check on me and treat me with an array of homeopathic potions—arnica, Rescue Remedy, magical salves. She performs Reiki. She applies ice. She confirms the bones are intact. After she leaves I accept more consolation from Bob, up from his nap, who again delivers the verdict that I will survive.

With this promise, I retreat to my room where I have some remedies of my own, remnants of Peter, a stash of intoxicants to help him float through his weekends at the ranch. I fish out some Kratom he's left behind, a head shop staple made from the leaves of a plant grown in Thailand, said to have properties similar to those of Vicodin. I wash down several capsules and follow up with a few hits off a joint. Finally, I sit in my bed, stoned, wiped out, shoulder throbbing, hoping for sleep to descend.

This is not to be. My phone rings. Peter's brother Scott's name appears on the screen. The breakup is just a few days old and talking to him will only upset me further. But my rational thought that I should let the call go to voicemail is muffled by my shock and my stupor. I answer. We ramble for a spell, he, too, obviously high on something, probably heroin, his drug of choice.

I whine to Scott about the breakup, about how I am destroyed beyond repair by his brother. I share these thoughts because they are true, and also knowing Scott will relay to Peter that I have been seriously injured physically and am in great emotional distress, too, magnified now by the pity party I whip up for myself recalling the many times I nursed Peter back to health, spent so much time in hospitals with him, and now, in my time of need, where the hell is he?

As the conversation wears on, I hear voices outside of my window. This causes confusion. The ranch house sits up a ways from the road, behind a closed gate, it is late at night, I am expecting no one. I tell myself I am being paranoid. The voices continue. I ask Scott to hold on, peer out into the darkness, and spot flashing lights, further scrutiny revealing these to be atop an ambulance parked just a few yards from where Tiny sunk his choppers into me earlier. Hastily, I release Scott from the conversation, stumble to the front door to investigate, my immediate thought being that my friend has decided I am more injured than I will admit, and that she has called paramedics to take me to the hospital. Preposterous theory, yes. But how else to explain the commotion in the front yard?

I step out into the dark night and find my friend, walking unsteadily, feet bare and bleeding, flanked by a pair of EMTs, the three of them accompanied by my friend's little dog. More confusion. *What the hell is going on here?*

Into the house we all traipse. Slowly the facts reveal themselves. Upon leaving me, my friend, turning onto a busy highway, had been T-boned by a speeding car. Her car spun and then rolled, then rolled again, eventually landing on its side. With much effort, she managed to climb a slim aluminum rescue ladder extended to her, slicing up her feet as she emerged, her shoes and phone disappearing into the ether during all that rolling. This is the reason for her second visit. With no phone numbers memorized and thus, unable to call anyone, but needing a place to stash the dog before being transported to the hospital, she had convinced the kind emergency workers to first bring her back to the ranch.

All of this unfolds in a fantastically chaotic style, giving me much insight and appreciation for the fact that paramedics have far more to deal with than physical injuries. My friend and I babble on and on as she wolfs down some arnica, freaking out her caretakers, they not knowing what she is putting into her system. "It's fine," she reassures them, and when they press for specifics, she brushes away their concern both for her well-being and the possibility of having their asses handed to them for allowing their charge to ingest a mystery substance. "It's magic," she announces, as if this will appease them.

We tell them over and over about my horse bite. They tell us over and over they have already heard about my horse bite, that this is about a car accident now, and to wrap up the conversation, no time to waste. They ask if I might follow them and drive her back home once she is released. With a major surge of adrenaline coursing through me for the second time in just a few hours, I have momentarily forgotten I am quite stoned. Still, my mind sends a continuous signal that I am not fit to drive, even if temporary amnesia will not allow me to access the reason why.

Finally, it dawns on me that I am under the influence. Without revealing this, I decline their request, claiming exhaustion as my excuse. I do take the dog. With this sorted, the trio exits, the ambulance pulls away.

It takes about a week before the intensity of that horse bite recedes, the brilliantly hued bruise finally fading, leaving only a small scar where Tiny's teeth sunk in deepest. My friend recovers relatively quickly, too. Still I am left with the challenge of convincing Tiny to use a halter, this task now made more difficult because of my newfound terror in his presence, and by the dismay this terror causes me. I can't fake tranquility around him, because he will still smell my fear. I must figure out how to be his friend again if we are to condition him for surgery. The prospect exhausts me, and I am already so exhausted trying to deal with my unending emotional torment.

Bob stands by me, watching my actions and reactions, coaxing me to follow him, my human North Star, to a place he swears I will get to, a place I try at least half-heartedly to believe exists, a place called Happy Again. We talk about Tiny, the need to find help to train him. On the bright side, this brings some variation to our morning conversations, so often focused on my broken heart.

Before too long, I inform Bob that I have at last weeded through a mountain of referrals and have finally come up with a possible solution for Tiny's stubborn halter refusal. When I lay out this plan, Bob scoffs. When, at first, I implement it, I am surprised to see a side of him I would never have guessed existed, had I not witnessed it myself.

TINY - PART II

SEVERAL FOLKS SUGGEST INSTALLING A GATE TO the open two-stall barn, to keep Tiny in close enough quarters to be sedated for surgery. Two different fence makers, however, warn of the foolishness of this plan. The barn, more of a lean-to, exists to provide shelter from thunderstorms and shade from the blinding Texas summer sun. The walls are thin plywood. The term *horsepower* obviously has its origins in equine strength, and Tiny's horsepower is Herculean, with the potential to be deadly. We fast determine that, given his feral tendencies, he might thrash upon being injected with a sedative, experience an adrenaline rush great enough to put a hoof or two through a gate or wall, injuring himself, and quite possibly, any humans unfortunate enough to be nearby.

Several horse lovers volunteer to work with him, but they're all amateurs and we need a professional trainer. This forces me to admit that the cavalier attitude I exhibited when I invited Tiny back to live at the ranch, the idea that horse ownership couldn't be that hard or expensive, is dead wrong. The price the vet names for surgery isn't outrageous, nor is the standard hourly trainer's fee. But the number of hours potentially required to tame him, along with any unforeseen expensive complications that might arise post-surgery, give me pause. I have no idea how I will pay for all of this.

Fortunately, a solution comes quickly, when a band of writers I have performed publicly with over the years offers to stage a one-night revival of our popular show, *The Dick Monologues*, with all proceeds going to the cause. The tickets sell out quickly, filling the Tiny Medical Fund coffers, leaving me to switch my focus to locating the right trainer. Now my ignorance trips me up. If I know nothing of horses, how will I be able to tell a good trainer from a poor one?

A neighbor strongly recommends her friend Rachel, and so I begin an email exchange. Her no-nonsense tone leaves me a little edgy, not because I shy from bluntness but because I intuit that, like me, Rachel might be stubborn, which though relatable, might also cause problems if our respective stubborn styles do not mesh. Rachel lays out her terms with no uncertainty. She will meet Tiny and, if she believes she can help him, I absolutely must commit to not letting anyone else interfere or work with him in any way other than her established protocol, which involves positive reinforcement only.

I'm a fan of positive reinforcement so no issue there. But despite her straightforwardness, I am a bit fuzzy about what I perceive to be apprehension on her part. Why would she even think I would bring in a second trainer? The idea makes no sense. Is she a control freak? And if so, will this cause a bout of wild defensiveness on my part and send the entire plan to Hell?

Rachel shows up for the initial consult accompanied by Lil, her enthusiastic teenage assistant. The horses are fenced in that day and keep their distance. As she is in her messages, so Rachel is in person. We stand together, alternately calling for the horses and exchanging information, Lil beside us listening in, Bob behind us sitting in his golf cart. I emphasize repeatedly my ignorance, this self-deprecation offered both because it is the truth and also to inspire Rachel to like me, to make it plain I will defer to her. That people-pleasing thing once again a form of armor.

This is when Bob, to my absolute surprise and concern, reveals an unfamiliar side. My eternally agreeable, oft-grin-ning, surrogate father now frowns when I look back to gauge his opinion of the conversation. Clearly rooted in skepticism, his attitude is borderline angry garnished with a dollop of *Scram,* seemingly being beamed from his mind to Rachel's. I suck in my breath, consumed by an echo of that prominent childhood sense that something is wrong, that this discernible tension might easily give way to an explosion, and most importantly that it falls to me to fix things pronto.

Courtesy of years of therapy, I am working to nurture The Observer, an inner entity whose job it is to just take in what is happening before choosing to do (or not do) something about uncomfortable emotions. The Observer notes I am internally wincing at the threat of conflict between Rachel and Bob. The Observer notes a desire to magically make everyone like each other, if not to the point of a group hug, at least to the place of tension dispersed. The Observer helps to keep me from letting loose a verbal blurt of insecurity and agitation mixed in with pleas for everyone to get along. Instead, I just stand there, feeling this weird energy between Rachel and Bob mounting, wanting it to go away, wanting myself to just go away. I tell myself with as much firmness as I can muster that it is not my job to sort out this impending locking of horns, that they are adults, and to just let the moment unfold.

"What are you doing?" Bob asks suspiciously.

Rachel says, "Did you ever use positive reinforcement to train a dog?"

"No," Bob replies, gruffly.

"Well," Rachel says, trying again. "Did you ever have a job that paid money?"

"That's a stupid question," Bob snarls.

I understand she is just looking for an analogy to explain the reward system she intends to use to coax Tiny into compliance. I also understand Bob finds her words and tone condescending.

Somehow, we ease away from the brewing argument and Rachel and Lil explain how, using a feather duster, a clicker typically used to train dogs, and a fanny pack full of alfalfa pellets, they can teach me to teach Tiny desired behavioral changes. My homework is to gather the necessary supplies for our next meeting. Bob just looks on, unconvinced.

After this session, I walk the trainers back over to Rachel's truck and choose my words carefully. I explain that it is not my job to apologize for Bob's crankiness, but that I am surprised by it, and I hope they aren't put off. I feel guilty saying this, like I am betraying my best friend. Really, I'm still inhabiting a younger, scared version of myself, afraid if I can't establish peace then Tiny will never be trained, surgery will never happen, and he will die an untimely death. Well, all that and, let me be honest, my own argumentative streak notwithstanding, I cannot bear it when others fight.

Rachel uses the opportunity to explain that *this*—meaning Bob's incredulity—is what she meant by requiring no one must interfere with training, that she's met plenty of good old boy farmers in her day, and that they are, if I might loosely paraphrase, a pain in her ass.

It doesn't take long to realize the true problem though. Rachel worries that Bob, courtesy of his age and Midwestern roots, is an old-schooler who thinks the only way to tame a horse is to "break" it. In fact, Bob's aggravation goes beyond his doubt of her technique and the possibility that I might well throwing a small fortune down the drain. He is so attached to the horses, Tiny especially, that he worries that somehow Tiny will be hurt—not necessarily physically but perhaps emotionally—by working with this woman who, it is obvious, Bob thinks is very unusual and possibly a charlatan.

Though Bob's misgivings persist through the first few sessions, his umbrage eventually gives way to more of a light-hearted eye-rolling the more he observes Rachel at work. To our amazement, Tiny loves training and responds enthusiastically.

Every time Rachel and Lil visit, they go over the steps with me again. I take a Swiffer duster, to which I have duct taped the clicker to the handle, and reach through the gate with it. Tiny, a fast learner, immediately touches his nose to the fluffy end, at which point I click the clicker, pull the duster away from his nose, commend his brilliance, and swiftly hold out a flat palm full of alfalfa pellets to reward him. Over and over and over. Reach, touch, click, pull away, treat. Once every few clicks, I glance back at Bob. Before too long he is grinning, his develop-ing trust in Rachel mirroring Tiny's growing trust in me.

We practice this ourselves, too, in between visits from Rachel and Lil, both of us astonished at how Tiny obviously knows what he is doing, that the repeated nose-to-duster contact is no coincidence. Even before Rachel gives us the official greenlight, like eager children we begin incorporating the halter into this training, holding it closer and closer to him, alongside the duster at first, and then by itself. He does not shy away. He touches his nose to the halter. I click, withdraw the halter, heap on the praise, then offer a treat. He is eager to try again.

One day, for the entertainment of our Facebook friends who love updates on the ranch, especially those involving Bob, I con-vince him to be in a little video with me. As a friend records us, we stand in the kitchen, Bob on one side of the island counter, me on the other, Swiffer in hand, a bowl of cherries between us. The result is pure comedy genius, me explaining that I am the trainer and Bob is the horse, Bob stomping his foot hoof-like, before bending in to touch his nose to the duster, me then click-ing my approval and rewarding him with a cherry, a process we repeat several times, unable to control our laughter.

Despite his initial skepticism about this technique, the thing is, Bob has employed a similar tactic with me ever since he got here, and even more so since Peter walked out. Every single day he works to get me to focus on the positive. When I manage to shift into a less miserable gear, he rewards me with his infectious giggles.

One morning when, yet again, I wake up crying, which quickly escalates to bawling my eyes out, Bob listens, reminds me I am going to live through this, and coaxes me to be more positive. That day our chat is about the insanity of having a body that contains a mind and a heart that are fist-fighting constantly—the logical, data-collecting brain that understands the breakup is for the best duking it out with a tear-drunk heart that keeps yelling, *No, wait... this is all wrong. I have to get him back.*

Bob never says—as he really would be rightfully entitled to at this point, nearly two months into my nonstop crying jag, no seeming end to my whining—"Shut the fuck up and quit ruining my breakfast with the sobbing." He just goes over the facts for the ten millionth time: *It will get better. It sucks now. He shit all over you. He is a fuckface. You are so much better off without him. You deserve respect.*

A slower learner than Tiny, still, I keep aiming my heart to touch the target of the truth that Bob holds out, eager to hear the click, frustrated at how often my heart misses the mark, fails to connect with the import of his words. But my Bob is a Benevolent Bob, the most patient trainer alive, and he dedicates himself to seeing me through the process, until I can still myself enough to halter my emotions and allow him, with his kindness, to excise the tumors of grief from my heart.

HUGS

EXPEND A GOOD AMOUNT OF TIME AND ENERGY TENACIOUSLY heaping shit and guilt on myself for being so constantly down, especially in light of all I have. I know, I know— grief is an equal opportunity asshole that doesn't care how much you do or don't have. Grief takes down the rich and poor alike, the healthy and the sick alike, optimists and pessimists alike. Humans suffer—it's what we do. Inescapable. Even with this knowledge, even having scrutinized the ravages of grief many times both up close in my own life and from a few paces back watching others suffer, even understanding grief is unavoidable, still I find it frustrating, when grief is crashing over me now, to inventory all that my life holds, and not find a way to let gratitude outweigh sorrow.

At least, even though I am not experiencing gratitude on a cellular level, I can sometimes muster a bit of fake-it-til-I-make-it determination, force myself to engage in an imitation of optimism, try to make myself believe this will help eventually rebuild my crumbled psychic foundation. Bob is right by my side, an emotional structural engineering genius, helping me heal from the ground up.

Just as his shed contains an innumerable variety of specialty tools, so does his arsenal of love. He knows, like all good builders, there are very basic instruments to first to be employed, that you don't need a jackhammer to do the job of a flathead screwdriver. Bob's Basic Love Kit includes encouraging words, mischievous laughter, and plenty of hand squeezes and hugs. These may seem obvious choices, and those who have not been severely traumatized might find them also to be abundant and ubiquitous in everyday life. Not the case with me. Growing up starved for even the tiniest tidbit of security, I was brainwashed into believing love to be ever elusive, or, more accurately, not knowing the true meaning of love.

My family did not touch one another or speak affectionately. No hugs. No *I love you's*. Plenty of criticism. Plenty of prognostication that I was going to Hell and that a punishing God was out to get me. No matter what level of success I achieved (and, arguably, the list is long), the lingering effects of such early conditioning include that ever-present inner voice constantly chastising me: *Don't ever forget, you're just a piece of crap*.

In my thirties, when my friends Jill and Kathie teased me about my poor hugging skills, noting that at best I only used one arm, and that one arm only tentatively, never a full on, two-armed wraparound, I responded defensively, even though I knew they were not being mean-spirited. I also felt challenged to ramp up my hugging skills. With practice, I improved over time. I became a decent hugger, at times embracing total strangers upon pleasant interactions.

When Bob first came to the ranch, for weeks I greeted him verbally and chatted with him cheerfully, almost always staying on the surface. Hugs were only occasional, and it took quite a while before I could say, "I love you," even though I came to love him very quickly. Surely this hesitation to demonstrate affection harkened back to my own father, how the only memory of physical contact with him I could conjure was an elbow squeeze he gave me the day I flew away to college and, a couple of years before that, the time he hit me in the face when I came home drunk one night.

Every now and again during our early months together, perhaps once every ten days or so, I leaned down after saying goodnight to Bob, seated in his recliner, and gave one of those half-hugs I once relied on before learning the art of full embrace.

Time passed and a shift occurred as it dawned on me that I was allowed to hug him as often as I wished. With this revelation, we added daily hugs to our growing repertoire of affection.

These Bob hugs eventually come to transcend mere fondness when, Post-Peter, the reticence of my younger days rears its head, a weird physical manifestation of being deviously duped by a man I once allowed to hold me so tightly. Now I am allergic to nearly all touch, literally pull back from anyone who is not in my very closest circle. Even my most trusted friends take to asking permission before embracing me. When I agree, inwardly I still recoil, this whole mess made sadder by the fact that I desperately wish to be held like a baby. Bob is the one exception to my new phobia, the one who never needs permission to wrap his arms around me, the one I seek out for comforting hugs. More love medicine.

I move up another level in the video game of Father Daughter Love when it dawns on me that I can say to Bob *I love you* not only every day, but multiple times each day if I desire, and that this sentiment will be returned with enthusiasm. With this established, I next dare myself to practice calling Bob *Pop*, which is what Ellen and her brothers call him. It is a next step toward accepting him as my new father, my real father, not just a surrogate.

When, at first, I try out the term, I pull back. The word *Pop* feels thorny and complicated in my mouth. Though he is the best father I could hope for, the entire concept of *father* is so fraught that I remain afraid of the very thing I have both most lacked and desired my whole life, that which eluded me more than any other thing, which literally showed up on my doorstep after five decades of alternately wishing for it and giving up on wishing for it: a loving paternal figure. In my experience, names are tricky things. Very few people call me by my birth name, given by my father, because that name, though beautiful, is so upsetting to my ears, not a gift at all, but an agonizing burden, a reminder that whenever I heard it spoken as a child, I knew it was time for another dressing down. Can I teach myself to say *Pop* with ease, and hear it not as an alternative to *Daddy*, the word I most loathe in the English language? Turns out, yes, I can, but only after much practice.

There is another obstacle to getting comfortable with calling Bob *Pop*. Ellen might think me proprietary, that I am failing to honor that, no matter how close I get to Bob, he will always be her true father and not mine. This inspires a shyness in me, any desire to ask her about it tamped down by expecting that she might say something like, *"What? Are you fucking crazy? He is MY POP. He is NOT YOUR POP."*

This fear, not surprisingly, turns out to be unwarranted. Ellen puts me at ease immediately when at long last I find a way, nervously, to broach the topic. Like her father, Ellen has a giant, generous heart. Her parents created a magical, safe, second-family environment for many of their children's friends when they were growing up. Even in adulthood Ellen has many friends who turn to Bob as a substitute father. She assures me she is more than fine to have yet another friend share the Love of Pop. This provides the added benefit of observing how often so many of my fears are unfounded, and that asking for what I truly want brings me that very thing. With her blessing, I exhale. "Pop," I now call across the house when I am looking for him.

Pop. Pop. Pop. I say it all the time now. It feels so good. He makes a switch, too. "Right here, Hon," he says. "I love you, Hon." *Hon. Hon. Hon.* He says this all the time. I am fluent, at last, in the language of father-daughter love.

ADAPTATION

HENEVER WE HAVE RENTAL GUESTS in the main part of the house, Pop moves over from his regular bedroom, aka The Bridal Suite, into a tiny space next to mine, a place we jokingly refer to as The Crazy Uncle in the Attic Room. He never complains about these much closer quarters or having to share with me a bathroom that has no door, just a thin shower curtain hung wall-to-wall, that does nothing to muffle the sounds and smells of our daily constitutionals.

The more bookings we take on as business picks up, the more time Bob lives on my side of the building. In the early days of our cohabitation, this means he has to use my claw foot bathtub, a very expensive purchase made right after I sold my house in Austin and was living under the temporary and extremely false delusion that I had infinite sums of money at my disposal. Egged on by my lunatic first contractor, I chose a high-end model, envisioning long bubble baths becoming a daily luxury, never mind that running a ranch barely leaves times for a five-minute shower even on a slow day.

Eventually, this tub comes to represent not only financial wastefulness, but a terrible Peter memory, one of his cruelest moments, which occurred during one of the lowest points of our first year together, when his increasingly failing health rendered him incapable of walking across a room without the serious risk of falling. One night, as I prepared to take a bath, he asked to join me. This surprised me, as co-bathing held the promise of physical intimacy, and by now Peter had nearly no interest in anything of the sort, which I attributed to how sick he was. Hopeful that this surprise request meant we might be at a turning point, I helped him to the bathroom and into the tub.

The very next day was when he blurted out that when he thought about sex, he did not think of me, that he wanted a girlfriend who excited him, and that was not me. Shocked, sickened as I tried to process what he was saying, I demanded to know, if he was so turned off by me, why he had suggested the bath. To which he replied it was simply because he did not have the capacity to bathe himself. The tub never looked the same after that.

The bright side to this bad association is that any attachment I hold for the tub diminishes greatly. And since Bob can't safely navigate getting into or out of it, this waning attachment allows me to easily make the decision to get rid of it. We need something more practical, a shower with grab bars. I post on Facebook my plan to make this switch. Really, I am just seeking a buyer for the tub, but wind up with a steady round of virtual applause for what others perceive to be a selfless sacrifice in the name of Bob. Honestly, I love showers, and I especially love the idea of not having to look at that stupid Peter-tainted tub anymore. Not so selfless then.

The ripple effect of my action continues. I enlist my friend, neighbor, and plumber, Charlie, to come up with the cheapest solution for shower installation. Charlie delivers, not just getting the job done well and fast, but also keeping to my tight—okay, nearly non-existent—budget. As he works I can see that this project is not just another gig for him. He has grown very fond of Bob, and reminds us often that anytime we need help with anything, we are to call him. Charlie isn't the only one. This is the magic of Bob. Everyone who meets him sincerely wants to help us out, not because Pop is an old man, but because, like me, they enjoy basking in his zest for life.

Even selling the tub turns into a lovely event, when a young couple with three little kids napping in the back of their monster pickup truck pulls up, inspects it approvingly, and doesn't try to haggle. They gladly hand over the full asking price in crisp hundred-dollar bills. It's like we are all in on this tub-centric adventure together, every one of us benefiting greatly.

Which is very much how the acquisition of the tiny heater goes down one terribly cold winter night, when the main house is filled with a bunch of well-padded renters from Michigan. Bob and I both prefer hot weather, and the outside temperature, hovering at freezing, is unbearable to us. For the Michigan folks, though, it feels like the peak of summer. They crank down the a/c to subarctic. I nearly expect to find frost inside of the windows.

I suffer less than Bob with this conversion of our home to a meat locker, since I enjoy the great fortune of a mini-split climate control system in my room, separate from the unit that heats and cools the rest of the house. The Crazy Uncle in the Attic Room is at the mercy of the main system. I arrive home late from teaching in the city, exhausted beyond exhausted, and find Bob shivering like The Little Match Girl, no quantity of blankets sufficient to fight off the frigid blast shooting from the vent in his ceiling.

My first thought is that I will go out the next morning and track him down a space heater. But, not ten minutes after kicking off my boots and trying to settle in, guilt overtakes me. I cannot let him go through the night too cold to sleep. I drag my weary ass back up, re-boot my feet, and set back out into the night, to the Home Depot twenty miles down the road, arriving just before closing time. Due to the cold snap, there are no heaters to be found, but I do that magical thinking thing I do, staring at the shelves, not blinking, willing a heater to appear. This technique rarely yields desired results, but tonight the magic works. There, up on a top shelf, pushed back nearly out of view, I spot an out-of-box model that has been used for display or returned without its packaging.

I track down an orange-vested clerk and ask if I might purchase this Holy Grail, grateful for his affirmative answer. I look at the price tag: $109. My bank account is empty, a state my bank account is almost always in since I first opened a bank account, a state that running the ranch keeps it in. I have, as in an O. Henry story, exactly $109 available on my mostly maxed out Home Depot card. I head to the register hoping for a second miracle, that taxes won't push the price to the point of the transaction being declined.

The cashier greets me, and I return his hello, blurting out a long, long story. About my roommate Bob. About his age. About his inability to ever be warm. About the big group of big people from Michigan, with all their built-in personal insulation, and their thermostat-dropping antics. I explain that with just $109 in my account, I'm afraid the sale won't go through. The cashier immediately connects with my story, assuring me I have enough. With this, he winks slyly. Ah! We are in cahoots.

His first attempt to push through the sale kicks back the dreaded *Transaction Declined* message. His second attempt, conducted with an on-the-spot custom discount he creates, does the trick. Before he finalizes the sale, he asks, "Would you like the extended warranty?" I look at him, confused. He knows I don't have enough for any extras. He gives a little knowing nod. "You do want it!" he announces, adding in the warranty at no extra cost.

Mission accomplished, I drive the heater home and wrestle it into the house. Bob, huddled in blankets, looks at the heater. Disbelief registers on his face, followed by a big grin. He says it is the best gift he ever received.

The heater comes with an added bonus: a tremendous laugh factor. This is no ordinary space heater. Fashioned of pressed wood, it is designed to resemble a fireplace, fake orange flames flickering as an electric coil emits heat. It's one of the most comical things I have ever seen. Bob uses it all the time. Even in summer he cranks it up, whenever he is relegated to the Crazy Uncle in the Attic Room while a gaggle of wedding guests runs the a/c like they are doing cryogenics experiments and not merely trying to keep a bride from sweating as she steps into her gown.

The heater also doubles as a dining room table for us, one upon which we have shared many tomato sandwiches and more than a few games of checkers. There is no tangible symbol of the love and warmth between us any greater than our kooky little heater, the one that makes us giggle every single time we sit and stare together at those silly flames.

OF VAMPIRES & LESBIAN WEDDINGS

EVEN BEFORE THE RANCH REMODEL WAS COMPLETED, and long before Bob arrived and tamed the lawn, I began renting the house to short-term guests. Shortly after I started running listings on vacation rental sites, I received a message from Bryan, who said he belonged to a group that held monthly murder mystery dinners and they were scouting new locations. After a brief email exchange, we set up a tour. He arrived with several friends on a blistering summer day and, after showing them the interior of the house, we headed out to look at the reception hall and chapel. Of the latter I said, "It looks like a church, but it's secular. I don't care if you do Satanic rituals in there."

I wondered if, subconsciously, I was testing my potential renters, making unambiguous my stance on religion so that if they were uptight zealots they'd be on their way. Perhaps not the best business strategy, and I really was in no position to turn away any potential income at that point. Still, in my big picture dreams, I hoped to only attract laidback renters.

As the words *Satanic rituals* left my mouth, Bryan and his friends perked up. We ambled over to the chapel, which has no electricity and thus no air conditioning, and sat on pews in the sweltering heat. This is when Bryan revealed the true nature of his group. "We're vampires," he said, going on to describe the subculture of Live Action Role Playing, or LARP-ing, apparently very popular in the Austin area. They explained they hadn't mentioned this sooner because they sometimes ran up against resistance when scoping out prospective locales for their vampire games. They assured me they had no intention of engaging in actual satanic rituals, but that my joke had put them at ease enough to be more forthcoming about their plans.

By the end of our sweat-drenched conversation, we were all beaming like kids drunk on Kool-Aid. We enthused collectively that this was going to be an excellent fit. The first weekend they transmogrified the ranch into a vampire playground. The event went great and they rented again the next month. Soon, they were using the ranch once each month, pre-paying several months in advance. In return, I gave them a generous discount, grateful for their early adopter patronage. This is an arrangement that carries on to this day. Whenever I tell friends that I host regular vampire sleepovers, they demand details. "What do they *do*?" everyone wants to know.

The truth is, I still don't know exactly what they do. Because, as with all guests, unless I am asked to participate in some way— be that to perform a wedding or fix a toilet—I give renters full privacy, hiding in my room or going off-site during their events. I do sometimes catch glimpses of the vampires scurrying from one building to another, dressed in elaborate costumes. They tell me they are assigned characters to play for the evening. My knowledge stops there.

When Bob moved in, he acclimated quickly to the vampires. Every month, right before they arrive, we bust out our running jokes. How Bob is going to casually don a strand of garlic and wear it as he makes evening rounds. How maybe he should keep a wooden stake in his golf cart. One morning, after they checked out, I found a box of red wine they left behind and used a sharpie to re-identify the contents as Type O Negative Blood. We never tire of this silliness, and the absurdity of some of the things we do to pay the mortgage.

Bob loves the vampires as much as I do. They love him back and always take time to chat with him before their games begin.

He basks in their attention and reports back on how pretty the lady vampires are.

One Vampire Weekend overlapped with The Night of the Rattlesnake, and dozens of them were wandering around when I nearly stepped on the snake. As one part of my mind whipped through the options of fight, flight, or flee, some other part weighed how best to tell forty vampires that a six-foot venomous creature was fifty feet away, without freaking them out. At last I called out to them, trying to sound nonchalant, not at all succeeding in this endeavor. "Y'all?" I hollered, "There is a snake right here! I need everyone in the house, now! You will hear some gunshots!"

They took the command in stride, hurrying inside unruffled, to wait out the execution. I hustled down the driveway, to put some distance between myself and the snake. Well, mostly between myself and the sound of the gun. Standing there in the dark, hands over my ears, I looked into the well-lit living room and saw, frozen as if mannequins in some Macy's Christmas window display, a plethora of vampires decked out to the gothic nines.

BANG. BANG. BANG.

And then, like that, the vampires resumed their game. I apologized to them the next day, but they brushed off my words. This is the country, they reminded me. Snakes happen. Not my fault. How I love their unworried ways.

Happily, the majority of guests who stay with us are equally pleasant, though inevitably we encounter the occasional asshole or two. Such is the case with Rhonda and Karen, an angry couple, both Debbie Downers, women who engage in deception from their first contact, an email announcing they are planning "a little party," and need a place to host it. Something about this inquiry does not sit right with me. I have learned, from more than a decade in the wedding business, that couples sometimes look for sneaky ways to save money. For instance, instead of telling a caterer or florist they are having a wedding, they will use the word *party*, since rates for weddings are typically higher than those for, say, a retirement soirée, given that client expectations are commensurately higher.

I ask them to describe the nature of the "party," specifically if they mean *wedding*. This they cop to, explaining that yes, they are trying to save money by downplaying the event. I should cut them off then, know better than to get involved with deceptive people. Instead, driven by a need to build the business, I invite them for a tour. They are fussy from the get-go, all furrowed brows as they point out this or that perceived flaw around the property, as if they are hired consultants I have invited here to advise me that my chicken coop does not match the aesthetics of the Four Seasons. Nonetheless, they book the ranch, and add that they want me to perform their wedding.

Every time we meet, whether to go over the ceremony or the logistics of the ranch, they are in a sour mood. With me. With each other. Sniping back and forth. Reporting that one has been in a car accident, the other has a sick family member, their favorite cat just died. Valid reasons to be upset, yes, but not once do they exhibit any joy about anything, not even the prospect of marrying each other.

They rent the place for several days, a steal of a deal I make them. The morning they are slated to check-in, I get up early. I hate the mix of resentment and desire to please roiling inside of me, a combination that leads me to anticipate that they will complain about a pile of lumber behind a small outbuilding, even though this wood is mostly obscured from sight. Bob offers to help me move it. I squat down to pick up a two-by-four and stand up just as Bob is turning around, also holding a two-by-four. His board slams into my head and I fall to the ground, head throbbing, doing my best to downplay the pain, not wanting to upset him. I flounder to right myself, unsteadily rise to my feet and resume the task, which, on account of the accident, takes longer than anticipated, leaving me unable to move the lawn-mower away from the house before the bitter brides arrive.

I wave at them as they pull through the gate. They park, get out of the car, and as they draw nearer, I see both wearing faces full of the sort of desolation one might more readily associate with a major act of global terrorism than a wedding. Unsure what is perturbing them this time, I wait to hear the latest cause for their disgruntlement. "You cut the wildflowers! We wanted wildflowers! You said there would be wildflowers!" They are actually crying.

Had I promised them wildflowers? What kind of lunatic would promise something so impossible to guarantee? Perhaps I said it was *very likely* the wildflowers would out? In truth, just the day before, the field around the chapel had been vastly abloom with beautiful, bright flowers, a sea of vibrant colors. Also, in truth, I remember watching Bob astride the mower, and I sort of remember mentioning something about maybe mow-ing around the flowers, and I also sort of remember him saying he didn't really care about the flowers, he wanted to mow the whole yard to make it uniform and nice. Which is exactly what he did, resulting in such a neatly trimmed patch of short green grass that a friend remarked the yard gave Arlington Cemetery a run for the money. Which is to say that, sure it's sad the flowers are gone, but dang the lawn looks tight.

Not to these women. Such negativity oozes from them that I, so warped with my people pleasing, so defensive at their criti-cism, so determined to avert a negative review, blurt out some very stupid words. "I'm just giving you your money back."

"We can't find another place in a day!" one of them wails.

"You don't need to," I say. "You have the wedding here and I'm giving you a 100% refund." Idiotic to be certain. But I just want them to shut the fuck up, and I want a refund to rob them of a chance to complain further.

There are problems with this plan. First, I don't have enough money for a full refund. I give them half and promise the other half soon. They say the other half "might not be necessary." Now the scene is set for a very tense weekend at the Tiny T. Worse, I still have to preside over their ceremony. Even during dark times in my personal life, I do whatever I need to do to get and stay grounded, focused, and present for a wedding, to bring my very best self to the occasion, to never forget that, never mind whatever personal drama I have going on, this is a very important day for the couple and so it is my duty to honor that.

Any cheer I attempt to bring to this union will be patently false, and if I can manage any smile at all for the sake of pictures, my smile will be purely fake. I kind of hate them now, my anger growing stronger when, once they get a grip on their crying, they begin to point out more problems. *"WHY is the lawnmower THERE?"* wails one. I want to tell her this is because I have just suffered a near concussion that has slowed me down. Instead I relocate it immediately. They move on to the next complaint, looking at the reception hall, which has been cleaned fastidiously. *"WHY are those there?"* moans one bride, gesturing at a pair of speakers in the corner, not seeing all that has been done to ready the place for their royal majesties. I lug the speakers out behind the barn and steel myself for their next round of demands, imagining this list will rival that of Martin Luther's church door manifesto.

The weekend continues, hostility hanging between us. I snap when I run into one of their guests on my side of the house, having ignored the DO NOT ENTER sign on the door between the kitchen and my apartment. An hour before the ceremony they still have not sent me their final script, despite repeated requests that they do so, so that I might print it and go over content. The wedding itself might as well be a funeral the way they frown through the entire thing. Another vendor confides that they lied to her, too, and that this event is much bigger than they said it would be, surely another misleading ploy to save a few bucks.

I am in such a rage after their ceremony that it nearly gets me killed as I race to an off-site wedding, and, turning onto the busy highway, find myself in the path of a speeding car that comes very close to taking me out. This happens so quickly that I cannot figure out if the fault lies with the other driver's poor skills and accelerated speed or if, maybe, I was so focused on my anger that I failed to see Speed Racer coming. Whatever the case, I am rattled, and my foul mood stays with me for days.

Bob to the rescue. It hurts him to see me hurting. It hurts him to think that his mowing caused the mountain of shit heaped on me by these ungrateful bitches. My strong, prolonged reaction to dealing with these angry women gives him another glimpse into my extreme sensitivity, how hard I find it to calm down sometimes. We sit in the Crazy Uncle in the Attic Room while the brides and their guests hold the main house hostage, eager for them to check out. We go over the ugly details of what has unfolded. I confess I don't want to give them the other half of a full refund, that those were foolish words spilled in anger, that I have shot myself in the foot, and want to rescind my offer. Bob listens and listens and reminds me repeatedly there is no pleasing some people. His words console me some, even if they do not tender a full cure for my angst.

When, to my dismay, the brides contact me the following week, saying they need to drop off things they have accidentally taken and pick up things they left behind, I swear I will hide in my room. *I will not confront them, I will not, I will not.* I compose a letter saying I have had second thoughts and decided a full refund is not fair, that I spoke in haste. I leave this in the reception hall with their forgotten possessions. But the sound of their car doors opening and closing proves too great a temptation and I cannot resist the urge to accost them, which I do, possessed by an unshakeable defensiveness.

No surprise, the conversation does not go well. They bitch me out. I bitch them out. On and on and on we go, all three of us occasionally using fake non-violent communication, sprinkling clearly angry words with hippie catchphrases like *I think what I hear your saying is that you are uncomfortable with...* when really I want them to fuck off and this sentiment matches their attitude toward me exactly. I do not fork over any additional dough. They leave in a rage. I wait for a scathing review to appear online. None does. I hold onto my anger too long, the only silver lining coming from the opportunity this affords Bob to keep reminding me that shit happens, you can't always get everything right, that he still loves me, and that yes, those women are awful, but certainly they are an exception, that the majority of our guests are wonderful.

He is absolutely right. We have the good fortune of mostly hosting extraordinarily kind guests. The spectrum of visitors is broad. One weekend we have a houseful of Christian Midwesterners, whose kids roller skate in the barn. Another weekend a hundred hippies take over, the smell of sweat and boiling beans pervading the house, accompanied by the sound of chanting, which Bob later reproduces, a twinkle in his eye as a gibberishy mantra spills from him, invented on the spot.

On two different weekends there are kink parties, involving elaborate props and equipment: whipping posts and whips, slut benches and handcuffs, blindfolds and paddles, sex wedges and dildos. I send Bob away these weekends, not revealing why, thinking the nature of the events might offend him. But Ellen's husband spills the beans the second time, and Bob jokingly laments having been banished. "I want to watch," he says, twinkling.

Regardless of our guest situation—be it a big wedding party, a group of thirty Danish students and their chaperones, or a punk rock record label that regularly rents the place for the South by Southwest music festival— all who meet Bob fall in love with him (those sour brides the sole exception). He is always equally pleased to make their acquaintance. Bob is a lagniappe, a bonus father/grandfather figure for all of them, posing for pictures, carting guests around in his golf cart, telling stories of his life, building a bonfire for a group of sorority girls when they ask, "How do you turn on the fire pit?"

Sometimes I ask him, "Did you ever think you'd be living at a ranch hanging out with vampires?" or "Did you ever think you'd be living at the Same Sex Wedding Capital of Garfield, Texas with a middle-aged punk rock roommate?"

"No," he laughs. "Did you ever think you'd be living with an old farmer?'

And then I laugh. No. No, I never thought that for a second. But how happy I am that I do.

SELF-HELP, BOB HELP

N THE LATE '90S, A MAN I'LL CALL PINOCCHIO CONSUMED TEN hellish months of my life, more if you consider additional time wasted fretting over him once we split up. For nearly twenty years, until Peter came along, Pinocchio very easily held the title of Worst Boyfriend Ever. Like Peter, Pinocchio was a fan of regular breakups, body shaming, and head games. Like Peter, he held a spell over me that I seemed unable to break, the economics of being regularly dismissed by him causing my mind to go into the same Diminished Supply/Panicked Demand effect seen in empty bottled-water shelves at grocery stores and snaking pump lines at gas stations during hurricane season in Texas.

Each of them led with tragic stories of ferocious childhood trauma, pursued me aggressively, and hooked me in with impressive bedroom stamina early on. Then, not long after the start of each of these relationships, Pinocchio and Peter exhibited other similarities in the bedroom, using sex as a weapon rather than a road to intimacy. I was, without understanding what was happening, put on the Random Rewards Sex Diet, no seeming rhyme or reason to marathon monsoons interspersed with extended droughts, bumper crops of orgasms supplanted by fucking famine. One sure bet: in each relationship, I had little to no say in when we congressed.

Pinocchio cheated on me repeatedly, and repeatedly I took him back. Sometimes he told me how much smarter this other woman was, and how much smaller, too, as if my juicy curves were an appalling detriment to his overall well-being. Sometimes he announced a number after sex, this indicating how many times we had now performed the act to date, going on to add where I now fell in the hierarchy of past lovers he'd had, regarding frequency of copulation. Whenever I beat him at Scrabble, Pinocchio, brutally competitive, would have sex only if I promised to stay awake after for another game, so that he could beat me and not go to sleep a loser. As if he weren't already a total loser. (To my credit, I never threw a game.)

On more than one occasion during sex, Peter stopped me to tell me I was "doing it wrong." My kissing was unacceptable. When I smiled with pleasure, he complained that this creeped him out. One night, misunderstanding a cue from him, I moved the "wrong" way, netting me an angry lecture that frightened me and killed the act midway. Like Pinocchio, Peter also played the comparison game, telling me how, though his previous girlfriend was batshit crazy, at least they'd had super-hot sex, and in her, unlike with me, he'd had someone he couldn't keep his hands off.

Sexual dysfunction was not, however, the most trying part of these relationships. Severe depression was. The cyclical depression that has plagued me since adolescence cannot, of course, be pinned on these men. Bad brain chemistry much credit for that. However, their abuse served as external stimulus, setting into motion bouts of depression so severe that suicidal ideation haunted me during my time with each. My refusal, or more accurately my seeming inability, to extract myself from these relationships at the first sign of abuse, depressed me even more.

Pinocchio urged me to go on anti-depressants. He took them, swore by them, and said I would benefit, too. I resisted. For one thing, growing up blue-collar, stubborn, mistrustful of doctors, and steeped in stigma around mental health care, I had little interest in seeking a diagnosis. For another, in fact I had, just after the divorce that immediately preceded Pinocchio, tried Prozac, which sped me up, caused constant shitting and weight loss, and made me feel even crazier than the crazy I felt when I finally caved and sought the prescription.

Peter never proposed anti-depressants for either of us and shut me down when I mentioned that he might give them a try to help assuage his unrelenting negativity. The more cantankerous he grew, the more desperate I became. I raged on in my journal, interminable passages about how I had to find a way to escape the abuse, followed by self-doubt as I countered myself, falsely reasoning that there were better alternatives, that if only I could come up with some combination of needed changes, we would figure it out, or more accurately, that I would figure it out for both of us.

This warped thinking, the belief that staying was mandatory and leaving meant giving up, sent me down a path seeking solutions in various forms. I loaded up on self-help books, dropped hundreds of dollars monthly on not one, but two therapists, and pursued a variety of healing modalities from Tai Chi lessons to Traeger massage, a technique involving a therapist jiggling my limbs like Jell-O, rather than digging into my muscles. To try to erase the movie in my mind of Peter fucking another woman, I devoured the book *Radical Forgiveness*. I studied *The Four Agreements*. I read *Chakras for Beginners* and determined that Peter and I were coming from very different places energetically—him the lower red and orange root chakras, answering to basic animal survival and desire hungers, and me, the higher energy chakras, the blues and greens, seeking spiritual connection and enlightenment.

I found hope—if not for the relationship then for coping with and treating my PTSD—in a book detailing the physical manifestation of emotional and psychological trauma. I put into practice as best I could suggestions found in *The Handbook to Higher Consciousness*, peeling away the hippy-dippy 70's lingo, focusing instead on core principles that seemed reasonable enough. I was like a pit bull being trained to fight to the death, set on a treadmill with a kitten dangling just out of reach, in this case the role of the kitten played by the false promise that I could find a way to have a true, loving, non-abusive relationship with an angry, emotionally shutdown man. In short, I was a fool fanning the fire of my fantasy with rampant denial and futile hope.

At the height of this frenzy to fix things that could not be fixed, I was at a wedding one day when I encountered a self-styled shaman. Cara, a member of the catering team, spotted me meditating before the ceremony, introduced herself, and asked why I was there. Upon hearing I was the officiant, she dramatically declared, "Ah, you are a priestess!"

This amused me, and we struck up a conversation in which she explained she was a healer. We exchanged contact details and she followed up with an email. I found her website interesting, the story of how she had made major life changes after serious trauma very compelling. I set up an appointment for what I thought was going to be a Thai Massage, massage being one of her offerings, massage being said to help more than sore muscles, to help release ancient trauma held in the body.

Cara arrived at the ranch and instructed me to lie down on a rug on the stage in the barn. It quickly became apparent there had been some misfire in communication. Massage was not her order of the day. Instead she chanted and launched into some magic routine, words and gestures, the particulars now forgotten, the overall combo very woo-woo, oddly incorporating a little plastic figurine of one of King Arthur's knights, and not at all what I was seeking. Still, I wished to not to be ungrateful for her help—if nothing else the placebo effect of having attention paid to my need to heal was nice. But there was also such an air of goofy New Age to the whole thing, even for me, a fan of chakra alignment and energy work. I did get a useful takeaway, though. I saw, at last, that I was exhausting myself psychologically and financially in pursuit of an elusive fix to my Peter pain. In this way, as well as in my pursuit of peace with the man himself, I realized I was not much different from Peter and his constant pursuit of a chemical fix to sate his demons.

Worn out from all these pursuits but still not ready to give up on finding a cure, I slowed down with the self-help tomes and massages, quit Tai Chi, and focused on therapy. For talk therapy, I saw Victoria, who got me through my last divorce and then coached me when the relationship after that fell apart. For somatic work, I found a trauma specialist, Leslie, with whom I connected very quickly. She employed a technique called Natural Processing, not unlike EMDR, which involved her tapping on my knees while I described physical sensations in my body. This sounds odd and admittedly looks rather ridiculous, but a growing body of remarkable research quantifies the amazing success rates of this method to relieve PTSD.

My work with Leslie commenced while I was still involved with Peter and she listened patiently—though in hindsight I wonder if not without subdued exasperation—as I ticked off long lists of grievances, including his heavy drinking and incessant weed-smoking. I insisted to Leslie I want to help him, I did not want to give up, that my love would prevail. She recommended that I look into Al-Anon, which I dismissed, making an excuses about my phobia of being in group settings.

Our sessions were fascinating. Once the tapping began, I often writhed and flinched as acute shooting pains radiated down my back and inside my skull, sometimes along my ribcage. I saw blobs of color, cloudlike and pulsating, inside of my closed eyelids. Frequently, I found myself crying as I flashbacked to recent Peter trauma and ancient childhood trauma. Though I showed up at Leslie's office greatly troubled for most appointments, by the time we finished each session, I felt better. Or at least slightly less nuts.

After Peter dumped me, I arrived for my appointments an inconsolable mess. I insisted I wanted him back. I slumped in my chair and bawled my eyes out. I could not ground myself in reality, could not see Peter for who he truly was: an abusive drug addict with zero capacity to love me and no desire to change. I kept revisiting our earliest days together, when making changes was the primary reason he offered for wanting to get close. I clung to this, in spite of all I knew to the contrary. I spilled out complicated reunion scenarios to Leslie who surely saw the futility in these schemes, but who listened without judgement, and just kept tapping on my knees until, once again, I noticed that, despite the fact the emotional pain did not seem to be receding, my anxiety lessened greatly.

I came eventually to understand this quieting was contingent on the fact that, even if I thought I missed him, what I surely did not miss was occupying every single day, as I had for the duration of our relationship, with wondering what would set him off next, strategizing how I might soothe him, apologizing for things for which I owed no apology. I also noticed my father's voice, urging me to kill myself, had gone silent. I was hardly happy to be alive, but I was making progress.

Often, I lamented to Leslie that I fetl so stupid, so naïve, so childish, coming to her session after session to talk about this man who disrespected me at every turn. What was my problem? What were my problems, *plural*? Why had I wasted so much time, energy and money on that relationship and why, now, could I not just accept that he was gone, and that this was for the best? Why had I wasted so much of my life getting involved with, talking about, and obsessing over abusive men?

Consistently and supportively, Leslie repeated the same answer. *Attachment.* I was attached to Peter, she said, or at least to my idea of Peter. I had been attached to the others, too. I had been attached to the Original Abuser, my father, by both blood and brainwashing, told so many times by my mother that he yelled at me *because* he loved me. That screaming equaled love. This imprinting had proved too strong to break. My loyalty to

Peter, my desire to make it work with him, all my vain attempts to fix the unfixable centered on attachment she explained. She also consoled me, pointing out that attachment itself isn't a bad thing. Humans are built to seek connection. What I needed to learn was *healthy* attachment.

In my Leslie-fueled, Google-enhanced post-mortem after Peter's departure, I fall down the rabbit hole of Attachment Theory. The studies make astonishing, troubling sense, capture who we were together, including detailed descriptions that spell out my contribution to the nightmare. I come to believe Peter is Avoidant Attached and that I am Anxious Attached. This combination is anything but unique. The descriptions of these two types and their dynamic so closely match us that the articles might as well include our names. I am oddly comforted to find that body shaming is a classic weapon of avoidant types, used to push away their partners, as they convince themselves that another, better—nay, *perfect*—mate is out there waiting to be found. Of my type, I am sad to read the anxious attached will do almost anything to keep the avoidant engaged, including starting arguments, which I have done so many times, not consciously recognizing this as a trait or a pattern.

These articles on attachment depress me at least as much as they enlighten me. Defeated, I cry to Leslie and Victoria that PTSD has ruined any chance for lasting happiness, that it will haunt me always and fuck up any possibility of ever having a healthy relationship. These women, my fairy godtherapists, soothe me, gently correct me, promise me I can heal. I try to hear them. After all, the articles do offer hope that one might, with effort, shift from being anxious attached to securely attached. The key ingredient to such a shift is to attach to someone already securely attached, and slowly work inside of that relationship to accept that the absence of drama is not a fluke, not boring, not wrong, but the very thing that defines healthiness. Rather a tall order for one so long steeped in chaos, mistrust, and abuse. Still, I do not push the idea away, just set it up on a shelf in my mind and look at it from afar, wondering if I really might learn to break out of a lifetime of relationship sickness, figure out how to live differently.

Enter Pop, a classic Wizard of Oz lesson right in front of my face, if only I can stop perseverating on Peter's rejection, betrayal, and abandonment long enough to tap my cowgirl boots together three times and repeat, "There's no place like Bob."

Because here he is, and here he has been all along, every single day since his arrival, my steady, my constant. I did not see this at first because I was still too busy running around like a headless chicken, trying to solve the unsolvable, pouring every ounce of myself into finding true lasting love with Peter, who was having none of it, spurring me to try harder still. The more he pushed me away, the less he showed up, the more it began to register, very slowly and subconsciously at first, that I *do* have daily, consistent love. Love from a man. Secure attachment in the form of this father figure who shows me what true love and respect are every day.

But Bob can't do my work for me. If I am to slay or at least tame the beast of PTSD, stop letting it run the show from sunup to sundown each and every day, I must apply myself, keep chipping away at it. How tired I get of hearing that happiness comes from within, that we are on our own. We aren't on our own. There are guides to take us down the river, people with prior experience, people with professional skills, people with sincere compassion, who have navigated the rapids before us, who can help us skirt known rocks that, though submerged, are knowable, mappable, and skirtable. Who can teach us how to become rock spotters. I have these guides in Leslie and Victoria, in a group of unconditionally loving friends. I find further guidance along other avenues I pursue, even the kooky New Age stuff. The advice in all the books I wolf down, too, is useful.

But Bob. Bob is, among all these people and words, the linchpin of my healing. His steadiness, his non-reactivity— all the times when I fear that he will criticize me for my foolish choices only to hear him instead say, "You never disappoint me, hon,"— help me gain footing on solid emotional ground. In Bob I Trust. He holds my heart gently no matter what. He makes me feel secure. I pay attention. I want to memorize the feeling, keep it with me, tap into it, make it my new reality. This is the gift of peace. This is the gift of true love.

One weekend we host a wedding at the ranch that stretches over days. The bride and groom and many family members check in the day before, and the party starts early as they decorate the barn, carries over the next day to the wedding and reception, and then the day after, music blasting most all of the weekend, people asleep everywhere including around the yard. It is on the morning after the rowdy reception that, as I head out to do chores, I spot two guests in Bob's golf cart. This immediately sounds an alarm inside of me—no one is supposed to use the golf cart except for Bob. My superpower of being able to tamp down and even shut out warning signals kicks in and, at first, I try to pretend I am not seeing what I am actually seeing.

After a few moments, I recognize that, as the venue proprietor, I have an obligation to confront the interlopers and warn them away from the cart. As I double back to initiate this uncomfortable confrontation, I note that now the two drunk men are on the ground, examining the undercarriage. I feel sick. I move closer. I see they have hit something, and hard, doing serious damage. I start out evenly, saying they can't use the cart, then take a closer look. Alarmed, I ask them what happened. They downplay the damage and insist the cart started without a key. They are bullshitting me—it might be easy to hot-wire but will not simply start up without some finagling. As for the claims of not knowing what happened, the smashed front indicates there is no way they could have been involved in such an impact and not have felt it.

Furious at both the wreckage and being lied to, I also notice another feeling. I am too petrified to tell Bob. Though nothing in his demeanor indicates it, I convince myself he is going to flip out. This, too, dates back to my father, who once, in response to a can of soda spontaneously exploding, acted as if one of us kids had thrown a live hand grenade in the kitchen. The sense that I am always in trouble follows me through to adulthood, and now I think Bob will freak out as my father always did. I cannot find a way to tell him about the cart.

In other people's worlds, an incident like this surely would not cause the high stress I have as I attempt to parse various scenarios flooding my mind. Here again, the PTSD is doing the driving, hijacking my senses, sending my thoughts spiraling into the darkest places, anticipating that Bob will be inconsolable and that the blame will fall on me. I message Ellen to ask for help.

Ellen promises me that Bob will be okay. Still, the knot in my stomach tightens. But as Ellen predicts, Bob, though bummed out, takes the incident in stride. "Shit happens," he says, a phrase he is quite fond of. Then he adds, "We'll fix it." And we do, the newly married couple apologizing and paying for repairs, the repair guy coming out to the ranch quickly and making it all better.

Living with him, watching him easily handle every crisis great and small, including the protracted crisis of my Peter-shattered heart, gives me a burgeoning stability. I have been living in the kind of confusion one experiences upon removing roller skates after skating for hours, feeling oddly off kilter until the body re-acclimates to walking, not rolling. Walking, of course, is the natural state, rolling around is not. My mind has this reversed. I have gone around in circles ten million times trying to make sense of life with Peter, a situation that will never make sense. Bob helps me get the skates off, takes my hand, shows me how to walk again. "We'll fix it," he says again. And again and again and again.

RV

N LATE 1985, I BEGAN DATING MY FIRST ABUSIVE BOYFRIEND, Matt. We met in college and got involved quickly, establishing a cycle of fighting and reconciling early on. The drama was nuts, even by my standards. One night I curled up on the floor of his dorm room crying, literally banging my head against a wall. Another night, at my birthday party, jealous of the attention I was receiving, he, pouting, lured me away to his place. We argued, it escalated, and he threw me across the room. I landed on a bicycle and sported a derailleur-shaped bruise on my ass for a week. We finally parted ways when I discovered I was pregnant a month after graduation, and he, after discussing the matter with his parents, said glumly, "You don't want to get married, do you?"

I beat a hasty retreat to my parents' home in New Jersey, a terrible choice but the only one I seemed to have. There, I had a devastating miscarriage, followed shortly after by a call from Matt, who'd heard the news from a mutual friend and who, during the call, confessed that he'd had an affair with a co-worker while we were together. All of this—the miscarriage, the breakup, the infidelity, my father's consequential shaming of me over my choices and his insane insistence that I should return to Matt—sent me spiraling into a major depression intensified by wild drinking binges. I thought I might never recover.

With all of this going on, it might seem a minor detail, but I was also upset over the fact that Matt got to keep the 1967 Volkswagen camper we had purchased together. Foolishly, I allowed him to be listed as sole owner on the title, though I had paid half. I loved that camper despite how many vicious quarrels we had in it on a month-long road trip. I vowed one day I would have another camper.

This story returned as I explored the thirty-one-foot RV Peter and I purchased after our post-England reunion. While lacking the compact engineering wonders of a VW camper, nonetheless it was a home on wheels and I adored it. It had a slide-out wall that created a relatively spacious living room. There was a full kitchen, master bedroom, and second bedroom with four tiny bunkbeds—one for each of our dogs I joked. Peter came up with most of the cash to pay for it and I kicked in a couple of thousand. The idea was that we would use it as an apartment on weekends he came to visit, to give us private space away from rental guests in the house. As with the VW, again I made the error of not including my name on the title.

Friends helped me haul the beast to the ranch and set it up. I felt cautious optimism that maybe this would be the thing that finally helped us to step into lasting devotion to our relationship. Sure, it was a tin box, but it also represented commitment, "our place," separate from his apartment and mine. My hope was tempered by an equal measure of dread, and I confessed to Chuck that this might be the biggest material symbol ever of how I was constantly overexerting myself to try to salvage the unsalvageable.

The Friday night Peter was to arrive to first see the RV in its place, the hours wore on and he failed to appear. Ellen and Bob and I stood by the chicken coop, looking across the yard at it, as I lamented Peter's growing remoteness and increasingly erratic behavior. I explained the RV was supposed to help us, to be a love nest, to make things better. Bob observed curtly, "You don't need him in it for it to be a love nest."

Peter eventually showed up late that night and things settled down. Not one to smile much—he was so proud of the tough guy scowl he told me he had been refining for years—he grinned uncharacteristically, absolutely beamed, as he surveyed his domain. To others, the RV might have appeared to be just an unsightly, oversized metal and fiberglass crate doomed to deteriorate over time. To Peter, it represented ownership. This was his castle. He swaggered around as if he were to the manor born. He stepped back out to his car and retrieved several guns, excited at the prospect of a weekend of target practice. His happiness brought me some relief, my apprehension about the relationship quieting momentarily. Perhaps the RV *would* move us in a better direction.

We did have a couple of good weekends in the RV, which I decked out with original art, nice dishes, and my best quilts, and stocked with all his favorite food and drinks. He added more art and filled the second bedroom with tools, weapons, and ammunition. But the bad times didn't stay at bay for long, and soon enough we were back in full-on Hell Mode. He resumed withdrawing. I grew more insecure. I wanted to leave him. I could not leave him.

On we dragged through the nightmare then, until, at last the final dumping. Which leaves me facing off every day with the sight of that RV, a hulking visual reminder of Peter. Memories of our brief time spent in it spin around my mind. This is the last place we ever had sex, him, as always, utterly incapable of intimacy, thrusting and grunting, aping what he clearly thought were porn star moves, accompanied by an actual porn playing on the TV, a biracial gangbang—his favorite—which he watched intently as he hastily finished his business, as if I were not even in the room with him, as if I were a hooker or a blowup doll.

The next week, on Sunday afternoon—as it turned out, our last day together as a couple—I was lying snuggled against him in the hour before he had to head home, when he blurted out that if we attended a concert together, people would want to know why he brought his mother. This he immediately followed up with wondering if I would ever dye my silver hair or wear makeup to look younger. I found his latest round of body shaming particularly ironic. Though I had six years on him, he was the one who, despite not yet being fifty and envisioning himself a stud, appeared truly geriatric with his unkempt gray beard, a face far more wrinkled than mine from years of practiced frowning, the bulge of his soft belly hanging over his unmuscled stick legs, and a neuropathy-related limp that caused him to walk in a manner that made Bob seem like spry Pheidippides by comparison.

I hate the RV now. Hate not just the bad memories it triggers, but also its reminder of how foolish I was, how many insults I put up with, how much disrespect I protested but continued to take nonetheless. I want it gone. Getting rid of it is not so easy, though. I go inside to take pictures to post so I can sell it. No surprise, Peter has left it a mess. I gather his trash and, not for the first time, mop up his piss from the bathroom floor. This latter task, when revealed to Bob, gives us a moment of shared deviant laughter as I send up gratitude for the piss, noting I will use it as a focal point anytime I slip into thinking I miss Peter. "You cleaned up his mess again," Bob says, and shakes his head sadly.

We thought we'd paid a decent price for the RV but, attempting to sell it, I learn otherwise. Flaws that seemed negligible—a small tear in the outside wall, a rusted-out water heater, an air conditioner that needs Freon—leave me on the receiving end of nitpicky critiques and lowball offers from a parade of Craigslist nut-jobs who take their time explaining what a piece of crap it is. Peter, though he had been thrilled with the RV and not opposed to the purchase price, now berates me, texting angrily that I should have let him haggle when we bought it. We debate whether he should haul it away and sell it, an unlikely prospect given logistics—he has nowhere to park it—and the fact that he is often too lazy to brush his teeth or shower, let alone orchestrate having an RV towed away. Besides, this would also involve having to see him, and by now I have an army of friends ready to physically keep this from happening, with Bob leading the charge.

Still—and this is so incredibly detrimental toward any forward motion—the RV becomes an excuse to maintain contact with him, leading to still more heated phone calls and long text exchanges, one stretching over eight hours in which he notes, quite unrelated to recreational vehicles, that we should never have been lovers, that he has located a drug dealer selling an amazing new strain of his favorite poison, and that he had not "banged" (his word) another woman to hurt me, but only because it was what he "needed to get through the day." I, fool, participate in this back and forth, the breakup still fresh, my mind still so warped that a part of me continues to want to reconcile, still hopes he will go to rehab. He liberally salts these conversations with emotional jabs, accusations, and putdowns. The abuse continues. As does my willingness to take it.

So, yes, the RV remains a wide-open door to agony. Not just the agony of continued communication with Peter, but the compounded agony of watching myself engage in highly addictive behavior. No, I do not resume drinking. But I am inhabiting the role of dry drunk now, my addiction being what I am incorrectly defining as love for Peter, a false sense that I will die without him, and my craving for contact, any contact, even text messages telling me that he regrets having been my lover.

Mornings during rounds with Bob, I gesture at the RV, once briefly viewed as a love nest and possible solution to at least some of my relationship problems, now just a hulking abominable memento of Peter. I say, "There it is still. I fucking hate that thing."

Without fail, Bob mirthfully offers the same answer every time. "I could blow it up for you," he says, grinning at the prospect. I laugh and tell him that's not necessary, but the thought of watching it be blown to smithereens cheers me.

Months pass, I still haven't made the sale, and any patience for the RV is gone. At least I am no longer in contact with Peter, having finally, thankfully, come to understand that any input from him is just going to make me emotionally sicker, and I am already far too sick from having been with him. I will find a buyer. I will have Chuck take Peter the money so I don't have to interact with him. Then my last bit of business with him will be finished.

Finally, a large family comes by, crowds inside the RV, and after a group huddle announces they're in. They make a small deposit and sign a piece of paper saying they will be back in thirty days with the balance. I go along with this unideal arrangement because it's not like I've had any other takers at all. Twenty-nine days later, they tell me the deal is off. Now I really am ready to blow it up.

Then I remember an earlier discussion with my friend Bubba about how his father is staying with him and how this situation is taking a toll on Bubba and his live-in girlfriend. I suggested then, partly in jest but with a serious undertone, that Bubba might move Big Bubba out to the ranch. "I'll start calling the place Yes Country for Old Men," I joked.

Now I call Bubba to revisit this idea. I explain my situation. Looking at the RV is constantly triggering my PTSD, I can't sell the damn thing, but maybe if his dad moves in I'll be able to look at it differently. Bubba brings Big Bubba, an old cowboy, out to have a look. I pull Bubba aside and explain a few things about the potential sale, such as that he will have to do all negotiations with Peter, whom he knows in passing, that I prefer he not mention me at all, and that the money handoff must not involve me. Bubba hears me out and is amenable to my terms. Big Bubba says he likes the RV and he likes the ranch. We have a deal.

They leave with Peter's contact information scrawled on a piece of paper, along with a list of numbers—what he paid, what I paid. I tell them I don't care about recouping my share. I just want Peter paid off so there is nothing left to tie me to him. This means I am about to lose thousands of dollars. I don't give a rat's ass. I can always make more money. This is a chance to be done with the RV, which sounds incongruous, as it will remain parked in my yard in direct view of my bedroom window. But to my eyes it will appear different, I am certain. I will see it now as a place for an old cowboy to live out his days. I will see it as an act of service to my wonderful friend, who can now have his space back and know that his father is happy.

Big Bubba's move-in day arrives. Bob is up and at 'em early, but he is not sporting his typical bright morning smile. I ask what's going on. "Big Bubba is moving here today," he says, petulance in his voice and on his face. "He says he's bringing his tools. There ain't no room for his tools in my shed."

His tone is reminiscent of the day he first met Rachel the horse trainer. He is now, as he was then, on guard. It's not that Bob is ruled by the old saw about change being hard—obviously not, given he moved to the ranch nearly nine decades into his life. But he does like the life we have together now, which has gotten even better with Peter gone, and he doesn't want any more potential headaches interrupting our fun. I assure him that Big Bubba will not use an inch of his shed space, not even for one screwdriver, not even for one screw for that matter. There is plenty of room in the RV for tools and, if Big Bubba wants a shed, he can get his own.

Bubba and I laugh, speculating how or even if Big Bubba and Bob will ever get along. Bubba promises it will happen, that his hermit-like dad will start to come out of his RV more and more and that he and Pop will acclimate to this new Two-Rooster dynamic once they start chatting. "It's like introducing cats," Bubba tells me. "They're wary at first. They'll get used to it."

Then he reminds me of the movie, *Step Brothers*. Will Ferrell and John C. Reilly star as two deadbeat grown men whose parents marry, and the four of them live together. Ferrell and Reilly hilariously get in the sorts of squabbles more like those between much younger siblings. Bubba and I adopt a phrase from the movie as an inside joke to refer to Big Bubba and Bob. "*Don't touch my drum set!*" one or other of us will say faux-peevishly. We never tire of this routine.

Little by little, Big Bubba comes out of his shell. He's most interested in the chickens and, intent on being flock master, moves an aluminum trashcan full of scratch just outside his door. This setup doesn't last long, as Tiny starts taking off the lid and helping himself to the feed, a funny trick, except that eating all that corn at once could kill him. Big Bubba secures the lid with a lock and chain, which nets him a loud rattling outside his window day and night as the ever-persistent Tiny refuses to give up his quest. Into the RV the can goes. The girls, inspired by Big Bubba's generous daily feed disbursement, readily switch their allegiance from Bob—whom they followed daily for months, leaving gifts of eggs in his golf cart, behind his grinder, and on his lawnmower—to their new friend.

Bob doesn't seem to mind much. Once he sees how much Big Bubba keeps to himself and realizes our dynamic duo status is intact, he lets go of whatever worries he had. As Bubba predicted, Bob and Big Bubba warm up to each other and make time most days for a brief chat, swapping tales of their youths and conferring on ranch improvements. The latter results in long lists of things they need from Home Depot and thinly veiled requests that I run into town and fill their orders for these supplies so they can execute their grand schemes. Bob will say, "I'm just going to drive into Bastrop," which we both know he shouldn't be doing, driving at his age on a dangerous highway. Still, he wants me to know he's *willing* to do his own errands.

I always reply, as he knows I will, that he isn't driving anywhere, to just give me the list, which is written in handwriting worthy of a medical degree, tool names that might as well be written in Latin, things I'm unfamiliar with because, I some-times surmise, he is using brand names from the 1930's. Nine times out of ten, I can't find whatever the hell he sends me after. The underpaid, orange-aproned clerks rarely seem able to deci-pher the list either, but maybe this is just passive-aggressive apa-thy on their part. Tough to decide which is more annoying—the ones who don't have the patience for these lists or those that exclaim they know JUST what Bob wants, then load up my cart with items he will later explain are all wrong. Necessitating, yes, another fucking trip to Home Depot to return it all and try again.

These runs increase in frequency because the more Big Bubba gets situated, the more he discovers things that need fixing in the RV. He's nearly blind so even if he had a vehicle, which wisely he does not, his driving would make Bob's seem, by comparison, on par with Mario Andretti at the top of his game. One day Big Bubba rides with me on a Home Depot run and we talk about broken hearts in a way different than Bob and I do, but still, I note that I seem to be collecting old men with wisdom aplenty to console me. This pleases me. As does an extra stop on the way back home, because Big Bubba and I both need ammo, him for his .410 shotgun and me for my .22 rifle. Perusing shelves of bullets, I wonder at how much things have changed in two years, how I have gone from gun-opposed to ammo-seeking, how I have two ranch mates whose cumulative age totals 160 years.

I might have poor choice-making skills when it comes to romantic partners, but it's starting to look like I have excep-tional skills in picking men to live with platonically. I relate to these guys, appreciate their need for solitude and their respect for my need of the same. I dig their manners, their kindness, their old school ways. I am so grateful for their gratitude that I let them stay rent-free. Yes, I am helping them by providing a cool place to live at no cost. But they know far more than I do about running the ranch. The trade-off is more than fair.

Nowadays when I look out the kitchen window and see the horses grazing near the RV, I do not have the visceral urge to puke, as I did back before Big Bubba moved in and all I could see was a piss-soaked monument to years wasted with an ungrateful, diabolical man. Sometimes I don't notice it at all. Or, when I do, I no longer see the last place Peter body shamed me, the last place he used my body for his gratification with no concern for mine, the place where some of the very last words I said to him were how disappointed I was in myself, not for my inability to please him, but for my inability to leave someone so barbarous. I see instead a cozy little home with a cute little deck Big Bubba built. I know he's inside smoking hand-rolled cigarettes and listening to country music on the radio, that the chickens are hiding beneath the trailer, keeping safe from hawks, which Big Bubba likes to shoot. Best of all, I see the absence of Peter, and with that absence comes a growing serenity.

GUS

I N THE MIDST OF ALL THE BREAKUP MADNESS, A QUIET HERO PRES-
ents himself. I am in the tattoo shop where I have been
acquiring extensive ink for years. The artists, Chuck
and Bubba among them, are like brothers to me. They
have watched me regress from ever ebullient into a
wreck of a human being courtesy of Peter's abuse, never heed-
ing their ongoing counsel that I get away from him, whom they
all know. On this day, only a few days after the dumping, I am
doing my best to put on a good face, failing miserably. My poorly
disguised sadness lifts a little when Gus comes in.

Gus is grinning that same broad grin as when we first met, a
couple of years before, at one of my book readings, our introduction brief. A few months later, we bumped into each other
again, another quick hello and goodbye. Our third encounter
came shortly after my birthday in January of 2016. I am a huge
fan of birthdays, mine especially, this being the one day each
year during my childhood that I did not have to fight for attention, when odds were decent that my father's hatred would be
less pronounced. Consequently, I always, purposefully, make a
big deal out of my birthday.

To celebrate the occasion in 2016, I invited a large crowd out
to the ranch to eat cake and take in the beginning stages of the
property makeover. Peter knew how important this party was
and yet announced he was skipping it, which hurt, a lot. The
hurt escalated, a furious argument ensued, and Peter refused to
budge. I was so enraged that I broke up with him, which in turn
mostly ruined my celebration as, unable to focus on anything
but my pain, I was a crap host that night.

A few days after that glum affair, I arrived at the tattoo shop and saw Gus, coincidentally also a regular, standing at the counter. He beamed at me. I drew a blank. He was familiar but I could not recall his name. I smiled back brightly, desperately flipping through my mental Rolodex, until Chuck, standing behind him, saved the day, mouthing, "*Gus. Gus.*"

"Gus!" I said. We hugged. He presented me with a half-dozen gourmet cupcakes. This floored me. It also confused me. How did he even know about my birthday? I supposed Chuck told him. But he barely knew me—why had he gone so out of his way to be this thoughtful and kind? The gift, not just of cake but of acknowledgement, would have moved me under any circumstances, but given Peter's refusal to celebrate me, I was especially touched. *This* was how it was supposed to be. *This* was what Peter should have done. Peter lured me back into his life a few weeks after the birthday breakup, texting from a Houston hospital where was scheduled for emergency back surgery the next day. He was scared, he said. He needed me. I was at once reluctant and gravely concerned. I asked Chuck what I should do. "Go to him," Chuck said.

I put everything on hold and rushed to Houston, crawled into his bed, held him. After surgery I took him to the ranch so I could care for him, as he was incapacitated. We maintained our status as exes, though I treated him with the love and attentiveness of a dedicated partner. This set the stage for our first reunion, a second round of pain. Sometimes I lamented Peter's mistreatment of me to Chuck, who reminded me that he had warned me not to date him, often adding, "You need to hang out with Gus more. That's the kind of guy you need—a nice guy."

Mild indignation visited me whenever Chuck said this. Not because the advice was bad—Gus *was* the kind of guy I should be with. He was always happy to see me, and the feeling was mutual. But I didn't even want to joke about dating someone else, the mere idea inspiring a sense betrayal, groundless but uncomfortable nevertheless.

This unwarranted guilt again consumed me when Gus made another shop appearance on February 14, 2017. While I am mostly opposed to stupid holidays—and I hold that Valentine's Day is rather stupid—I told Peter in advance that I did want him to call and wish me a happy one. Instead, midday, I received a cryptic text message, urgent and angry, saying something bad had happened at work and that he would be going silent.

Peter was a big fan of ghosting me when he was angry, long episodes of silence during which he refused to take my calls or answer my texts, compelling me at times to, in his words, "blow up" his phone with repeated attempts to reach him. Which in turn led him to accuse me of being crazy. At least on this day he warned me that he would be disappearing. Given by now my self-esteem was totally trashed, I chalked up as progress his communication to say he wouldn't be communicating. I reminded him that I still wanted a Valentine's Day wish, which he begrudgingly sent, and then: nothing.

I fretted about him for the rest of the day, and wondered what had happened. Wondered, as I did every other day, if he was planning to break up with me. I worked myself into quite a state trying to guess what was going on. I messaged his daughter, who lived with him, to ask her to make sure he was okay. Then, The Bomb dropped. His daughter replied saying she had some important news she was afraid to share. I called her immediately. She revealed she had found a meth pipe in Peter's room and that she was moving out.

A meth pipe? A motherfucking meth pipe? Shock set in. How could he have hidden a meth addiction from me?

Fortunately, I happened to be driving to therapy during this call. I stopped by the tattoo shop first. I was so shaken and the shop had always been a grounding place. Chuck took in Peter's daughter's news and instructed me to come back after therapy.

During therapy, Leslie tried to get me to understand the urgency of the situation, the need to get out. I tried to listen. I couldn't hear her. I was determined not leave Peter, but instead try to convince him to go to rehab. First, though, I had to confront him about using.

I tried repeatedly and unsuccessfully to reach him after therapy as I drove to the shop. In the midst of these efforts, a friend of Peter's called in. When I told him about the meth, he voiced surprise that I was just figuring this all out. I was equally surprised at his surprise. "You knew?" I asked. He said of course he knew and explained that every time he saw us together, Peter's pupils were dilated, and he exhibited other obvious signs of hard drug use. Well, obvious if you knew what to look for, which, never having even thought about using meth, evidently, I did not.

By the time I arrived at the tattoo parlor my head was buzzing, no clear thoughts possible. Chuck consoled me, saying with a wink, "Gus is coming in!" This irritated me, as it always did. I was so over Chuck teasing me that I needed to leave Peter—his best friend for crying out loud— for Gus or anyone else who would treat me better than Peter, which, it was finally dawning on me, was pretty much any other human on earth.

Sure enough, Gus strolled in, smiling that big smile of his. Gus smiled so often it made me wonder who could be that happy all the time. I took in the whole of him—clean-cut, classically handsome, soft-spoken, and quietly confident—and it was impossible not to note that before me stood the anti-Peter. Also, he was genuinely excited to see me, something else that differentiated him from the man who was supposed to love me more than any other. Gus invited me to catch some music with him at the club next door. On any other night I might have agreed, but this night, in a wild panic, I felt I must get home, get through to Peter, and get to the bottom of this meth business. I declined politely. As he had before, again Chuck stood behind Gus, this time mouthing, "*GO! GO!*" stopping just short of kicking me.

I don't know why I relented, but I did, following Gus up a narrow staircase to a tiny listening room, bathed in pink light, womblike. We chatted before the show and as he answered my questions I felt like I was in the movie *Sliding Doors*, which follows the protagonist down two paths—life if she goes with the bad guy and life if she goes with the good guy. It was as if Chuck had paid Gus to read from a script designed to dazzle me. I discovered we had many common interests including—I found this odd—a passion for rescuing Great Pyrenees dogs.

The singer, Curtis—a friend of my son's since they were three, now a man of impressive talents—started singing beautiful original tunes. In that moment, I had an opportunity to be happy, present, and loved by the kind man standing beside me and blown away by the musicianship of this singer-songwriter I used to babysit twenty years before. Instead, though not a single word or gesture between Gus and me hinted at anything except friendly interaction, unease filled me. I should be with Peter, wherever he was, however miserable we were. It did not seem right to be with this kind man enjoying myself, on Valentine's Day of all days, when my boyfriend was in crisis, shut down, and struggling with addiction problems far, far greater than those he confessed to when he first wooed me, when he claimed he wanted help slowing down drinking and smoking weed, acted as if these were his only indulgences.

By the fourth song, about a terrible relationship, I could no longer hold it together. Sensing I was about to cry, I begged off like Cinderella at 11:59 pm, ran down the stairs, disappeared into the night, sat in my car in the dark, crying uncontrollably at Peter's deception and, also, an undeniable attraction to Gus. Peter finally answered his phone and, after a long pause, admitted that he had been doing meth throughout our relationship.

Also coke. And pills. When I asked why he had kept these secrets from me, why he never told me the truth about the extent of his addictions, he said simply, "You never asked." As if the fault lay with me for having failed to ever inquire: *Say, Peter, by the way, are you by any chance a meth head?*

By this point though, I was so inextricably enmeshed in Peter Hell, such a victim of Stockholm Syndrome—even though I was not yet aware that this was the case—I did not cut and run. I took the news calmly. I was supportive. I promised we would get through this together. I heard in Peter's voice astonishment that I was not going ballistic.

My calm was not real, of course. More a symptom of shock than acceptance, it was the calm of disbelief and denial, which I had to sustain if I was going to save this relationship. And because I was so sick by then, so entirely under his thumb, I was more determined than ever to figure this mess out, to help him get better, despite now having irrefutable proof that I had spent the entirety of this relationship with an unrelenting liar who deceived me every single day. Information that led me to look back over it all, like watching *The Sixth Sense* a second time, after being told all the characters are dead, and having *aha* moment after *aha* moment—*Oh! That time he yelled at me? That time he slept for 72 hours? That time he didn't call for days on end? That time I rushed him to ER when he woke me in the middle of the night sweating profusely and moaning in pain? Oh! I see now. I see! He was ripped off his gourd on meth or in withdrawal.*

Gus messaged me several times over the next few days after our night out. Nothing flirtatious. Just follow-ups to my Valentine's Day suggestion that I would like to pick his brain about an idea I had, inspired by Bob, to develop the ranch into an alternative retirement community. Gus works in real estate and I figured he might have some smart ideas to share.

I replied that I did want to meet up, but that now was not a good time. I explained I was worn out from having spent a year taking care of Peter, that his health was failing miserably, and that I was depressed. I did not mention the meth. Gus said he was happy to chat anytime, just let him know when things settled down, which, of course, they never did. Still, a few weeks later, I invited him for coffee. Our conversation was again easy and upbeat, his advice sage. We swapped a few more stories that revealed how much we held in common. And then, again, I disappeared, still nervous about my internal reactions whenever I was around him.

Now it is early June 2017, the breakup so fresh, and here I am in the shop lamely trying to smile. There Gus is, again smiling easily. I pull up a chair and we chat as Chuck tattoos him. Gus is brilliant and so swift-witted that I laugh despite my pain. I text him after leaving. *Thank you.* I say. *You are loved,* he replies.

A couple of weeks later Peter comes to retrieve his things from the RV. Waiting for him to arrive, though I have barely eaten in days, I think I am going to puke. Or faint. Possibly both. For the first time since I've known him, on this, the last day of our acquaintance, he is punctual. I pour out my heart, beg him to reconsider. I am so out of my mind that I hear things fly from my mouth that are beyond fucked up, and yet, as if possessed not by my true self but rather some poltergeist, I cannot stop. I say I don't even really care about the meth so much, only that he hadn't told me about it. I say he can set the schedule, see me just once per month. I say I will do anything to keep him.

He says he is possibly willing to try a cooling off period, that he can probably honor my plea that he not run out and fuck someone else as he had after a previous breakup. I request that if he does move on to another woman, that he tell me. He says he is so lost, that he is contemplating going to rehab or quitting his job. I ask him if he will please still attend a concert with me, two weeks hence, for which I long ago purchased us tickets. He says he'll think about it. When at last he gets in the car to go, I lean in and kiss him, tell him I love him. He does not pull away.

A couple of days later, I call him to ask again about the concert. Even knowing with certainty his answer before he reveals it, when he says he won't be going, I am crestfallen. I mull what to do with the tickets. I can give them away. I can sell them. I can invite a friend. All reasonable options. And then I think of Gus. I dare myself to invite him. He is so positive. I need positivity. I need good, solid, easy company. Desperate for validation, I want to share time with a man who, I already know, truly cares about me. One I am sure is safe. Plus, he'd already messaged me a week earlier to say if he could ever be of service all I have to do is ask. I text him now, tell him about the concert. Instantly he accepts my invite and asks if I will please have dinner with him beforehand.

When concert day arrives, I go shopping for new clothes. I feel like my entire wardrobe has been sullied by having been in Peter's presence. I need everything to be different. Back at home, I try on my new green dress and model it for Bob. He is so excited in his approval, enthuses how pretty I look. Shy gratitude fills me. Peter dedicated so much energy to making me feel ugly and undesirable, and vestigial insecurity from this constant debasement tempts me now to protest Bob's compliments. For the rest of the day he follows me around, gleeful. "*Spike has a date*," he sings out. "*Spike has a date!*"

This is certainly not a date. I can't foresee ever dating again, and surely not now, given my current state. But it is fun to listen to Bob be so ardent in anticipation of my big night out. I laugh and cry simultaneously. I am a complete and total mess, sure that I am about to subject Gus to an evening of torture. I fight the urge to text him an over-explanation of my fears, to warn him what he's in for. He already knows that I am distraught. I do my best to keep a lid on my crazy, my phone in my pocket, to not wallop him with hourly updates of my fragile mental health.

He picks the perfect restaurant. Not too big. Not too busy. He is waiting at the bar when I arrive. I have been so conditioned by Peter to expect a late show or no show that this moves me. Gus greets me enthusiastically, jumps up to hug me and kiss my cheek, admires my dress, and the host leads us to a patio table.

I look straight at him. "I'm really sorry," I say. "I might cry. A lot."

Gus smiles. "Not a problem," he says. "I already came up with a plan if you do." He gestures around at the other diners. "If you cry I will drop down on one knee and propose to you in front of all of these people."

Hearing myself laugh as I do at this silly threat startles me. This is a letting- loose I haven't felt in longer than I can remember. My laughter is obnoxiously loud, and it sounds like a foreign language coming from a place inside of me I have forgotten exists. I order a big meal and eat every bite. Another startling act. By now I have so little an appetite that the food on my plate could last me a week. It is gone in half an hour.

There is not a single uneasy moment between us. I ask Gus if he is a fan of Jason Isbell, the singer we are going to see. He answers that he has no idea who Jason Isbell is, he just wants to hang out with me. We have a wonderful time. When we part ways, he asks me to let him know when I have gotten home safely, which I do, touched by his concern.

Inside, I find Pop waiting, fighting off sleep, up extra late, eager to gossip about my evening out, demanding all the details. "Did he kiss you?" he asks, with a sly grin. I remind him this wasn't a date. He chuckles. Another first then, my new father excited for me the way my old father never was. I can tell Bob is hopeful that Gus will, if not become my next boyfriend, a good boyfriend, that at least maybe he will distract me from "that guy who shit all over you."

The next day Gus replies to my thank you text saying anytime I need a companion he'll be delighted to step to the front of the line. I take him up on this and, in no time, we start hanging out frequently.

One invitation I extend to him is to see The Dick Monologues fundraiser for Tiny's medical expenses. I have prepared a savage piece going into meticulous detail about Peter's escalating abuse and the burning shame of having stayed with him. I feel reckless inviting Gus, and I have an ulterior motive. Bob insists Gus is courting me. I'm not so sure, but if he is, he needs to know how fucked up I am, my monologue a warning shot across the bow.

When Bob announces he plans to attend the show, too, I try to dissuade him, knowing it will crush him to hear these new details of what Peter did, things I purposely have withheld to shield him. Bob holds my hand as I cry and tell him I don't want to hurt him by asking him to stay home, I just want to spare him pain. "I want to be there for you, hon," he says, squeezing my hand. I cry harder. I relent, advance apologizing for the secrets I am about to reveal publicly.

Gus sits next to Bob at the show. Nervous, I stand to read my piece. The audience gasps and hisses audibly. My friend Carol covertly snaps a photo of Bob, wrapped in a fuzzy blanket to fend off his constant coldness, watching me perform. This picture includes Gus by default. In it, the pair looks like father and son, heads tilting at just the same angle, paying riveted attention to me.

After the show, Gus joins the cast and some other friends, Bob among them, for pizza. Everyone loves him. Again, *Sliding Doors* comes to mind. Again, I think this man is the anti-Peter. At the end of the night he walks me to my car and thanks me and I blurt, "I invited you to scare you away."

"You can't break me," he says, and smiles that big broad smile of his.

POSITIVITY

HE NEXT DAY I NOTICE A STRONG SENSE OF RELIEF. The catharsis of finally sharing publicly the abuse Peter doled out has the added benefit of forcing me to at least start to truly admit what happened, what I allowed to happen, how brainwashed I became in the grips of Peter, how unable to break away from him despite many interventions by friends, warnings to myself in my journal, and the assistance of two therapists. I realize just how much I have kept from my closest friends and, to an extent, from myself. Classic denial.

Now, with much of the truth out in the open, I am waking up. Finally. There will be no getting sucked back in. Peter will never again be a part of my life, which, sadly, so often I had wished for after he left. What part of me was so broken that I thought I wanted that? Oh, I have been so fucked up for so long.

Bob and I sit at the kitchen table drinking coffee, the beautiful light of the morning sun shining across us. He gets a mischievous little grin on his face and announces, "I had a talk with your friend last night."

He is, I know, referring to Gus and I flinch. "What did you say?"

"Oh, nothing. I just told him if he ever hurts you, I'll kill him." With this his grin broadens. I feign horror but really am pleased at his protectiveness. I also know without having to ask that Gus surely took this just the right way.

Gus and I text daily, checking in throughout the day, and go out often. I love our time together and the steady, easy rhythm of our friendship. I also feel tension over these very same things. I find myself getting very attached. Even knowing Gus is a bona fide good guy, worry will not leave me alone. I understand now, as I had not when it was happening, a major tool in Peter's belt of seduction had been constant contact, the onslaught of his flirtatious messages diverting my attention from serious red flags.

I wonder now if I am acting addictively with Gus's messages. Are they a distraction from all the work I still need to do? Am I just using him, to avoid dealing with my internal chaos?

There is something bigger nagging me, that proverbial saying about things that walk and act and quack like a duck. Our time together resembles an incredibly traditional courtship. Gus never tries to lay a hand on me. He opens my car door, pulls my chair out at restaurants—fine dining establishments he selects with care—pays for every meal, helps me put on my sweater. I am amused at how we are more like sixteen-year-olds in the 1950s than modern day middle-agers. All of this causes confusion. Is he interested in more than a friendship? Am I?

In truth, I am glad Gus never asks for more. Our laughter remains easy, the events we attend diverse and fun. When I am with him, I am fully present. And when I am alone, times I fall back into my pit of misery, I message him. Always he replies swiftly, consoles empathetically, encourages me to keep my head up.

Gus makes time for Bob, too, taking both of us out to eat. Bob loves clutching Gus's arm for support as we enter and exit restaurants. Afterwards, when we are home, Bob, still holding out hope Gus and I will start dating, says, "I can barely get my arm around his bicep!" As if I might be swayed by the fact that Gus is so ripped he makes Michelangelo's *David* look like a couch potato.

One day I set out to grocery shop at the mega HEB up the road, queasy at the prospect. I am so fucked up by the food aversion caused by my eating disorder that the idea of all those aisles crammed with so many choices paralyzes me. Nourishing my body remains a huge battle. I must remind myself that eating is not optional, it is essential. Besides, Bob also needs to eat, so even if I can make excuses to not feed myself, these trips are still necessary.

As I walk across the parking lot, suddenly deeply buried memories resurface and flash across my mental screen. *Peter and I are in my bed having sex. He pauses, hovers over me. Then, with no warning, his hand crashes into my face. His eyes are angry. Shocked from the pain and unexpected violence, I say nothing, just look up at him, dazed, hurt, scared, confused.*

This sickening flashback unleashes a torrent of other repressed details. I recall how I tried to make sense of this savagery, flailed around for excuses for him. How, more than a year into our relationship, he revealed his affinity for porn, insisting this was not an addiction (yet another lie I will come to discover later). How I told him porn wasn't my thing but agreed to watch some with him anyway. How he said he wanted things kinkier in the bedroom. How I agreed to this, too. How he liked to have two porns going at once, one on the monitor above his nightstand, the other on the jumbo screen on the wall. How I did not protest. How I actively participated in some crazy requests.

And, with all these memories, another: Thinking, while my ears were still ringing from the impact of his heavy palm, *Maybe he's acting out a porn fantasy, maybe this is my fault for not explicitly clarifying smacking me upside the head is never okay.* And then, another memory still of how, when he hit me *again* in the face during sex on a different day, I wondered if maybe my failure to protest the first time might be to blame for this second assault.

Memories of his sadism loop in my mind as I wander in a stupor up one aisle and down the next, feeling certifiably crazy. Peter is gone, yes. But the stain of him might well be permanent. Am I doomed to squander the rest of my days rehashing the inestimable ways he purposefully hurt me?

Gus, as if psychic, texts in a hello just as my anxiety crescendos. I reply that I am on the verge of a full blown panic attack.

I do not give him the specific details—it will take me a while before I can work up the nerve to describe that bedroom brutality to this loyal protector of mine. I merely tell him where I am and that I am very scared. To which he playfully replies that, statistically, HEB is an incredibly safe place. I exhale slightly. He urges me to do a reality check of my surroundings. I heed this advice, name in my head the things I see in front of me—*freezers, dairy, juice*—still feel off, but no longer in immediate danger.

After that episode Gus says anytime I need a grocery store escort, he will be happy to do the honors. I like this idea. We meet one Saturday at a different HEB, one I never went to with Peter, hoping the change will alleviate some of my malaise. Gus is in no hurry, puts no pressure on me, walks beside me. I explain a bit about my eating disorder, the constant struggle to put food in my body. He listens, makes some suggestions, and we select hummus, tabouli, protein bars, and individual serving packs of peanut butter—healthy, ready-to-eat items that requires no preparation.

This thoughtfulness, this desire to help me recover and gain strength, the way he walks beside me, is infinitely more intimate than anything Peter and I ever did together. Gus, ever humble, dismisses my gushing gratitude. He's just happy to help, happy that I am working on getting better.

Gus, Bob, Ellen and I make a plan to see a screening of the classic movie *Giant*, playing at the historic Paramount Theater in Austin. Bob and I have watched so many old Westerns on TV together, not a genre I would have pursued on my own, but with his shared encyclopedic knowledge of actors, directors, and shooting locations, I now take in these flicks with great appreciation. Seeing the epic *Giant* on a huge screen will thrill him. It will thrill me, too. In nearly three decades as a Texan I have somehow managed to miss it.

Bob and I head into town early for the movie, both of us dressed up like it's Country Bumpkins' Trip to the Big City

Day. We stop at a huge candy shop packed to the rafters with all manner of old-fashioned and new-fangled sweets, stocking up on far too much to easily smuggle into the theater. Then we drive north on South Congress Avenue, over the Colorado River, floating in Bob's trusty old silver Buick, beholding the sparkling pink granite capitol, majestic on the horizon, on our way to the Stephen F. Austin Hotel, next door to the Paramount. Inside the hotel, we take a seat in the bar of The Roaring Fork restaurant, where Gus and Ellen are slated to meet us for a pre-show meal. Bob orders a big fancy cocktail and I look at him in his checkered shirt, with his cool beverage and his big smile. I am relaxed, happy even, slowly reclaiming parts of myself that left the building when I was with Peter.

The Roaring Fork aesthetic leans heavily on Old Texas—cowhide rugs, longhorns mounted on plaques, paintings of the Wild West. We crack up when Gus arrives and reveals that he, too, has brought some candy—big boxes of Swedish Fish—to secret into the movie. Dinner is splendid. I am with friends. They are happy to be with me. We are laughing. I am safe. I easily eat a substantial meal. All of this had once been normal, taken for granted. Now it all feels new, and I am astonished. I am waking up some more now, remembering how I used to feel before Peter swept in and left me on constant edge.

We wander down to the Paramount after that hearty meal, Bob hanging onto Gus's bicep, me taking in this scene with joy. Sinking back into our plush seats, rummaging through pound upon pound of candy, we wait for darkness to fall over us, to escape into the saga of Texas rancher Bick Benedict Jr., played by Rock Hudson, his beautiful wife Leslie, played by Elizabeth Taylor, and that burning hot troublemaker, Jett Rink, played by James Dean in the last film he made before his premature death.

The cinematography is breathtaking. Sitting in that sold-out room with a bunch of Texans, we laugh collectively at the inside jokes about our state. Though I am able to stay mostly present, occasionally my mind drifts, as it still annoyingly does every day, to what being with Peter has done to me. My eyes stay on the screen but my thoughts flit around, settling at last on the concept of suspension of disbelief, how this is required to truly enjoy a movie. From here, I jump to how I suspended my disbelief as Peter grew exponentially crueler the longer I remained, his rages and insults more frequent, more harsh. Blocking out the times he hit me in the face, the way he looked at me with hatred in his eyes as he struck me—this was surely the most staggering display of my denial in action. I must stop disbelieving, must stop downplaying and making excuses for him, must admit it really happened, all of it. Because no matter how badly accepting this truth hurts, acceptance is absolutely crucial if ever I am to heal.

During one scene, Bick and Leslie's daughter Luz, who is madly in love with Jett—by now an obscenely wealthy oil-man, raging alcoholic, and pathetic shell of a human—listens to another character spell out the extent of her lover's depravity. She responds dismissively, "Oh, he must be ill," as if he merely has a chest cold, not a permanent mental affliction. I lean over and whisper to Gus, "She's my spirit animal."

How that scene resonates, denial in the extreme. There was never a time Luz did not know that her boyfriend was bad news, a total mess. Watching her minimize Jett's madness is a virtual slap in my face now, provoking a reaction stronger than when Peter actually struck me, when my response was silence followed by excuse-making. I am forced to reckon with another truth: Even if I had not known the full extent of his addiction—the meth, the coke, the pills, the porn, all of which he kept hidden from me—I *had* known from the very start he had some serious substance abuse problems. That was, after all, what had brought us together, his false claim of a desire to live a cleaner life, his request that I, sober, help him to do so.

Despite the emergence of all these disturbing facts I had shut away in the recesses of my memory, the evening is otherwise perfect. The more time I spend with Gus, the more relaxed I become. Bob, too, is pleased to see me in the company of a man who respects me. How happy we both are to have Gus in our lives.

Just one thing mars the evening. Standing in line for the ladies' room after the movie, I glance at my phone. My stomach twists as I see a text from Peter. With the exception of one extremely brief text I sent him, I have had zero contact for a month, since the day he came to retrieve the last of his things from the RV and leave piss on the floor for me to clean up one final time. The exception came the week before, when Hurricane Harvey crippled Houston. Despite concern for his well-being, I successfully convinced myself not to use this as an excuse to resume our rancorous communications. But then, his aunt in England, still a friend, sent me multiple messages, saying Peter was not replying to her queries, she was very worried, wanted to know if he was safe, and was wondering if I had heard any news from him.

Wanting to bring her peace because she had always been so kind to me, I broke down and texted him after her second or third request. I was brief and to the point, noting that contacting him was a bad idea but that his aunt was freaking out. He did not reply then, though the aunt sent a follow up, letting me know he had finally called her. Now, in this beautiful theater, on this otherwise wonderful evening, his name appears, and with it, a days-delayed response. More upsetting is the upbeat tone and content of his words, acting like we're old friends just catching up. He tells me about his brother. He hopes Bob and I are doing well. He says I am not to worry about selling the RV because, he assures me, "We'll figure it out." As if there is a "we" left.

Reading his words, my hate for him swells. Hate that—as if sensing I am out in the company of a truly good man, one who gives me love and kindness freely as he never did—Peter must horn in on my joy and proprietarily piss on me, like I am his territory, like I am his bathroom floor. I do not reply, but the damage is done. The poison of this fake nicety leaks in, another setback, one that thankfully lasts only a few days, but that's a few days too many. I have given him more than enough of my time. I want him gone. I want him to leave me alone. Some days, I wish he would just die.

I leave for Europe not long after that jarring, fake-nice text from Peter. Because, no matter how empty my bank account is—and after all the money I spent trying to please Peter with ludicrous lingerie, fine food, expensive gifts, helping pay for his incarcerated brother's lawyer and his daughter's therapist, caring for his cousin upon her release from foster care, and traveling weekly to see him, I am basically fund-free—I always find a way to travel. I am hopeful that a change of scenery will further quiet my grief and confusion because, though I am waking up a little more each day, my head is still in a thick fog. Frequent flier miles get me to London. From there I hop over to Italy to go on holiday with my friend Garreth and his kids, my favorite children on the planet. Garreth graciously picks up the tab on all of my food and lodging.

We explore for a few days in Rome and one in Cambridge before parting ways. I take a train back to London to meet up with another great friend, Raz. We linger in pubs and catch up and I allow myself to be consoled. I book a tiny hotel room in Kensington, roughly the size of a monk's cell, exactly as I prefer accommodations when traveling solo. I am cocooned in that closet-sized space, safe, able to see every inch of the place.

My last two days in London I walk till near collapse, twelve miles the first day and thirteen the second. These fantastically exhausting urban hikes perk up my spirits noticeably, as does Gus's virtual company. We text constantly, messages flying back and forth across the ether, London to Austin and back, me bemoaning my lack of sense of direction, sending a steady stream of photos of all I am seeing. A lush green park. A palace. A statue. Another palace. Gus cheers me on when I describe bursts of exhilaration I feel, the scales tilting now from anger at being discarded to gratitude that I am free from constant abuse. My crippling emotional pain is at last dissipating, hopefully for good.

All of this—the grocery store trips, the texts and long emails we swap while I am away, and his steady, steady love—stirs something in me, which I recognize and enjoy, but which also scares the bloody hell out of me. I am not just *getting* attached to Gus. I *am* attached to him. Very attached. I continue to remind myself that I am to remain curious and open-minded, to not force his hand or my own. If he wants more from me, that is up to him to say. If I want more from him, then I need to figure that out and say so myself.

Each time worry taps at my heart, I silence it and tell myself that one day I will be able to play reverse connect the dots to understand why Gus is who he is to me. Even if I were healthy enough to step into a romance, which I most certainly am not, after all I have been through with Peter, I'm not sure I ever want to let anyone in that close again. The thrill of being in charge of my itinerary, of needing consult no one, of going when I want, where I want, of sitting in an elegant Indian restaurant solo, flush with gratitude at my freedom, happily spent from all the walking—these things stimulate buoyant feelings. I spent years alone before Peter came along and ruined everything. I enjoyed those years alone. I had not felt like some self-pitying spinster. I felt like a character Kate Chopin might create, a woman who only wants her independence, not some relationship with a domineering brute bogging her down.

Somewhere in all our correspondence, I carefully broach the topic of our deepening attachment. To my great relief, Gus assures me he is not coming onto me. He wants a friendship, nothing else. I do not have to fret about the complications of saying *no* if he asks for more, because now I know he will not ask for more, for something I am not ready for after Peter's reign of destruction.

Maybe, on some distant level, there comes with this now-defined boundary a whiff of remorse, like the Neil Diamond song about how in another time and another place we could have been something else to each other. But that thought drifts away swiftly, easily, and of its own accord. Gus tells me that he firmly believes we're always where we are meant to be, and that whatever happened to us, even the bad shit, shaped us into who we are. He continues to remind me that, like Bob, he will always stand beside me, and he will always stand up for me.

BODY MODIFICATION

GROWING UP, ONE OF THE INNUMERABLE RULES IN our house was that you were not allowed to get your ears pierced until you turned sixteen. Once I hit that milestone, I began a lifetime of body modification that waxed, waned, then waxed again. In my late teens and early twenties, I perforated my left ear to the point I was surprised it didn't fall off. I got my first tattoo in 1988 at Sunset Strip Tattoo Parlor in LA, a little cow with the inscription, *Born to Graze*. My next tattoo, another cow, was inked in 1995. Then, a little over a decade later, at first in an unplanned fashion and then with focused intent, I began transforming my body in a major way.

In 2006, to celebrate my second impulsive marriage, I visited a tattoo shop to have my new husband's name inscribed on my body. Not just his name. His name splashed across the depiction of a washboard, to honor that he played one in a band. I had envisioned something small, but when the artist applied the stencil to my upper left arm and I noted how large it was, instead of requesting she downsize it, I thought, *What the hell, my love is big and so shall be my message to the world.*

When the marriage imploded less than a year later, I reasoned that this tattoo marked part of my journey, that I must keep it. Maybe there was a little self-punishment intended, too, part of the price I had to pay for my foolishness in both getting married and getting his name permanently etched upon my being. Later, I rethought this self-flagellating belief and off to the laser removal shop I went. The technician explained that several sessions would be required, that each would take about sixty seconds, and that she could stop for as many breaks as needed if the pain proved too much. Multiple pain breaks? For a sixty-second procedure?

As the lasers hit my skin, crackling and burning, I wanted to howl. The pain of removal was infinitely more intense than the pain of application, and that had taken more than an hour. Also, I discerned no fading effect whatsoever. A better strategy was in order because no way in hell was I going to do that four or five or ten or however many more times it would take for results that were not even guaranteed. Upon bemoaning my unwanted tattoo and the unsuccessful laser treatment, I got word from a friend of a friend that Bart, an artist who co-owned the shop where I'd received the washboard, was a genius at cover-ups.

I set up a consultation. Looking at the heavy black lines forming the washboard—their thickness, their darkness, and the amount of real estate they took up on my arm—Bart said he needed some time to come up with a plan. Several weeks later he called me in to show me some sketches. Amazed at his proposed solution, I was eager to start.

The result was more than a gorgeous tattoo extending from my shoulder to just above my elbow, featuring brightly colored flowers and a bird of an invented species that sprung fully formed from Bart's imagination. The process took around twelve hours, spread over multiple appointments. All that time spent in the shop excited me. I liked the vibe. I liked the artists. I liked the ink. I *loved* the ink. I also loved the endorphin buzz that kicked in while the needles buzzed away on my skin. I returned for more work, this time a quarter-sleeve on my right arm featuring some of Henry's childhood artwork. I became hooked on the needles, the pain, the results, the smell of the green soap used liberally in the shop.

Upon returning from a transformative trip to London in 2013—my first visit to England—I popped into the shop for a small memento tattoo to mark that journey. As I waited for Bart to prepare, Chuck approached me to chat. We'd met years before but had never had a real conversation. We stood by the photocopier and Chuck looked me straight in the eyes. "You need to hang out here more often," he announced.

This struck me as a strange statement. It also appealed to me. A day or two later I sent Bart a shy email and relayed Chuck's invitation. I wasn't sure if he really meant it, or if he'd just been flirting. I confessed to Bart that hanging around a bunch of men might do me good. Just a few months out of a nearly six-year relationship, I speculated that I might never in this lifetime figure out men, but that maybe regular time in their company would help me understand them better. Bart said sure, I could come hang out.

I showed up a week later, both excited and shy. I sat quietly in a corner knitting, wondering if all this was too weird. Chuck walked in, smiled, told me to put down my knitting and participate. Then we stepped outside and talked for a while. Chuck is a gifted storyteller. He is charismatic, clever, and uniquely beautiful with auburn hair, bright blue eyes and a roguish smile. I felt an immediate attraction as he spun elaborate tales and asked me about myself, listening intently as I answered.

From that first October day onward, I come in one day each week, help greet customers and answer the phone. Thus, Man College is born. I write a blog about this adventure, full of faux life advice sarcastically doled out by the artists. Chuck and I fast form an extraordinarily tight friendship. We go out nearly every week for dinner or to hang out in bars where we people watch and make up outrageous stories about the patrons. I am in awe of the way he unabashedly loves me, listens to me, dotes on me. Such attention is crush-worthy and I am something like smitten, which does not go unnoticed by my new companion who, rather than recoil or make a big deal about my unrequited love, just keeps hanging out with me until my heart settles down.

Chuck gets serious with a woman he's dating but does not push me away. We continue going on adventures, sharing secrets, entwining our lives. One night, very late, we sit on a bench outside a concert hall after taking in a Nick Cave concert so charged with sexual energy I tell him I'm surprised people didn't get it on in the aisles. This leads to one of the most humorous and telling moments of our love, when we note how fortunate we are to have never fallen in bed together. How easily he could have seduced me. How wise he was to not have. How grateful I am.

Hanging out at Man College brings close ties with the other artists—including Bubba, whose father eventually moves into the RV of Doom—and with Bart's wife Doris Ann. Before long I count these people as true family. They love me at my bubbliest. They love me when I lose my shit over Christmas, which I do every year. They love me, too, steadily but worriedly, as they watch for nearly two years as I sink deeper and deeper into the Peter Hole, as he dismantles my self-esteem, as I fail to leave him despite their urging me to do so. What counsel they have for me is almost always couched in kindness, if not handed out with kid gloves. Chuck is especially displeased. He is the one who introduced me to Peter, the two of them best friends for nearly thirty years. He is the one who warned me over and over and over to never get involved with his friend, joking but not joking that if I fail to heed him, one day it will end, and he will be forced to choose one of us and banish the other.

There's a saying about how, if you hang out at a barbershop, you'll eventually get your hair cut. The more hours I log at Man College, the more ink I acquire. I have full sleeves now, several tattoos on my legs, and a full back piece, from my neck to my waist, that took nearly forty hours to complete. I take pride in not crying, in learning to breathe into the pain of needles piercing skin. I come to theorize that getting tattooed relates in some peculiar way to my eating disorder in that, while extreme discomfort is involved, this pain is a conscious choice, unlike the pain of my childhood, which came unrequested and over which I had no control at all. In an odd way then, the chosen pain of hunger and tattoos is a sort of antidote to the unchosen pain of my father's abuse.

On the first day of Autumn 2017, on the cusp of my fifth year at Man College, I receive the most painful tattoo I have ever gotten. Bob accompanies me. This is not his first time to escort me on an adventure that involves calculated masochism. Weeks earlier, when the stone on my nose-piercing popped off, he went with me to the piercing parlor to have it replaced. That Bob was game for this amused me. As I once posted on Facebook a picture depicting me pretending to give him a tattoo at the shop, on that day I posted a picture of us under the neon PIERCING sign and joked that we were there to get matching septum rings. As ever, Bob's legion of online fans went wild. Taking the joke to the next level, a friend photoshopped an image portraying Bob and me sporting thick bullrings, looking at each other with tough guy expressions. I posted this picture, too, and again his fan club shouted with virtual joy. That prank provoked spontaneous giggling between us that lasts for weeks.

Because I did not learn my lesson from the washboard episode, today's tattoo is another cover-up. Nine months before, on his birthday and in this very shop, Peter and I got matching tattoos featuring his nickname. His mark on my body, me eagerly and impulsively choosing to allow a permanent tribute to him on my flesh, not stopping to think he would never even consider getting a tattoo honoring me. My stupid belief that, like a ring he had once given me, this his-and-her homage to *him, him, him* indicated some true commitment to *us*, some promise we would stay together forever. How happy we were that day, posing for pictures side-by-side, showing off these tattoos. How unhappy I was after he left me, angrily contemplating how I would have to look at that tattoo every single day for the rest of my life.

Unable to bear that idea, I planned, shortly after the breakup, to have it inked over. Then, still lost in denial, I second-guessed myself, and kept it just in case he came back. At that point, I was still fantasizing he might check into rehab, get clean, acknowledge the errors of his ways, promise my love was worth more to him than his addiction, and commit to make amends for the rest of our lives together. How I clung to this vision, even knowing subconsciously it would never come to pass. *But wait—maybe it will!* I told myself to focus not on how the tattoo was a tribute to Peter, but more a reminder of the conversation the artist Jeffrey and I had when he gave it, a fascinating romp through our personal histories. How, when he finished, and Peter came to take a photo, before I could stop myself I said, "Don't get my stretch marks in the picture," a statement I immediately regretted, as it spoke to how much I had internalized Peter's body shaming. Of how Jeffrey silenced me in that moment, saying "You earned those marks." Of how right he was, my beautiful son living proof of his observation.

As more time passed though, I returned to the original plan of covering up the tattoo. By then, nearly four months on my own, the repercussions of Peter's destructive ways were becoming clearer. The trauma, though quieter, still consumed me. The mental anguish was bad enough. But the physical challenges were equally trying. I was terrified at the thought of any man ever touching me intimately again. I had allowed Peter full access to my mind, body, and spirit. Examining how this played out in the end, my body shrunken and afraid all the time, I desperately wished to reclaim myself, most especially this patch of skin defiled by a tattoo that matched one of his and, to my greater dismay, that celebrated him.

I do not fully disclose to Jeffrey my reasons for getting this cover-up. I hint that I have been body shamed and note that in general I just want to forget Peter, and that transforming this daily reminder of him will help with that. I ask him to come up with a design, saying flowers always bring me joy, but other than that I have no specific ideas. In no time, he offers a fix—he will craft a cleverly placed poppy over the existing ink. Poppies, he tells me, are about pain numbing and forgetting. I do not add aloud, but think: *Yes, and they represent drugs, too.* With this red flower, then, I can have a symbol of both forgetting the man who harmed me and never forgetting that at the root of so much of that harm was his addiction. Perfect.

Jeffrey instructs me to lay on a the table on my side—"Like a fancy French lady," as he puts it. I close my eyes under the bright light and he begins. For the first time since my first tattoo in 1988, I cry in pain as the needles dance across my skin. Extensive experience has taught me that there are many sensitive areas on the body and some hurt much more than others. But this spot is the most tender I have ever had worked on. I'm not entirely ignorant to this going in, of course, since obviously the original tattoo is in the same place. But its replacement is a much different affair, lots of heavy outlining followed by a good bit of color. I struggle unsuccessfully to maintain my composure.

Led Zeppelin pours out of the speakers. Bob sits on a chair at the foot of the table. Joe and Bubba sit nearby, sketching art and chatting with me, small talk to try to distract me, until at last, I cannot speak another word, so hard must I focus on breathing, which at times I seem to forget how to do. During most sessions, I easily connect with the buzz, both the literal vibration of the needles and the rush of endorphins that floods in to alleviate the pain. While I have a moment or two of getting into that zone now, mostly I am awash in agony so great it easily finds a place on the list of Most Painful Physical Experiences Ever, right behind giving birth and being bitten by a half-ton horse.

Clutching my face, weeping, I reject Jeffrey's suggestion that we take a break, insist that we forge ahead. Externally I stay as still as I can. Internally I writhe. I think back to the nightmare of childbirth and tell myself over and over and over *I must breathe through this, I must not ask him to stop.* In an odd way, I like these flashbacks of labor. I am rebirthing my own self here on this table, taking a big step toward re-owning my body, which I foolishly entrusted to a man who time and again insulted and abused it.

Though my eyes remain closed most of the time, occasionally I peek at Bob, seated down by my feet, sometimes watching, sometimes nodding off. I am moved by his presence, his willingness to sit by me and observe my pain, as if by being here he can absorb some of it. And he can. He does. Always he carries me.

Two hours after starting, Jeffrey turns off his tattoo machine, wipes the new ink clean with cold liquid green soap, and I recoil like a wounded squirrel being poked with a hot, pointy stick. I joke with Joe and Bubba that at last we have come upon a way to shut me up, just hit me in the ribcage with a million buzzing needles. At last the endorphins kick in, and despite some lingering pain, giddiness arrives. I am high from internal chemistry and the joy of reclamation. Then off Bob and I set for a night on the town, dinner and a concert in the park.

IMPERMANENCE PART II

AN HOUR AFTER GETTING THAT POPPY TATTOO another bomb drops. One that shatters me still more—which seems impossible. One that reveals several new truths about Peter's infinite capacity for duplicity, facts that send me plummeting back into sheer hopelessness, that voice urging me to kill myself returning in full force, louder than ever before.

Bob and I are sitting on the patio of Lucy's Fried Chicken. It is a lovely evening and despite the residual pain of the needles cutting into my ribs, I am relatively happy courtesy of the endorphin effect and knowing never again will I have to see Peter's nickname on my body. I feel present. I feel the shift that has occurred after the passing of three months since the breakup, an interval reached two weeks before, one my son and Garreth both correctly promised would be a big turning point. Then, just as Bob and I are about to dig in—how nice we are eating a big meal—I receive a text message from my friend Carol, asking me to call her as soon as possible. Never having had such a request from her before, I break a personal rule and phone from the table, afraid she is having an emergency. As delicately as she can, she breaks it to me that Peter is in a new relationship, being flaunted on social media by his new girlfriend. I fight the urge to vomit.

I knew this day would come, figured he was probably already out getting drunk in sleazy bars and hooking up with women he deemed more aesthetically worthy of riding in his midlife-crisis mobile. Women who favor makeup and hair dye, flimsy lingerie and tight skirts. Women willing to drink and drug with him. Speculation and confirmation are different beasts though. A rage tears through me at the news of this rebound, and a second rage on top of the first, rage born of the fact that, after finally starting to feel like myself again—my upbeat pre-Peter self—and in the immediate wake of having taken a big step toward reclaiming my body, now I am hit with another gut punch. Carol does not intend to upset me. I understand she is trying to prevent me from being blindsided by randomly stumbling upon the information. I have blocked Peter from my social media and done my best to remove all photographic evidence that he ever existed from mine. But we still have mutual friends and acquaintances, and the dark side of Facebook is that it affords ample opportunity to be caught off guard in this sticky Venn Diagram.

Bob listens as I tell him the news. My ribcage aches. My heart is exploding. I find myself tumbling into the hole of believing that all progress I have made through therapy, self-reflection, and fourteen weeks of being apart from Peter has vanished in an instant. But a little background voice urges me to at least fake continuing with the joy Bob and I have begun our dinner with. "You're better off without him," he reminds for the umpteenth time. I listen. I tell him I know. I tell him I believe him. I mean it. And yet.

I am knocked down again. Bob and I follow through with our plans, finish our meal, enjoy the concert, we really do, but now I am only half-present at best, as I ruminate on this latest news. Back at home, with only her first name to go by but with sleuthing skills honed over twenty-seven years as a journalist, I locate the new woman's Facebook page in less than a minute. I see her announcement to the world: IN A RELATIONSHIP. I look at the date on the post and see she put it up twenty days after he discarded me. *Twenty days. Not even three weeks.*

I scroll, find a picture of the two of them snuggled together with a gloating caption. "I sure do love this man!" she boasts, punctuating her proclamation with multiple goofy smiley-face emojis sporting hearts instead of eyes. I scrutinize her. Ah, yes. Dyed hair and makeup, the very things he asked of me, because he wanted me to be someone I was not and would never be. I scrutinize him. He is stoned, pupils dilated, and looking miserable, his signature scowl in place.

I fluctuate between fury at them and self-hatred at my inability to close the window. I scroll through the comments on her posts and see that his family is gushing over them as they had once gushed over me, and I feel sicker still. These are the same family members who, only recently, sent me lengthy messages to tell me how fucked up Peter is, how I was the best thing that ever happened to him, that leaving me was a huge mistake on his part, and how very sorry they were about the way he treated me, especially after all I did for him. How keenly it hurts to see them rush in and support this new union, not only the public slap of it, but because knowing what they know about his drug addiction, they should not exalt, they should warn her to run away. But no. I am erased from their lives like I never existed. She is this year's model. They fall at her feet.

Something else hurts so much more. I feel with certainty this is the same woman he fucked the year before, the one he told me about the night of the rattlesnake. When he confessed, Peter steadfastly claimed that dalliance had been a one-night stand with a random stranger picked up in a bar, that they got a hotel room. He insisted their tryst had been awkward, and, weirdly, overshared that he had not been able to ejaculate, I suppose his implication being she turned him off. He said he regretted the whole thing, with the exception being that sex with her had crystalized that he only wanted to be with me. He said they were not in contact anymore.

I had already discovered, after he left me, that the one-night stand woman was, in fact, no stranger at all, but a coworker, this news spilt by Peter's brother Scott, during one of his phone calls to see how I was doing and tell me what a grave error Peter had made in letting me go. Scott, always high and loose-lipped, dished details entirely contrary to what Peter had sworn, explaining how he had just flown to Houston from Los Angeles, and had been irritated that Peter blew off their reunion to be with this woman instead. How he was more irritated still that Peter asked him to drive his Camaro to the woman's apartment, swap it out for his work truck. Scott described in detail having been terribly upset with all this, and how unhappy he had been that Peter coerced him into complicity in his shitty behavior, demanding he never breathe a word to me. So much for brotherly confidence.

Seeing the picture of Peter and this woman, confirming in her profile details that she works for the same company he does, means that if she *is* the same woman, Peter never stopped being in touch with her. It's entirely possible and most probable they never stopped actually touching. At the very least they saw each other in the office regularly, surely spending more time in each other's company than Peter and I ever did, as we conducted our relationship living more than a hundred miles apart. Had they been cheating all along? So many questions fill my mind, so many scenes assault it. I picture him confiding in her, inventing stories about how terribly I treated him, soliciting her sympathy, duping her as he had me, and in doing so, grooming her to be my replacement.

I want to not believe any of this. I entertain the possibility that maybe the coworker Scott identified is a different woman. If I confront Peter and demand the truth he will just spit out more bullshit lies. I, fool, dig around some more, salting my gaping wounds. On a public page Peter created allegedly to promote positivity, a page of which he made me a co-administrator, I see that the two of them had flirted openly, something I missed as it was occurring. I find a comment he made on one of her posts there, a movie quote, the exact same one he once used to woo me. I look at the timestamp and see he left this for her precisely *one hour* after telling me he when he thought of sex it was not with me. Now I flash back to the black lace underwear I once found in the trunk of his stupid car, how he held those panties up and asked if they were mine. They were not. Informed of this, he mumbled an excuse, saying that they must belong to his daughter. I wonder now—*Why would his daughter store her lingerie in his car?*

This final straw, this hammer-to-the-head wakeup in the form of this woman's boastful social media posts and the little mushy heart emojis he responds with, spark further epiphanies still that the entirety of my relationship with Peter had been one never-ending series of lies. A total scam. I had been taken, used, fleeced, drained of all energy and resources, and then discarded by a sociopath. This does not strike me as the sort of truth that will set me free. This truth feels like it will kill me.

Why am I torturing myself digging up confirmation of this affair? Why not just say—*Hey, no surprise that he's an even huger asshole than I realized?* Why not thank the Baby Jesus or the universe or whatever for my freedom from an obviously manipulative sadist?

How I wish it worked like that. A mental snapping of fingers, a pulling back of shoulders, head up, a dignified march forward. But this is not how the fallout of Peter's abuse plays out. I cannot now, as I had so often when we were together, even try to pretend his sustained, clearly calculated villainy has not happened, or that maybe it wasn't so bad. Now I know he cheated on top of every-thing else. Imagining confronting him, I can just hear him mutter-ing some technical excuse that they had not started dating until he had officially left me. But this, too, would be yet more bullshit. I look again at her announcement of their relationship, again note it is dated twenty days after he ended things with me. *Twenty days.* The math here is not algebraic. If they made their union public in fewer than three weeks then, doubtless, they conspired in advance. The lack of discretion, this public display of hers, was surely meant to reach me. Who does something like that?

Though the knowledge does little to soothe me, I actually know exactly who. Someone incredibly insecure. And, I speculate, someone who had been his mistress for some time, who had been eager all along to go public, let the cat out of the bag, to prove to the world *she* was "his girl," not me. Now she no longer has to hide it. She thinks social media notices equal proof of commitment from Peter, just as once I had thought a ring, a co-purchased RV, and matching tattoos proved his commitment to me.

I am not jealous of her. I feel sorry for her, knowing what she is in for, that her time with him will be far greater punishment than any comeuppance I could conjure, if I even had the energy to hate her and wish her ill, which, oddly, I do not. I know Peter, his bag of tricks, his skill at eliciting sympathy as a means of seduction and then sadistically fostering insecurity as way to keep the upper hand. If he hasn't yet begun to make her life a living hell, I know it will only be a matter of time before he does. Imagining her looming suffering, I recall a quote in the Capuchin Crypt in Rome, the resting place of thousands of monk skeletons: *"What you are now we used to be; what we are now you will be..."*

I see she has a young daughter. My heart aches knowing this child will watch her mother be tortured by Peter, that she will suffer lifelong damage as a result. I remember times my own son had, as a child, witnessed me on the receiving end of abuse from various shitty men. How he has carried this hurt with him into adulthood. I look again at the picture of the two of them. I see that triumphant smile of possession on her face. She might likely be very nice, perhaps empathetic, assets in everyday life that will turn to detriments during the time she serves with him and he uses her up then discards her, as he did with me. I am irritated that she rationalized cheating with him, but I also know his powers of persuasion, and have little doubt he held her tightly, swore he was leaving me for her, and that I was such a bitch, making it so complicated for him to escape my grip. How clever he always was with me, too, whipping out the pity card to secure my love.

Knowing all that I do, knowing how much better off I am without Peter, still only goes so far in comforting me. In truth, uncovering his cheating leaves me feeling tortured anew. When, for a moment, I slip into anger at this other woman, I hit the brakes swiftly on that emotion, again remind myself that she is a victim, too, that I do not need to wish her ill will, that she is now living in Hell, kissing his ass, making his dinner, soothing him every time he complains about anything, which is always. He will look for her vulnerabilities and exploit them. I see she is quite plump and know he will shame her, too, for not being supermodel thin, for that double chin of hers. He will play on her insecurities, manipulate her, and even when she makes changes, which she will, he will in turn, as he always did with me, move the goalposts, find other vulnerabilities, exploit those, too, until, like me, he will at last tell her she is unbearably crazy, ugly, undesirable, and replace her with whatever other woman he is surely already lining up, keeping waiting in the shadows.

By midnight I am drained from my detective work. Still I scroll. Twelve-thirty. Ready to drop and yet somehow still wide awake. A very bad combination. My reptilian brain has taken over. This is exactly, *exactly* how I felt the night of the rattlesnake, after hearing Peter confess the one-night stand, which I am now confident was anything but. Now I have a face to put to the heretofore blurry figure in the movie looping in my mind of him fucking someone else. I cannot sleep. Now I understand why I had, all those times, brought up the dalliance after promising not to, crying about how betrayed I felt. My intuition had been spot-on, his angry outbursts claiming that my inability to let go of the past was the problem a load of horseshit. She had never been in his past. She had been in his office, right there, by his side, the two of them colluding.

I stare at the ceiling. I fantasize messaging her, telling her of Peter's meth and coke and pill and porn addictions and describing how he hit me in the face. Twice. Of sending screenshots of our last long text exchange—eight more hours of my life lost to him—in which he defensively claimed to have kept his meth use secret and, in the exact words he used to describe his relationship with her, "banged another woman," not to hurt me but just to "get through the day." A punishing part of me wants to point out to her the date of this conversation and the many other times he called and texted and emailed me *after* they went public as a couple, but before I found out about it, insisting he needed time alone to better himself, dangling before me a conceited "offer" that if I were lucky, he might just show up a year hence and sweep me off my feet. To let her know of his trip to the ranch five days after she updated her relationship status, that long talk during which he sat so close, let me go on and on about getting back together, his promise to consider a cooling off period, that he might be willing to renegotiate the relationship. About how, during this lie-fest, he never mentioned her, cleverly omitted that she even existed, just took the ego strokes that came with my begging, did not pull away when I kissed him goodbye. And how, in doing all of this, he was, in his own fashion, now cheating on her with me. Such depraved irony.

How will his new victim react if I do this? How will she feel knowing that he has remained in touch with me and communicated at length, saying he still loves me, that perhaps he will return? What will she think, learning that he is playing both of us?

Fuck him. Fuck him. Fuck him.

My mind switches tracks, and once again memories rush in of the untold times I cared for him when his body was so broken he could barely move. How he took advantage of me on so many levels. I futilely try to calculate all the time and money I spent, thousands and thousands of dollars and hours lost, never to be reclaimed. I think of how he shit on me and shit on me and shit on me, taking until I had nothing left to give, us some real life version of that disturbing children's book, *The Giving Tree*, then, monstrous insult to measureless injuries, yelling at me that I was toxic, codependent, too nice, overly helpful, and to blame for everything, before walking away.

My anger surges, my spiteful desires expand. I will myself to call up as many self-soothing strategies as I can from all of those self-help books I once read to try to salvage the relationship, the nightstand stack a teetering tower, ever-growing with each new Peter hurt. I so do not want to be consumed by petty vitriol.

I am consumed by petty vitriol.

Once again rattled beyond measure, I cry. Finally I close my computer, crawl under the covers, and drift into a fitful sleep, waking up at horse-feeding time, too tired to tend to this task. I fumble around for paper and a pen, write Bob a note asking him to proceed without me, and leave it in the bathroom sink where he will be sure to see it. I lie back down. Sleep will not come. I get back up and find him, announcing I will go on feeding rounds after all.

I watch Bob at the counter, fixing his coffee. He asks about my ribs. I tell him they hurt, a lot. I tell him the renewed Peter pain hurts even more.

"I know," he says. And then, again, the refrain of the summer. "We'll get through it," he promises.

I tell myself he is absolutely right. I feel so sick, but vow I will not let this latest tsunami pull me under as so many previous waves of grief have. Coffee finished, we make our rounds, chuckle at the chickens, putt-putt in the golf cart across the yard to the barn, Tiny and Queenie flanking us, these mighty beasts unconcerned with my heartache, only hungry for their breakfast. I remind myself of all I have gotten through already. I am going to get through this, too. Bob is going to help. Because that is what Bob does. He helps. Always.

ONE STEP FORWARD, A HUNDRED BACK

AM BACK TO FEELING LIKE SHIT MOST MINUTES OF MOST WAKING hours. But maybe the work I have been doing in therapy has not all been for naught, as Peter taunted me it was, causing me momentarily to question if he might be right, before realizing his real beef with my seeking help was that it forced me to clearly see and acknowledge the truth of his abuse. I notice a speck of determination, nearly imperceptible, in the far reaches of my mind. Though I remain nauseous most of the time, I believe Bob now in a way I found impossible in the immediate wake of Peter's departure, back when I awoke suddenly so many nights, sitting bolt upright, disoriented, jolted into consciousness by a shooting pain in my chest, wondering if I was literally having a heart attack. Those days, when Bob told me I would be okay, I might tell him I agreed, but really, I could not conceive his prediction ever becoming a reality. Now I am determined to apply his advice: *Makuna Hatata.* I have got to put this crap in my past. I must.

Progress is blemished by backslides. Temptation gets the better of me. I send Peter a brief, biting email, admonishing him for being an ungrateful asshole, for cheating, for lying about cheating, and for parading his not-actually-new relationship online, where he knew I would find out about it. Part of me thinks I should feel regret for this relapse, for taking his stupid bait yet again, for contacting him, for letting my inner angry teenager drive the car of my emotions. And part of me thinks, *No, I don't regret it. Fuck him. Who will stand up for me?* I will not lie back and take the abuse anymore. I will modify my body. I will modify my heart. I will modify my spirit. I will erase this cruel man from my mind for good.

This determination to go forward, to get present, to not ruminate on the abuse, is noble but, rather than gaining momentum, as time passes, increasingly my efforts seem fruitless. With each passing day, the more the news sinks in that Peter betrayed me even more than I could conceive possible, the greater my despair grows. Flashbacks of him hitting me in the face resurface. I cannot shake them. I am appalled at these memories. How had I let that happen? Again I ask myself: What part of me is so damaged that I would allow myself to stay—that I would create reasons to stay? Gus consoles me over and over and over. He points to studies explaining that I am not alone, that so many victims stay with abusers in part because, for as wrong as it sounds, they know what to expect. Like Bob, he promises me I will survive and thrive. I repeat these promises to myself, but find little consolation.

Shame. Confusion. Sorrow. Pain. Anger.

Over the course of the next few blurry weeks, I make choices. I am unable to discern whether the choices are good or bad, helpful or harmful. I feel intoxicated, impaired, overwhelmed, and driven by my rage and my grief. I lash out furiously on Facebook, posting open letters to Peter and his new victim. I detail, at length, the abuse I suffered at his hands. Though I have blocked both of them, I am sure that mutual friends will alert him, that he will find a way to see these words, just as his new victim intended her announcement to reach me. This, in large part, is what drives me. I anticipate the triangulation will likely get him off, as he misinterprets my outcries as a catfight for his love. I don't care. I take pleasure in shaming him now the way he so often shamed me.

On the other hand, I also wonder if this public dressing down might inspire him to smoke a bunch of meth, speed to my house in his overcompensatory muscle car, his teenage boy music blaring, and shoot me with one of his many guns. My fear and hypervigilance grow. If he comes after me, I will not hesitate to defend myself. How have I come to this—being opposed to guns entirely before meeting him to fantasizing blowing him away should he try to hurt me?

The most agonizing choice I make is to tell my son and Bob about Peter's physical violence. Henry had watched me endure more than one abusive relationship when he was little. Now I confess to him that not only had I again gotten mixed up with a dangerous man, but this time the brutality had escalated from psychological to corporal. I choke out the words, "He hit me in the face," and sob uncontrollably. My son, a compassionate man now, listens intently and responds softly, "I love you," he says. "I'm sorry that happened."

When I muster the courage to come clean with Bob about the full extent of Peter's abuse, we are sitting in the golf cart, having just finished our morning rounds. I tell him about the hitting. He takes in the news and is silent, pausing momentarily before angrily murmuring, "Son of a bitch," under his breath. He reaches for my hand, squeezes it. We sit very still for a long time. I cry. I always cry. I am, it seems, back to never not crying. I tell Bob what I have told him ten million times before. That I am so sorry that he has to see me so sad. That I so badly want him to see the joyful me, that a joyful me really exists, buried under all these layers of sorrow. That I hate he has yet to see this true me, the happy me, the self-confident me. The me that Peter found and, inch by inch, reduced to rubble.

Bob just keeps holding my hand. After a while, he says, "I'm glad I can be here for you, hon." I'm glad, too. More than glad. I tell him a truth—that if he were not here with me, that if I were alone at the ranch, I might not have made it. Because, though I have always pushed away suicidal ideation, perhaps being all alone for long stretches trying to deal with this latest fallout might have been a last straw. I tell him his steady presence is the daily reminder I need to stick around, to get better.

Meanwhile, back over on social media, it takes very little time for the Facebook chorus to weigh in with their opinion on my rants about Peter and his new victim. Resoundingly the verdict comes in from many others who have had the misfortune of going before me, who have dwelled in their own circles of Hell dealing with nearly identical abusers. Peter, they reveal, is a classic narcissist, possibly a sociopath, or a combination of the two, known in psychology lingo as a narcopath.

A narcissist? I had been with narcissists before. So how did I miss this about him? Back to Google I go for the next phase of my post-mortem. I read several articles on Narcissistic Personality Disorder, equally shocked and fascinated at how precisely Peter fits the profile. Once, back when we were still together, after describing him to one of my therapists, I wondered aloud if he might be a narcissist. She said she didn't think so. This memory comes back and with it the sad knowledge that, so in the grips of Stockholm Syndrome had I been, I had described him inaccurately.

I realize how, foolishly, I had thought my marriage to a narcissist more than a decade prior, and the therapy to address that pain, had inoculated me against getting involved with another one. Now, I see all too well that my blinders had not been successfully removed. Not even close. As I let this sink in, as I devour all the research people share with me about the predatory nature of narcissists, as my blinders finally, *finally* do fall off, I awaken still more to the reality of Peter's mendacity.

The more I read, the more appalled I become. I now understand that Peter had, as all narcissists do, waged a very calculated campaign to destroy me, that he took perverse pleasure in causing me pain. I learn that the man who came onto me so unremittingly to seduce me into a relationship with him was a total imposter, non-existent, a character created to lure me in with love bombing, as he insisted I was the most amazing woman he had ever met, heaped upon me gifts and false words of love, and fired off infinite stupid texts full of lovey-dovey emojis and terms of endearment.

Then, once he hooked me, the boundary-testing began: body shaming, ghosting, getting wasted all the time, all of these actions angering me, as he knew they would. I protested, yes. I threatened to leave. Once I did leave. But Peter understood how to lure me back, using hoovering, another classic technique, sucking me back in with his personal crises and, once in a while, just enough more love bombing to convince me true change was on the horizon, that I just needed to give him some more time. At which point he would smash me back down, seeing forgiveness on my part not as compassion but as weakness, and an indication of just how much he could get away with. He made no secret of this even, often saying what he loved most about me was my willingness to put up with his bullshit.

The tactic of offering random rewards was a specialty of Peter's. My rude awakening about the cheating helps me to look back and see so many examples of how he employed this strategy. The time he showed up hours after he had promised to, and bedded me down immediately, whispering in my ear afterwards, "See? This is what you get when you don't complain about me being late." The time he clung to me like a baby after a particularly nasty fight, his lips pressed to my ear, desperation in his voice, confiding, "I would die if you ever stopped loving me." The ring he bought me. The times he pretended to be earnestly seeking work in Austin, so he could come and live with me. And that motherfucking RV. What was up with that? Why invest thousands into an alleged love-nest when he knew he was going to leave me? All tactics of confusion I see now. Such cold comfort.

Now I drag myself through the days. Ironically, because I am no longer busy putting out Peter fires, tending to his constant crises, I finally have time to read, to knit, to relax, to take care of myself, to spend time with friends. But my agitation is so pervasive I cannot find the concentration or energy for any of these things that used to bring me joy. He has moved on to his next fix. I am stuck perseverating on the abuse, the shock at realizing how evil he truly is, my PTSD flaring out of control and causing me to loop and loop and loop.

Yet another anvil falls when at last I attempt to talk frankly with Chuck, who introduced me to Peter, warned me away from him, then watched in disgust as I dismissed his warning and became a dark shadow of my former sunny self in the company of his best friend. So many times Chuck told me to just get out, that Peter was trouble, and my desire to make things work the ultimate Fool's Journey. The longer I stayed with Peter, the more my friendship with Chuck sputtered. Now it seems broken beyond repair. He is so angry that I did not listen to him. I am so hurt that he has pulled away.

Peter told me, more than once, of his great jealousy over my intimate friendship with Chuck, whom he considers a brother. He also told me of his lifelong jealousy of his biological brother, once even awkwardly joking, before he introduced us, that surely I would prefer Scott, just as he said their mother had. It occurs to me now that Peter's inferiority complex might well have been what inspired him to seduce me, that this seduction was not born of desire for me—how many times he told me he found me repulsive—but rather to show his Chuck, his chosen brother, that he could steal me away, and in doing so prove he was, for once in his life, top dog. Had the whole thing then been a sham, a pissing contest initiated by insecure Peter, a sick, sick man pursuing me for sick, sick reasons? I could easily enumerate far less plausible theories.

The more I fell apart over Peter when we were together, the more Chuck withdrew from me. For years I had confided in him, sought counsel, found comfort. Now, in tremendous pain, I feel unable to go to him, once one of my greatest confidantes. He is so upset that two of his best friends hate each other. This I understand. I also understand now that I have always loved Chuck more than Peter, a love uncomplicated by romantic entanglement and nurtured by reciprocity, of which Peter was incapable. I am devastated at the thought of losing him. I want so badly to put this Peter shit behind me, to resume my easy friendship with Chuck. When I am at the tattoo shop, a place I used to laugh all the time, things are tense more often than not. Somedays Chuck smiles, hugs me, says he loves me. Most days, though, he is distant and dark. This feeds my fear that our friendship is doomed.

The terrible conversation, the latest blow, comes while I am driving to a wedding way out in the Hill Country, way too much alone time on my hands, ruminating on my Chuck angst and crying. Peter robbed me of my dignity, self-esteem, appetite, and so much time, money, and energy I will never get back. Now my foolish choice to be with him has, it seems, cost me my cherished friendship with Chuck. I cannot take this. I call Chuck and tell him I need to discuss this matter now. He pushes back, lashes out at me, calls me stupid, yells that my suffering is all my fault. I tell him I am feeling suicidal. This, too, he dismisses with rage.

As his words sink in, I wonder if, at last, I really have reached my very darkest hour. I honestly don't think I can take the pain any longer. I imagine checking into my hotel room and offing myself. I remind myself that this thought is false desire. I do not want to die. And besides, it would be incredibly rude to leave such a mess for an unsuspecting, underpaid housekeeper to find. I think of Henry. I think of Bob. I try to think of myself, the profusion of love all around me, so many friends, so many pets, my amazing ranch. All very valid reasons to live. I think, bitterly, of Peter, and how if I heed the voice telling me to step off, then he will win. My father, too. These hateful men, tag-teaming in my head and heart, forever willing me to die.

I also think about how hard I tried to forgive Peter, to take into account that his traumatic childhood shaped the sick man he became. I had used this excuse a million times to give him a pass as he abused me more and more. But the literature I read about narcissists informs me that, to a one, these monsters hook their victims with incredibly sad tales, usually on the first date, knowing their sob stories will cause an instant chemical reaction in their targets, an actual biological switch-flipping, an internal voice insisting, *YOU MUST CARE FOR HIM. YOU MUST REMOVE HIS SORROWS WITH YOUR LOVE!*

These stories, then, are bait narcissists use to secure a new supply to feed their sadistic needs, and later as excuses for being incapable of change. They "can't help themselves" because they are "too broken from childhood trauma." They blame their cruelty, cheating, and violence—exhibited once the honeymoon period ends and when they are called on their shit—on their partners, claiming they are driven to such behaviors because these victims "aren't being understanding enough." So, yeah, it's always someone else's fault. Sadly, because this happens incrementally over time, the victims are gaslighted into self-blame, and wind up constantly apologizing for things that aren't their fault. The cumulative effect of these cycles, to which I can testify with great authority, is that eventually the victim loses all self-esteem. At which point the narcissist hurls further accusations, tells the victim she is too needy, and how repulsive this is. Then it's discard time, and whomever they've been cheating with—because narcissists are notorious for cheating, there is almost always another one already on the hook—gets moved from side project to shotgun seat.

I look back over some of the more obvious narcissists I have been with. One told me, during our first conversation, that his parents had forced him to do something that resulted in his infant sister dying. Another opened with the tale of how his sister had shot dead their mother and then herself. The narcissist to whom I had been married began softening me with tales of how he had been widowed and left alone to raise his daughter. And Peter? He told of being taken away from his father at four, moved from England to the States, never seeing him again as he died tragically a few years later, and how his mother had overdosed ten years after that, and how even before this, he had been surrendered by his mother to the state, raised in foster homes. An underdog addict, I could not resist such tales of woe. I wanted to make each of their lives better. Instead, being with each of them made my own life so much worse.

Peter deployed so many other tricks, too. When he was especially evil, when he couldn't gaslight me into thinking I was just crazy and misinterpreting his mean actions, he would fall back on this one: "Sorry. I'm just an asshole." This was simple reverse psychology, trotted out to confuse me into forgiving him some more, though I did not see the ploy for what it was, and so, often, fell for it. Even times I agreed with him, said yes, he really was a huge asshole, almost always I qualified my agreement by saying, "But you're also so good. Look at all you've done." And then, as he knew I would, I ticked off the ego-stroking list I had down pat, about how he had raised his daughter (never mind how much his drug addiction had fucked her up), how he had survived his childhood (never mind that I had survived mine, too, and yet did not use my trauma as an excuse to maliciously hurt others), how he was trying to get sober (utter bullshit I realized too late).

I dig and dig, desperate to make sense of the insanity, despite knowing I am engaging in self-harm, ripping opening wounds that haven't healed in the first place, as I inventory more and more examples of how he calculatedly stole from me everything he could. He said how jealous he was of my accomplishments, of how easy I made it seem to have so many friends and a fun life.

Now I wonder if, in wooing me, he thought he might become kind and successful by osmosis, proximity a magic potion, a shortcut to joy. And when that did not happen, he punished me for having what he did not, took from me and destroyed the very things he once claimed to admire: my happiness, my friends, my life.

I find myself firmly entrenched in unmitigated despondency. Having lived fooled by his lies for years, I no longer trust myself to know what truth looks like. I had made myself believe in Peter. I had made myself believe he loved me. He fed these lies. Understanding that I had been so wrong for so long makes me question my sanity and my future. How will I ever again let another man near me?

I wobble. I cry. I sleep terribly. But I make myself get out of bed each day. And every single morning, there is Bob, asking, "How are ya, hon?" Reminding me to hold on.

DANTE

N EARLY NOVEMBER, MY OLD YELLOW LABRADOR, DANTE, begins exhibiting signs he is approaching the end of his life. He cannot catch his breath and pants constantly. For a day or two I opt to take the path of denial, hoping the matter will resolve itself. It does not. I contact a mobile veterinarian and arrange for her to come assess the situation, explaining my greatest desire is that if he is, in fact, close to death, perhaps we can find ways to give him a little more time. In my correspondence, I own that this wish is selfish, and emphasize I will need her guidance to help me make the truly right choice for Dante, instead of choosing what is best for me.

The appointment is scheduled for a few days later, and on the eve of the vet's arrival, it becomes increasingly apparent her job will be not to prolong Dante's life, but rather to assist him in easing through his final transition. I spend the entire day in bed with him, grateful for the incredibly rare occasion of an empty calendar. I observe him panting incessantly. Some moments I aim for normalcy, dive into my computer while he snoozes beside me. Other moments I stop typing and scrolling, wrap myself around him, and bawl my eyes out.

Dante, unwavering in his ever-pleasant disposition, receives both my actions and inactions with the same response. He smiles his just-happy-to-be-here smile, exhibiting no signs of pain, and keeps right on panting. This cheerfulness is his signature, and his greatest talent is demonstrating life in the present moment.

I wake up the next day knowing with near certainty that this is Dante's last morning with me. I offer him a can of wet food, surprised and happy to see him scarf it down. A big clue that he is at the end has been his greatly diminished appetite of late. Food had been Dante's first true love always, his recent waning interest a sign that cannot be ignored. His last few hours are spent in good company, as he joins me in the living room for the writing workshop I lead, and all the attendees heap love on him and do not raise an eyebrow when I lie on the floor and spoon him.

Workshop wraps, the clock ticks closer to the Hour of the End. Bob has been working outside in his shed, but now comes in to get some lunch. He finds me still on the floor with Dante and says, "One day you'll have to do that for me."

He means this as a joke, a little gallows levity before the grim task of saying a final goodbye to Dante. Even as I understand on one level his intent, my brain makes no time to process his remark or its true meaning. A sharp pain shoots through me and I cry out in anguish, tears that had only recently ceased now returning in a torrent. Bob recoils, a look of horror on his face.

"I'm sorry, honey," he says. "I didn't mean it."

I leap up to hug him. "Don't apologize," I say. "I know you didn't mean it."

This begins a short back-and-forth that reminds me of the gift-giving ritual I witnessed on my trips to Japan, each gift given spurring another gift given in return. Bob explains he was kidding. I explain I didn't mean to react so strongly. He apologizes again. I apologize in return.

Bob approaches Dante and tells him he is a good boy. Then he tells me he cannot be present for the death because, he assures me, I do not want to see him cry. After lunch, he retreats back outside to his man cave and Henry's father, Big Red, arrives to help me through. Though we split up before our son turned three, Big and I have always maintained a close friendship, which has included co-parenting the ten dogs I have adopted over the years. He has attended the deaths of many of them, crying with me, holding me, holding the dying dog, being a steady presence.

Now he sits next to Dante as I stand and begin pacing the house, this pacing much like the pacing I did upon being bitten by Tiny, when I was driven by shock, denial, and a desire for escape. I should stay right beside Dante, but I have to put some of my anxious energy somewhere. So as Big holds vigil, I dash down the hall, make some beds, come back to check in, dash back down the hall, make some more beds, until, at last, the vet arrives.

Dr. May appears to be barely out of her teens. She is the perfect mix of pragmatism and mercy. Looking at Dante, observing his panting and the bulging fatty tumors that are likely pushing on his lungs, she says she can do diagnostics, including exploratory surgery, but this might well result in nothing other than great financial expense and reveal only that his time really has come. We all look at Dante. We know. I make the official call, which is always the very hardest part. Once I tell her to retrieve the medication needed to release him painlessly, ironic relief washes over me. No, I do not want him to go. Yes, he is ready to go. I need to let him go.

Sluggish from the anesthesia she administers first, Dante falls into a heavy slumber. Dr. May then injects the heart-stopping medication as Big and I cry and cry and hold him and thank him for all he has given us and wish him fair sailing. Once she pronounces him dead, the vet slips out. Big holds me. We continue to stroke Dante, who appears only to be napping, save for the fact the sound of his labored breathing has now ceased.

When other dogs departed, we quickly sent their bodies off for cremation. This time, because the dog undertaker is out on other calls, Dante remains for hours. Big Red stays for a spell, then leaves me to sit an abbreviated shiva alone. I observe how I am not freaked out by Dante's still body, the way I had felt with the other dogs. Someone once told me that death is not an emergency. I let that message sink in now, have gratitude for a little extra time with him, continuing to thank him for all of his love. When the undertaker arrives at last, I am able, as I had not been with other dog corpses, to help him heft Dante's enormous body onto a stretcher.

The following day, noting I continue to feel relief more than anything else, I wonder if this is just denial, if grief, which has already been torturing me for months as I try to wrap my head around all of Peter's deceit and abuse, will pummel me some more. But there is a palpable difference in the loss of Dante versus the departure of a violent man. Dante has only ever been steady on, full of love, in the moment, loyal always. I provided him with the very best life I could— true of my time with Peter, too. Unlike Peter, though, Dante appreciated the love, did not take advantage of me, never bit the hand that fed him. This is what allows me to know that I really am at peace with his departure. Ours had been a true, heartfelt, reciprocal love. There were no unresolved hurts or disputes between us, no betrayal to reckon with, no confusion to try to futilely sort through.

One day, not long after Dante dies, I head to the tattoo shop for an appointment with Chuck. He has been working periodically on my left sleeve over the course of a year, and now he is going to finish it. This appointment has been made, canceled, and rescheduled a couple of times already, due mostly to Chuck's busy schedule. But we both know there is a bigger reason. Things are still not right between us ever since that phone call when he yelled at me that I was so stupid for having gotten involved with Peter. An apologetic text message sent immediately after that call, asking him what it will take to heal us, netted me a one-word reply: *Time*.

A few weeks after that, when I could take his silence no longer, I said as much and he agreed to meet with me, a meeting that started with a promising hug before quickly dissolving to anger as I extracted a piece of paper, upon which I had made a list of topics, most of them detailing what Peter had done. Chuck's temper flared and he asked if this was about Peter or about me and him. I replied it was all intertwined. When I told him that he needed to know that Peter had hit me in the face, and more than once, Chuck laughed. This was a surreal moment, and I tried to convince myself it was nervous laughter, the inappropriate sort you hear at funerals. I told him it was not funny at all and continued with my diatribe. In the end we both calmed down, if only slightly, and I asked him if we could please navigate our way back to true friendship. He said we could. We stood to hug again, and I said, "I love you." He offered silence in response. I asked, "Do you love me?" He said, "I do. But sometimes you're hard to be around."

When I arrive for my appointment, a couple of weeks after this conversation, Chuck seems chilly. I ask him if he is up for finishing the work. He says he is. I lie down on the table. I toss out a few light topics—ask what he is reading, how his life is. He answers monosyllabically, and I know him well enough to understand he is not happy to be with me. My tension mounts. Besides my sorrow at what has become of us, it is never a good idea to give or receive ink when one or both participants are in a foul mood.

We take a break and step outside. He observes me post a picture of our session on Facebook and snaps at me for not asking his permission first. I point out that I have been posting pictures of my sessions for four years, that this is promotion for the shop, and not once before has he complained. He snarls back an angry retort. I demand to know what is up.

Now the truth pours out of him. He barks at me. "My girlfriend hates you," he says. Then, of Peter, he adds, "My best friend hates you. I'm tired of defending you to them." He goes on to say that I have been a shitty friend, he doesn't know why I hang out at the shop, and he doesn't know why he has been roped in to working on my sleeve, when he's only ever done a few tattoos on me.

I am both affronted and shocked at these aberrant statements. He is the one who, all those years before, extended the invitation to spend regular time in the shop. He has done at least fifty-percent of the ink on my body, and I have a lot of ink. I respond with my own blur of words, chief among my retorts that his best friend is a piece of shit that hit me. This pulls from Chuck an explosion of bitterness, and repeatedly he tells me he doesn't believe me, that I am lying, that Peter never hit me, or that, on the off chance he did, it is because I asked for it.

Now I am shaking with rage. He says it's time to finish the tattoo and I look at him like he's just proposed we go on a five-state killing spree. There is no way I am letting him finish my tattoo. There is no way I will let him near my body ever again. I am done with him. I am done with all of the repercussions the shit storm called Peter. I rush into the shop to retrieve my things and see Chuck return to his station and put gloves on. "Let's finish it," he growls.

"Fuck you," I say. *"He hit me! He hit me! He hit me!"* And then I march out the door.

It takes me a few days, but I am surprised to find myself able, rather quickly, to step back a few paces from my Chuck consternation. I still have moments of white hot anger at the things he said. I have moments of self-righteousness, too, a desire to send him a card saying SORRY FOR YOUR LOSS, ASSHOLE. I am furious he did not tell me sooner that he didn't want to see me, that he said we could salvage our friendship, that I believed him and kept showing up, not knowing how much he despised me. I am so embarrassed by this. But there is something bigger, something that outpaces these moments of pain and rage.

A lesson I learned from Dante long ago revisits me. When I adopted him, when I was told how ill-behaved he was, and when all of this proved to be untrue, I wondered aloud to a friend why I had been so misinformed at the pound. This friend had done animal rescue work and explained that sometimes people incur such guilt over surrendering their pets that they make preposterous excuses for giving them up. That sometimes they make themselves believe the stories, to alleviate their guilt.

I call up the story Dante's humans fed the shelter when they gave him up. How they likely invented this negativity about him, the most pleasant dog I ever lived with, to convince themselves they were off the hook, that they had no choice but to give him up. I tell myself that Chuck, always a gifted storyteller, has come up with a narrative to keep his head from exploding. He needs a scapegoat for his pain. I have been a scapegoat my entire life, in my family of origin, in employment situations, in friendships gone awry. Now, here we are, a perfect storm. His loyalty to Peter crosses many decades. He does not want to accept that his friend is the sort to crash a hand into my face. He needs plausible deniability, just like Dante's people did. He told me long ago one day he would wind up choosing either Peter or me if I made the error of getting involved.

Now, his decision is made. He chooses Peter. And he chooses his girlfriend, who for years has held a grudge against me, dating back to when I first got the ranch. I had so badly wanted to sell Chuck five acres—long before I ever thought about moving to the country, he dreamed of buying land he could camp on, roam around, build a house upon. But the acres he asked for were in the middle of my property, an impossible proposition with the potential for complicated legal entanglement down the road. I offered him a different section instead. Chuck, miffed, was not interested. His girlfriend never forgave me for this, never stopped to take into account that if our situations were reversed, there is no way in hell they would ever sell me a center parcel of land. Too, I suspect that, like Peter, she had always been jealous of the friendship Chuck and I once so easily shared.

Of all the collateral damage that being involved with Peter

causes, losing Chuck is the most incomprehensible and far, far more painful than losing Peter. Chuck had loved me in a way unique to any other love I had ever experienced. I once thought him my platonic soul mate. Now the friendship is over. Easily this is the most crushing, most devastating blow delivered by having let Peter into my life. And yet, I forgive Chuck. I miss him. I see in him what I see in so many of my siblings who, to this day, deny the abuse of our narcissistic father. How very personally I used to take their denial, thinking they were all calling me crazy, shunning me, until, finally, I came to realize, no, really what they are doing is whatever it takes for them to survive.

It's like Peter has smeared gallons of steamy wet shit all over every last inch of my existence and I will never be able to clean it all off. But Peter also taught me the humiliation that comes with begging a man to take me back. What an excruciating lesson that was. I will not make the same mistake with Chuck. I do not call him, or text him, or try to come up with ways to fix things. I honor his request to never see me again. I abruptly stop going to Man College, no longer comfortable in the place that brought me such happiness for so many years. I am again unmoored, astounded at what my involvement with one wicked man has done to my life.

BIRTHDAY

ANTE DIED THREE DAYS BEFORE BOB'S EIGHTY-ninth birthday. A month before his big day, I began posting requests on Facebook, inviting his followers, who are smitten with him, to send him cards. I'd conducted many social media campaigns over the years: soliciting photos of friends meditating to celebrate my fiftieth birthday; inviting financial assistance for those with medical needs; raising funds for my writing projects and the purchase of my tiny chapel. Always the outpouring of support floored me, bolstered me, raised me up. The response to this latest call proves to be the most moving of all.

The cards pour in, addressed to me, so as not to arouse suspicion should Bob check the mail. Each features a letter B written on the back to indicate the true recipient. I had stated a goal of eighty-nine cards, which enthusiastic senders surpassed swiftly. Each day the count climbs. One hundred. One hundred and ten. I lose track after one hundred and thirty. The bag I store them in literally bursts at the seams.

Looking at this bulging, torn bag, it dawns on me that perhaps I have gotten too carried away, as I have done unintentionally but so often before. If I am this overwhelmed by the response to an effort of which I am aware and orchestrating, how will unsuspecting Bob react to the onslaught of well wishes? Will it be too much?

Perhaps it is the need to boost my spirits the day after Dante's departure that leads me to present Bob with this surplus of greetings a couple of days in advance of his actual birthday. I wake up very early, before Bob, arrange all of the cards on the stage in the Molly Ivins Pavilion and take a photograph the lot of them to share with the senders, to show them their collective awesomeness.

Back inside the house, I find Bob at the dining room table. We drink coffee and exchange our good mornings, our daily reports on how we slept. Then, I announce that I need his help with something in the reception hall. He says he'll meet me out there. I hurry back over and position myself by the stage, ready to record his reaction. That two-minute video is one of my very favorites ever. Here comes Bob, approaching on his little scooter. He parks it outside the door, gets up slowly, pushes open the door, and steps into the room.

"Hey Pop," I call out, keeping the camera trained on him. "So, we have something here for you." I go on to remind him he has a lot of fans and direct his attention to the stage. "Those are some birthday cards for you," I gesture. He literally recedes a few steps, as if the force of so many greetings is pushing him backwards.

"Aw hell," he says, taking in dozens upon dozens of cards. I explain the surprise and urge him to approach the stage, which he does with a slow shuffle. "Makes me want to cry," he says, getting very choked up.

"You make everybody happy, Pop," I say.

To which he responds, "I don't ever intend to offend anybody, 'cause I don't want to be offended, you know?"

The video ends with him bending down to scrutinize rows upon rows of envelopes. He opens some gifts that have also been sent, among them a t-shirt emblazoned MADE IN 1928 ALL ORIGINAL PARTS and a pair of socks emblazoned with *I Fucking Love it Out Here,* which fast becomes his mantra, him repeating it many times over the ensuing weeks. Big Bubba, out tending to the chickens, sees us inside and comes to find out what's up. Bob shows him the bounty, holds up his gifts, points to all the cards, the two of them amazed at the generosity of strangers. I photograph them, amused again at how Bubba's prediction that they would find a way toward companionship has come to pass.

After the big reveal, I dash off to perform a wedding and return later to find Bob in the Crazy Uncle in the Attic Room, sitting on his bed, opening cards. So many cards. His Wranglers are covered in sparkly red glitter. He holds up one after another, tickled that some people have included money—one-dollar bills, five-dollar bills—as if this were his eighth birthday, not the last year of his ninth decade. The cards are clever, funny, heartfelt, poignant. Several people have added messages addressed to me. One card leaps out of the bunch. An egoless do-gooder with a joyful spirit has photoshopped Chuck Norris with his arm around Bob's shoulder. The card is signed *Chuck Norris*. How we laugh and laugh and laugh over this, and Bob hangs it above the TV, so that every time we watch reruns of *Walker Texas Ranger*, which we continue to do with alarming frequency, we will see the picture of Chuck and Bob together, right above the small screen antics of Mr. Norris.

When his official birthday arrives, November 18th, I find myself raw and weepy all day. My crying at this point has become so legendary that the idea of building an ark to keep myself from drowning seems like it might become necessary. Most of these tears have come courtesy of the pain of Peter's infidelity and abuse. Today's tears are different.

I weep with gratitude that this man, against all conceivable odds, has shown up. That he is not some crotchety old fart to be tolerated, but a true, good, loving father. The father I have longed for my entire life, even long after giving up on the notion that I ever could have a good father. I have buried that longing down deep enough as to be barely noticeable, or, perhaps more accurately, I have integrated the pain of unrequited father love in a way that it has become a part of me, a pulse in the background only occasionally beating loud enough to hear anymore. This longing I finally, fully acknowledge only after Bob arrives to show me what is possible, to allow me to embrace with full-ness his tender father love, and in doing so to erase that longing and fill the lifelong void in my heart.

That evening, I drive him into Austin for some Lucy's Fried Chicken. We'd been at Lucy's the night I got the call about Peter's infidelity. Given how emotional I have felt all day, I wonder if yet another trip to Lucy's might trigger my PTSD. I push away that idea. I refuse to associate the place with anything negative. Bob loves fried chicken. This is his day, not mine. And besides, if I need to make some association, I also have the option to remem-ber we'd also eaten at a Lucy's on Father's Day—the first Father's Day ever that did not fill me with dread and loathing, but joy and gratitude. What a day that had been, starting with a gospel brunch at El Mercado—Mexican food and rowdy singing by The Purgatory Players, featuring some of Pop's favorite Austin musi-cians. After that, we lingered for hours poolside with Ellen and her husband Rick, Bob drinking cold beers and using his King for the Day privileges to forbid me from working, to make me relax. That night at Lucy's he'd been spotted by one of his Face-book fans, a beautiful woman who gushed over Pop and left him grinning and amazed to be treated like a celebrity.

On his birthday, we get rock star parking courtesy of his NEVER EXPIRES handicapped parking tag. Lucy's is hopping, packed with patrons, but amazingly there is one tiny table avail-able immediately, a postage-stamp two-top adjacent to another little table at which sits a mannequin dressed as Willie Nelson.

We sit, two under-eaters, peruse the menu, and order what for us amounts to a gluttonous feast. Chicken, mashed pota-toes, and a bourbon and coke for Bob. Macaroni and cheese and onion rings for me. I am pleased by my voracious appetite, apply ketchup liberally to my food and wolf it all down, amusing Pop with my gusto and speed-eating skills. I ask him for any knowl-edge he cares to impart, his secrets to a long life. "Hard work and good friends," he says, summing up the accumulated wisdom of eighty-nine years in five words. After dinner, he scoots over to the next table, sits down across from Willie, and our waitress sets up the pair with a couple of beers. For the millionth time since his arrival, I snap another priceless photo of my new father to share with Team Bob on social media.

Contemplating his steadfastness, as I do often, but especially so this night, sets still more weepiness into motion. This man has carried me through such trials. He continues to carry me. He never once admonishes me to "just snap out of it," understanding my recovery is a complicated process. Some observations he knows he must to keep to himself, let me reach certain unpleasant conclusions on my own, that all he can do is wait to catch me when I fall, knowing I will fall, knowing I will need to be caught, even if I don't always know this myself. I fall. He catches me. I fall again. He picks me up.

Reflecting on summer's cornucopia of sorrows, I reach back further, examine so many long periods of unabating grief I have known. I am fond of saying that grief is not a competition. It really isn't. Still, I have survived some people, circumstances and events that might have broken someone weaker. My mother's name translates from its Latin origin to *grief, sorrow, pain*. I like to joke that this, then, literally means I was born of grief and sorrow. The die was cast the moment I was conceived, sealing my fate as one destined to live a life enveloped in grief. How this has come to bear out over the decades, so many setbacks, so much heartbreak, such overpowering suffering.

And yet, I never forget so many people have suffered so much more than me. I have so many friends who have outlived their children, the death of a child roundly agreed to be the most torturous suffering one can experience. Everyone suffers at some point I remind myself. Suffering is the human condition. Suffering unites us.

If my entire life to date has been unintentionally dedicated in large part to studying the mysteries of grief, Bob is my greatest professor, my guru, my hero. He never complains. He barely speaks of his grief. He rides out much of that grief on the godforsaken lawnmower, bringing order to acres and acres of unruly grass as he brings order to his heart, his thoughts, his emotions. He understands he cannot dictate my journey. Now that I better understand what he saw and knew and kept to himself as he watched Peter destroy me, my awe increases. How helpless he must have felt as I crumbled, knowing, long before I did, ways in which I was exacerbating my own suffering, that there was no use in trying to stop me by being didactic, that he could only show me, through steady love, the way back into the light.

If you consider the principle of equal and opposite actions and reactions, mine has also been a life of immeasurable happiness, adventure and bounty, as if each time the pendulum swung fully in the doom direction, it swung back with equal velocity in the opposite joy direction. The love all around me, the people who embrace me, surround me, hold me up, see me through—there is no unit of measure great enough to quantify this abundance. Contemplating the stunning heaping upon me of kindness by friends and strangers alike is humbling. Perhaps, had I not suffered so profoundly, I would not feel such bliss, which, when it does visit, arrives waving a banner of jubilation high. Crazy examples of this abound, like a ranch landing randomly in my lap, made possible by loving, supportive business partners who have faith in my ability to make it thrive, even times I stumble.

Life with Bob also illustrates with crisp clarity the sunny side of this polarity. Where I once had the bleakest of fathers, now I have the brightest. Where once I felt trapped in a relationship with Peter, a man hell-bent on crushing me, robbing me of my joy, and shaming me into a puddle of insecurity, now I live with a man who loves me unconditionally and says so daily, who

respects me, who reminds me over and over and over the importance of not taking shit from anyone ever again.

How many times does Bob tell me, while squeezing my hand,
that I'm the strongest woman he knows? So many times. Always,
I cry, because always these words come when I feel my weakest,
think that—despite knowing from past crap relationships healing will happen—this time there will be no healing, that having
been stripped of all dignity by Peter, I will forever succumb to
the shame and the pain and the self-loathing he instilled in me
with his ongoing attacks on everything that ever meant anything
to me, namely the very core of who I am.

I tell Bob I don't feel very strong. He just pats my hand some
more until slowly, so very slowly, I begin to emerge from the fog.
My strength does return. I am wobbly but no longer falling constantly. Sometimes I hate when people assure me that I will be
stronger for having lived through Peter's abuse, that I will come
out the other side better than ever before. I liked my life just fine
before I met him. If I could go back in time, unmeet him, and
just be the way I was, I would do that, would skip this promised
Stronger Better Me everyone keeps talking about.

But of course, going back in time is not an option, except for
the irretrievable hours I waste revisiting the most unsettling
Peter incidents, so many incidents, the vastness of the pain only
finally clear in hindsight: the constant putdowns, the violence,
the brainwashing. These time trips do not allow me that one
thing I most desire, to go back and eradicate him entirely. Like
it or not, then, I must accept the new, greater strength being
foisted on me by virtue of the fact I choose to live instead of
succumbing to my father's voice urging me to die. I understand
that those telling me I will be stronger mean well. I also know
they miss the mark. I am not growing stronger so much for having survived that hell as I am growing stronger because of Bob's
love.

Bob watches me recover. I watch him watch me. He fortifies my growing strength mostly because he wants to see me happy, healthy, and smiling again. It also dawns on me that a powerful side benefit of this process has not escaped him. I realize that he is preparing me for that inevitable time when he is gone. That day when I go to wake him up to feed the horses, or check on him in his green shed, or wonder why he is sitting so still on the mower, and discover that he has died.

I dread this day. It is coming. But I also know that the man I will miss for the rest of my life is the same man who showed up to teach me how to continue on without him once his work is done. Because, I think, when the student is *truly* ready, the teacher *disappears*.

Maybe I'll be fortunate enough to live as long as Bob has. Maybe I'll be fortunate enough to come to truly understand and unquestionably believe what he works to show me every day. The possibility of great joy that exists even in the face of great suffering. The beauty found in being truly present in the moment. The simple yet fervent pleasure of watching the sun rise and set, its rays dancing across all these green acres, the light setting the horses' whiskers aglow. The amusement offered by squabbling chickens, games of checkers, and Chucky Baby. The uncomplicated culinary fabulousness of thick-sliced tomato sandwiches. The gift of appreciating what is right in front of me. And that, times I do lose sight of the present moment, to remember that looking forward is always, always a much better option than looking back. *Makuna Hatata.*

A few days after Bob's birthday, Thanksgiving rolls around. I jump from bed and greet him at the table where, as ever, he is drinking his coffee.

"ASK ME HOW I FEEL!" I demand.

"How do you feel?" asks the man who has, hundreds of times, received the static news that I feel like shit.

"I FEEL GREAT!" I nearly yell.

"Me, too," he says.

"I usually wake up crying on holidays," I say.

"Oh, is it a holiday?" he asks, having lost track of the days.

I laugh and laugh at this. Every day is Thanksgiving for Bob. He doesn't bother differentiating. If the sun is up, the lawn-mower running, and the horses impatiently standing at the door waiting for breakfast, these are reasons enough to be thankful.

I have no good explanation for my giddiness. In fact, I should be distraught, having been banished by Chuck just days before. I don't allow myself to plumb that line of thinking, to seek out sadness. Nor do I bother looking for an explanation for my joy. I am, appropriate to the day, full of gratitude.

After a lazy morning, Bob and I head to dinner at Ellen's house. My good mood prevails, a fascinating curiosity given that holidays usually find me angry, sullen, and often hiding in my room, avoiding others. The feast is fantastic, the company splendid. I dash down the street after a spell, to the home of nearby friends, Erin and Steve and their boys, with whom I have spent many Thanksgiving and Christmas dinners times I could rally and leave the house, feeling safe enough to do so because they always honor my dark holiday moods, never try to force me into false joy.

Sitting with this group, nine of us, having not been at this table in the two years, I am welcomed warmly. I understand now that I had unintentionally cut myself off more and more from the people and events I loved in my fruitless, time-suck-ing attempts to make Peter happy. These friends, like so many other friends, held the space for me. Now they welcome me back. They embrace me. We resume our witty exchanges and laughter, everyone acting like I'd never gone away into the dark-ness. In their company, I wake up some more. Driving home that night, I tell Bob how amazing it is to feel alive again, to feel good.

"You know," he says, "When I was younger, I used to think everything needed to be in order. Now I don't. You gotta let shit go."

With that, he asks me to turn on an interior light, so he can root around in his pocket and find a little bottle of nitroglycerin pills, which he extracts and opens, putting a tablet under his tongue. His heart is hiccupping and he wants to make sure it holds out. He wants to stick around as long as he can. That's exactly what I want, too.

EMERGENCY

FEW DAYS AFTER THANKSGIVING, I GO LOOKING for Bob, who, oddly, has not yet made it to the table for coffee. I find him in the Crazy Uncle in the Attic room. He looks worn out and a bit shaken.

"I had a really bad asthma attack in the night," he says. With effort, he stands slowly and works his way to the kitchen.

During our rounds to feed the horses, I can hear his breathing and it does not sound good. An audible ragged wheezing. I choose my words carefully, asking him if he will go to the Emergency Room just for a checkup, some peace of mind. We've been through this drill before, when he sliced open his arm on chicken wire, and before that when he overexerted himself in summer, his first in Texas, overestimating his ability to reckon with the brutal heat, winding up dehydrated and with a case of vertigo. That netted him a week of cabin fever, stuck sleeping upright in the recliner beside his bed, me on a tiny mattress on the floor, getting up in the night to make sure he was breathing, as one might with a newborn.

Given his age and—at the risk of sounding sexist—his gender, I would not have been surprised if, for either of these earlier medical crises, he had stubbornly refused to seek help. But Bob is a reasonable man. No, he doesn't like hospital trips. But he also wants to keep going. He is pretty good about seeing a doctor when he needs to. I am cautious in my request now, reminding us both that I recognize he is a grown man, I am not coddling him, but that I love him, and it is important that he tends to his health. He says a checkup isn't unreasonable. We agree we are in no big hurry. I have a wedding to perform and a ranch tour to give, and Bob doesn't feel bad enough to necessitate rushing to ER. Dawn, our friend, neighbor, and another of Bob's honorary daughters, drops her Sunday errand-running and comes to sit with him while I take care of business.

This happens to be the very day that an essay Ellen has written about Pop and me appears in the online edition of *Texas Co-Op Power Magazine*, the most widely circulated periodical in the state. In this beautiful piece, Ellen perfectly details the year-long adventure we've been enjoying together. Both of us are weepy at her account. As I stand washing dishes and Pop and Dawn sit nearby at the table where I have cried so many times, I watch him now choke up as tears fill his eyes. I have seen him a little misty once or twice before, but I have not seen him cry like this. Only later will I understand something more than his daughter's loving tribute lies behind his emotion.

When go-time arrives, Bob asks to return to the Heart Hospital in Austin, the place he received great care for his vertigo and terrible care for his chicken wire wound. I made such a huge fuss after the latter—publicly posting a long letter of complaint to the hospital CEO, who would not take my calls, letting him have it—that the CEO called both Bob and me to apologize. This is enough for Bob to give them another chance. He likes how small the hospital is, and that heart care is their specialty. We arrive at ER late in the day. Ellen meets us there.

The doctor on duty conducts a thorough evaluation, asking plenty of questions. Thankfully, I am standing out of Bob's sight-line when it comes time to discuss Do Not Resuscitate orders. I understand, I really do, that my time with him is limited. I also understand DNR orders are important. But, overwhelmed—it has been such a long, sorrowful summer, Dante's loss is fresh in my mind, and now this—I begin to weep. Soon, I leave to run to a grocery store nearby to fetch some snacks for Bob and Ellen.

There, wandering the aisles, the feeling of *Too Much* sweeps over me. I already struggle with grocery stores, and have only recently started to feel less anxious shopping for food, thanks to the loving assistance of Gus. Back to square one, then. I am confused and disoriented. I need crackers. I can't find the fucking crackers.

A thought pops in. *This is what it feels like to fear losing a parent you love.* Such a bittersweet moment, a wholly unique feeling for me, the daughter who exhaled with joy upon seeing my father in his coffin, not because he was no longer suffering but because he could no longer make me suffer, at least not actively. Once again, Bob is bringing me another first. I do not want to lose him. I am desperate for him to stick around. Just then, my friend Lize appears from nowhere. "What are you doing up this way?" she asks.

"Bob's in the hospital," I blurt. "He's having trouble breathing." With this I begin crying. Lize pulls me into a hug and I accept, grateful for the embrace, grateful that I can receive hugs again, no longer automatically recoiling from touch.

Feigning trying to pull my shit together, I try to get present and engage. "How are you doing?" I ask.

Lize smiles. "I'm fine," she says. "I'm not having any trouble breathing." She turns the topic back to me. I confess I cannot navigate the aisles, have no idea where the crackers are.

She takes me by the hand then and leads me to the crackers. This simple act moves me to my core, and is the first of countless kindnesses visited upon Bob, Ellen and me over the next several days as a team of doctors works to come up with a precise diagnosis and the best plan for treatment. Test results indicate that Bob has had a heart attack. Though relatively mild, still, this is a problem, one worsened by the fact that his kidneys are not functioning well. The kidney situation precludes a heart catheterization—the dye used in this procedure is stressful on the kidneys with the potential for full-on renal failure. Bob says he'd rather be shot than risk this, as it would necessitate dialysis and there is no way he wants that. Fluid on his heart and lungs causes further complications. A bad allergic reaction to a diuretic causes him to collapse, and he teeters on the edge of his bed, barely able to breathe.

The days drag on. Ellen and I tag-team sitting with him and giving each other breaks so we can try to get some rest. The staff showers Bob with attention. The CEO, whom I had called out in summer, comes by to say hello and have his picture taken with Bob. Bob's Facebook fans send hundreds of good wishes, many in the form of humorously hyperbolic Chuck Norris memes and adorable animal videos, which bring us much needed, healing laughter.

By the time they release him the following Friday, Ellen and I admit a shared truth to each other. We are both beyond spent. We had rallied during those Pop-focused days in the hospital, relied on adrenaline-fueled optimism. Now we are both ready to collapse. I need to get in bed and stay there. To sit still. To catch up on work. At the same time, I want to sit with Bob. He says he understands my exhaustion, he is exhausted, too. He rests in the Crazy Uncle room. I try to rest in my room.

Rest is not to be, though. The sink in the little bathroom we share when he is on my side of the house is clogged. Money, perpetually tight, is currently non-existent. If necessary, I will find a way to come up with funds to call Charlie and have him unclog the pipes. First, though, I attempt to resolve the issue myself. Bob wants to oversee my efforts. As he stands over me "helping," I recall a time when Henry was little and I asked him for an assist finding lost keys. He trailed directly behind me, getting underfoot, driving me slightly mad.

I don't want to banish Bob to his room, but I crave being alone. I am having a major hot flash. I am feeling very sorry for myself. And I cannot disassemble the goddamn pipes. I do manage to pry apart one section, remove some truly foul black matter—

sludge, hair, scum—and think surely I have solved the problem. My sense of triumph is short-lived however. I put things back together and the sink remains clogged. I remember the slogan for a handyman business in Brooklyn—*We Repair What Your Husband 'Fixed.'* At least I recognize an oncoming rage.

"Bob," I say, "I didn't get to meditate this morning. I need to meditate. Now."

This is true. Whenever I delay my daily meditation, I pay for it. I retreat to my room, assume half-lotus position, and breathe, pushing away a tangle of thoughts trying to choke me out. That I will never get my work done. That Bob might up and die on me any moment. And all the usual bullshit about Peter cheating and lying, which is getting quieter, true, but still haunts me. One thought I do not push away as I breathe in and out is a possible solution for the plumbing problem—maybe I can fashion a wire hanger to serve as a makeshift drain snake.

After meditation, I apply my technique. Though unsuccessful, with my concentration somewhat restored, I am able to discern the proper way to take apart the plumbing completely. At last, victory is mine. I scoop out more disgusting sludge, then reassemble the whole complicated pipe labyrinth, which seems to have been designed by the ghost of Rube Goldberg. Finally, the water flows freely again, the sink draining easily.

"I did it!" I announce to Bob.

"I'm proud of you, hon," he says. How I love these words. How often he says them, regularly and steadily enveloping me in praise and encouragement. Day by day coaxing me to believe in myself, he continues to repair the damage my father had done, heal the ancient wounds Peter ripped open. I feel much better. Still, I remain exhausted. Still, I am badly in need of time to sit still. I need hours and hours, days and days of rest. Collapse hovers, imminent.

Again, though, rest is postponed as, shortly after I fix the plumbing, wedding guests arrive to check in for the weekend.

A large, rowdy party, they announce their plan to hold the reception in a field adjacent to the chapel. No one has done this before. The field is spotted with piles of horseshit. It needs to be mowed. The guests say they'll tend to this, but landscape management isn't their job. I don't even find their requests unreasonable, I only wish they had alerted me in advance, so that perhaps I could have tended to the field prior to their arrival, earlier in the week, when I had some energy.

I retrieve a shovel and trash bin and walk across the front lawn to the field. I begin shoveling. For every pile of shit I shovel, four more seem to appear out of nowhere. I am overcome with so much frustration, more than a little self-pity. I am, by now, in the habit of telling myself, every time another task presents itself—clean the house, wash and fold sheets and towels and tablecloths, vacuum and mop the barn—that no matter how tired I am, I am so fortunate to have these jobs, that collectively they represent the unbelievable great fortune of living at the ranch. This is true now, too. I tell myself to buck up, keep going. As I shovel, and the sun shines down on me, my exhaustion does not exactly subside, but the frustration gives way to gratitude.

I realize that in the days prior, I had not dedicated nearly as much time to thinking about how much Peter hurt me. I look at all that horseshit and seize it as a metaphor for everything he represents. The cheating, the hidden meth and porn addictions, the physical violence, the yelling, the undoing of my self-esteem—this has all been pure horseshit. As has happened hundreds of times before, a list fills my mind of all the help I'd given him, and how greatly he had taken advantage of my trust, my resources, my love. *Horsehit, Horseshit, Horseshit*, I think, as I shovel another pile and then another.

Rather than sinking back into the hole of rage, disbelief, and grief, I smile, noting now I am digging myself out. The fog of the gaslighting is lifting. I understand with clarity how wrong he had been. I understand with further clarity how often he tried to pin his horseshit on me, accuse me of being the problem, insisting I was too nice, even when I was only doing what he had asked of me. Oh, he had asked so much. Demanded so much. Yes, I had been a fool to accommodate him, but loving him had not been wrong. Or maybe loving HIM had been. But the loving itself, the acts of love? These were not wrong. Of course they weren't.

I think about Bob, too. How his heart attack has brought me sharply into the present. Yes, in this moment, I am again reflecting back on all the hurt. Those days in the hospital, though, had been all about staying right there with him. I even joked that he staged the heart attack to finally convince me that putting the past behind me is the only way to go.

I also think about how much he does to keep the ranch running. This is never far from my mind, even on a typical day when he is up and about, outside working his butt off as he prefers. I tell him time and time and time again he does not need to work so hard, or even at all. Each time he tells me he knows this, but that working keeps him alive and happy. By the time I shovel two fifty-gallon cans worth of shit, I see the huge gulf between knowing how hard he works and actually doing the work myself. I am thirty-five years younger than him, physically stronger, and still this shoveling really takes it out of me.

When it comes time to mow the finally cleared field, I go inside to ask Bob where the lawnmower key is. He explains that the mower has a flat tire that will need to be filled with a product, Green Slime, to seal the leak. Furthermore, this will require jacking up the mower and pulling out the valve stem. I want to cry.

"Let me come help you," he says.

Impatient with exhaustion, I snap a little bit. "No,' I insist. "You have to stay inside and rest. Please, Pop..."

I am standing above him as I say this. He, seated in his chair, drops his head, his discouragement matching my own. I have seen him display this sort of defeat just once before, when he and Chuck were working to build the barn, each man with his own ideas of "the right way," Chuck overruling Bob, both of them quietly fuming. Now I start to weep. I do not want to hurt him. I understand he feels helpless and useless. I stand my ground, promising I will text a mechanic friend or ask our wedding guests to help. "I'm sorry, Pop," I say, then head back outside, leaving him there dejected.

With some effort, the father of the bride and I get the lawnmower tire sealed and inflated. I text Bob to let him know all is well and I will start mowing. "Go slow," he texts back. "You, too," I reply.

The mowing is not strenuous. In fact, I enter a zone of semi-Zen, riding so slowly I wonder if the guests are mocking me behind my back, thinking me stupid and incompetent as I snail along. But we have had incalculable fucking drama with this lawnmower. The last thing I need is a broken blade, another flat tire. Finally, I finish, and drive the mower back over to the shed.

Inside the house, I find Bob still in his chair, still glum. I sit on his bed, across from him. We look at each other. We both feel bad about many things. He wants to help. I want him to rest. I want to not emasculate him or treat him like a child. He wants to honor my fears of losing him.

"I'm sorry, Pop," I say. "I'm just so tired. I know you hate not working, but I really want to keep you around."

"I know, hon," he says. "I want to stick around, too."

Another hug. Another *I Love You* call and response. I retire to my room to finish a writing assignment, willing myself a second wind to get the job done. I do. Then back to Bob's room to sit with him and watch TV, to make fun of Chucky Baby, to try to get back to our version of normal.

911

AFTER MONTHS OF WORKING WITH TINY TO train him to wear a halter, he is finally ready for surgery to remove the cancerous tumor from his eye. Rachel, our trainer, comes over to help the vet, Dr. Huddleston, and his assistant EZ, with the procedure. Bob is nervous the night before and more nervous still the morning of, as we wait for everyone to arrive. Our vet is kind, skilled, and highly competent. Still there are risks. Tiny is enormous. If he thrashes he could hurt himself or any of us. The cancer may have spread too much to be wholly removed.

I have made peace with Tiny over the six months since he bit me, and every day I look at him with wonder, rubbing his velvety nose, grateful to have him as a companion. My love for Tiny and our other horse, Queenie, pales compared to Bob's. The horses are like children to him and he lavishes them with attention, talking to them and petting them throughout the day. As the doctor explains the procedure and warns us that if we are even slightly squeamish we should leave, Bob's tension is palpable. We both know that, though the odds are slim, we might wind up with a dead horse. He sits in his golf cart fretting. I stand a few yards away and video record the vet injecting Tiny and then very, very slowly, lowering him to the ground.

I have traveled the world, seen natural and architectural wonders, given birth, attended a birth, and stumbled upon surprise moments of dizzying poetry in motion both great and small. But I have never witnessed anything quite like the incredible spectacle before me now. Tiny is woozy and unsteady on his feet. The vet holds his head, one hand on either side of his nose, grasping the halter. He lowers Tiny's face to his belt buckle, focuses intently on him, reassures him again and again. This is a delicate dance, a human/equine ballet that takes less than three minutes but feels expansive. Time stops. Time stretches. We are in a surreal bubble, the bubble of Tiny, who slowly, slowly sinks to the ground, seeming to understand and believe the words of the gentle man telling him this is all going to work out fine.

Once he's on the ground, he needs to be rolled onto his side, a move that requires finesse so that he doesn't break a leg. EZ and Rachel now join the dance, one pulling on his tail, the other pushing him carefully until, at last, he is in just the right position. Dr. Huddleston kneels down with his instruments and begins to cut. I see blood. Rachel, as she has been doing since her arrival, reminds me to stay positive, that Tiny can pick up on my energy, and I must be focused on him, on a good outcome. I am slightly dissociating, which is serving me well. I do want to watch the surgery. I don't want to pass out.

I turn my attention momentarily to Bob and see he is hunched in the golf cart, bawling his eyes out. Rachel announces, "You know, I need a cup of coffee. And I need you to go make it. And I also need you to take Bob with you."

I immediately grok her true message: *Get Bob out of here.* He does not protest when I ask him to join me in the house. He can't watch anymore. By the time we return with the coffee, surgery is finished. The vet announces he has gotten the entire tumor, clean margins. He has not taken the eye because Tiny began to wake up and stir, and continuing to cut posed too much danger. Unbelievably Tiny slowly gets to his feet, looks around confused, and take a few tentative steps, like a newborn foal. Though he is disoriented and streaks of blood stripe his face like war paint, he is fine. He is alive.

We all exhale, Pop most of all. That afternoon we sit and

rehash the morning, marveling at the vet's skill, his dexterity, his bedside manner. Bob also can't stop talking about how much he loves Rachel, what a wonder she is. This especially pleases me as I remind him, teasingly, of that first day they met, when he had nothing but skepticism for her.

This is a story we re-tell the next day to Joy, a reporter from the local public radio station who comes to interview us. Ellen's magazine story about our life at the ranch has garnered quite a bit of attention and Joy wants to do a broadcast piece about the highly unlikely story of how an old Indiana farmer came to live with a middle-aged roommate with a punk rock sensibility, a ranch, and basically zero knowledge how to run the place. Here we are, yet again, at the old wooden table in the dining room, the scene of so much crying, so many cups of coffee, so many words of consolation as Bob nursed me through the summer.

We laugh easily as we describe our love, the impact we've had on one another's life. Bob lights up recounting how he threatened to kill Gus if he ever hurt me, adding how, now that he is the gate-keeper, never again will a bad man cross my path and trash my heart. When we get to the part about Tiny and his surgery, Bob starts crying again, overwhelmed as he recounts details from the day before. We show Joy around the ranch, Bob chauffeuring her in the golf cart. I beg off then, to head into town for an appointment.

When I get home, I let Bob know I am going out back to shoot with Joe, one of my tattoo brothers. I invite him to join us, knowing he'll decline, but wanting him to know he's always welcome. He tells me to go have fun, and I do. I am amused anew every time I take up a rifle or a shotgun, aim for the target, pull the trigger. Shooting, no matter how often I do it, remains so out of my character that Joe and I both crack up each time I squeal with excitement, which is just about with every shot I take.

I get more than laughs and skill improvement during these sessions. Over the nearly two years he's been teaching me about firearms, Joe counsels me on other topics, too. He is both a straight shooter literally and conversationally, opposed to bullshit, and always willing to call me on mine. During my time with Peter, sometimes I brought my bruised heart to Joe, who simply pointed out how obviously unhappy I was, and noted the solution of exiting was real and attainable. The night Chuck told me he wanted me gone from his life, it was also Joe I reached out to, as I sat in my truck crying and shaking, and realized I was too rattled to drive safely. He told me to meet him in a CVS parking lot nearby and, with great caution, I slowly maneuvered my pickup toward him.

What I most wanted to discuss with Joe was not Chuck specifically. I wanted to tell him that I felt powerless, that with Chuck's angry dismissal of me from his life, on the heels of all the Peter crap, I was experiencing a bottoming out. That I needed help. I was so over angry men yelling at me. I was so sick of being put down. I was so weary of how I reacted, let get to me false accusations and lies.

Though sober for eighteen years, I had only attended a smattering of Twelve Step meetings during that time, stubbornly wanting to recover on my own. I was finally studying the steps, listening to an audio recording of Russell Brand's book, *RECOVERY*, and it was this book that inspired me to seek Joe out, because he knows way more about sobriety, true sobriety, than I do. I told him I could not take this pain anymore, could no longer deal with being in toxic relationships. I had no interest in drinking, but still, I knew my addictive tendencies were what got me into the harrowing years-long Peter mess. I was, if only tentatively, at last ready to try to see, own, and hopefully eventually fix whatever part of myself that made me think getting and staying involved with Peter and so many other abusive men before him was a good idea.

Joe listened. Then he talked. I asked him if I should start going to meetings. He replied he couldn't tell me what to do but going certainly wouldn't hurt me. This gentle encouragement set me down a whole new path, one that scared me, but one I finally believed necessary. Immediately, in my first meeting, I found some comfort, which was mixed with terror as I contemplated that the eighteen years of sobriety I had amassed counted for almost nothing in some ways, given the work in front of me. I tried to push aside these obstacles I was obviously setting up for myself, to remember that no matter how cliché the words may have come to be, one day at a time was my only hope.

I have been to several meetings between that first one and this shooting lesson. I tell Joe where I'm at, that I am slowly adjusting to being around groups, but that the steps intimidate me. I whine that I don't want to make a list of people to whom I must make amends. I cop to being angry and self-righteous, with at least one foot still planted firmly in Victim Land. Joe responds with a mix of comic rejoinders and his signature directness. He never stops reminding me this is my journey and I can steer the ship however I see fit, that he isn't here to judge. But he certainly makes some valid points about my defensiveness, and does so in a way I can hear, even if I don't love the truth in his observations.

I am still so tired. Tired with a capital T. Wiped out from trauma and emotional pain. Wiped out from running the ranch. Wiped out from Bob's heart attack and Tiny's surgery. The thought of needing to still do more work to get better is daunting. But I am not conducting this conversation to try to persuade Joe or myself the Twelve Steps are a bad fit. I am relaxing into the safety of his presence, using this as an opportunity to confront my long list of fears, a big one being that this sobriety thing, if I am to do it correctly, is going to take a long time, a lot of effort. He reminds me the effort will be worth the payoff and assures me that if I apply myself, finding serenity, courage, and wisdom actually won't take long at all.

When Joe leaves, I let Bob know I have some business emails to answer and promise him some hangout time in an hour. Atypically, once an hour passes I do not convince myself to do just a little more. A voice in my head tells me to keep my promise, quit for the day, and have some fun with Bob, a decision that will prove to be life-saving.

I bound into Bob's room, announce I'm ready to head out to give Tiny his antibiotics, and ask if he'd like to join me. Now it's his turn to veer from the program. He says he's not feeling so good, and I should go on ahead without him. This sounds an alarm—he never misses a chance to be with Tiny and Queenie. I look more closely at him. He is sitting on the edge of his bed and I can see he is in pain, and that he is downplaying this. I ask if I can take him to the hospital and he nods. Not yet understanding a serious crisis is at hand, I continue on my trajectory of horse care, and swing by Big Bubba's RV to drop off his laundry, which I washed for him that morning.

Back inside, I find Bob struggling to breathe. I will myself into level, emotionless mode, and tell him I will pull the car up to the front door. Unsteadily, he shuffles tortoise-like outside, and painstakingly lowers himself into the passenger seat. Before we even reach the gate, I can tell this is a true emergency, one beyond my skill set. We need an ambulance. An idea comes then, swift and welcome. I will rush him to the fire station a few blocks away where, surely, they can hook him up to oxygen while we await EMS. A minute later he is begging me to turn off the heater, rolling down the window, gasping for air. Bob is never not cold, and it is this claim of being too hot on a frigid night that pushes my panic button. I leap out of the car at the fire station and tell them to quick bring oxygen. Bob slumps. The next half-hour blurs.

The ambulance arrives and the surreal dream state that often accompanies such medical emergencies descends upon us. Firefighters and EMTs are fussing over Bob. I am trying to explain to Ellen on the phone what is going on, though I am not sure myself.

I tell the ambulance driver I want him to take Pop to the Heart Hospital, because he likes it there and they know him. The ambulance driver pushes back, gets in my face, and says, menacingly, that if they don't take him to the hospital he has in mind, things might go very badly. He doesn't specifically say that Pop will die if I don't do it his way, but this message is strongly implied.

The hospital this asshole prefers is one where I once had a disastrous experience. No way in hell are we going there. As he pushes me, I now push him. Our confrontation escalates, the clock is ticking, and Ellen is crying, listening as I lose my shit on this pompous fuck. Even as the argument is occurring, I have a vague understanding that something at play here is an indication that my strength is returning. I had been so beaten down for so long by Peter, was so apologetic so many time when no apology was called for, that now I am overcorrecting. As Bob has told me so many times, I don't need to take shit from anybody. I am practicing this newfound skill on the ambulance driver, going ballistic on him.

I show him my GPS, which unquestionably indicates it will take the exact same amount of time to get to either hospital. He begs to differ, citing traffic jams. Never mind that my GPS takes into account traffic and, more to the point, the dude has *A FUCKING AMBULANCE*. With a *GODDAMN SIREN*. He can circumvent traffic.

How long does this argument last? Decades it seems. Finally, I get right up in his face. "*TAKE HIM TO HEART HOSPITAL!*" The ambulance driver, with a dismissive head shake and a *Fine, bitch, have it your way* look in his eyes, reluctantly agrees.

So, I am surprised and more than a little livid when I arrive at the hospital—having made it to town in a record twenty-three minutes, my pedal to the metal of Bob's 2005 Buick—only to be told Bob is not there. The ambulance driver stopped at another hospital, not his original choice, not mine, one that is literally five minutes away from Heart Hospital. I race back into the night and head to St. David's.

Cold comfort given the dire state of things, but I notice that I am acutely aware of my feelings, which are murderous, and, more importantly, I am also aware that this is not at all the desired state of mind to be in when I finally get to the correct hospital. I have to calm down. I suddenly remember that Gus trained as a paramedic. So averse am I to talking on the telephone, I have never, not once, called him. We conduct all of our conversations in person or via text or email. But I have got to get centered fast, I can't text and drive, so I call him now. So shocked is he to see my name on his caller ID, he picks up the phone and laughs, "Oh, this has got to be great!" His tone switches abruptly when I greet his cheerfulness with sobbing.

As he has done so many times, now Gus talks me in again, honors my anger, and stays on the line with me as I drive. Yes, he says, that driver was out of line, and tells me there are plenty of arrogant EMTs. Then he convinces me that I am capable of setting aside my fury, that I must focus solely on Bob's health, that this is the only thing that matters right now. His voice is like magic. My blood pressure drops. This is a very good thing because by the time I park and find my way around to the ER— and this hospital is like a fucking IKEA the way it is laid out so confusingly—the news is very bad.

Ellen and her husband Rick and I sit in the ICU waiting room for ages before they will let us see Bob. My eating disorder switches gears and I sit mindlessly plowing through bags of Bugles and pretzels from the vending machine, washing down all this garbage with a sugary ginger ale. Finally, they call us back, warning us that Pop is on a ventilator, and that this might be a shock to take in. I don't hesitate. I have spent plenty of time in hospitals, sitting with sick and dying friends. I don't care what he looks like. I have to see him.

The man who just that morning sat and laughed at the table telling his stories into a reporter's recorder is not the man in this hospital bed. He has a tube shoved down his throat and all sorts of gadgets strapped and taped to him, monitors beeping in the background. He is sedated but ever so slightly conscious, and I can see in his rolled back eyes that he is in great pain and very angry. He wants to rip the tube out. Having ascertained this, the staff has restrained him. He is tied down, arms Velcroed to the bed. Ellen and I stroke his hands, reassure him he will be fine, despite our own doubts.

Once again, we find ourselves as we were just two weeks before, meeting with a doctor, discussing DNR orders. I "sleep" in his room on a pullout couch "bed," something more suited to torture than rest. The next morning, after fitful jagged naps inter-rupted by nurses checking Bob's vitals throughout the night, I finally wake up, hungover with exhaustion. As happened so many times during the summer, I am now, again, brought to the surface by my own crying. It's been some time since this was the case. More flashbacks of Peter hitting me invade my mind along with a ghastly montage of so many other terrible things he did and said. A mental calendar appears, upon which I see, with humiliating clarity like I have not had before, that not a single month of our time together was without some majorly cruel move on his part.

I don't exactly shake this off—simply shaking off PTSD loops being impossible. But I do get semi-grounded very quickly. I rec-ognize almost instantly that I am having these flashbacks because being in the hospital is triggering me. Hospitals don't normally freak me out, which is why I have spent so much time in them, comforting sick and dying friends, unaffected as some are by the smell of isopropyl, the beeping of monitors, the sight of blood. But I sense two things at work here. One is the unbidden memory of being with Peter in the hospital numerous times, a thought fol-lowed by then recounting how much he asked of me, how much he used me, and how he then condemned me for helping too much. The other is the notion that my mind cannot handle the very distinct possibility that Bob is about to die, but still, needing to direct my attention somewhere dark, it has selected the next worst thing—recollections of Peter—in which I find no shortage of opportunity to focus the heavy emotions weighing on me.

I step over to Bob's bed. He looks so frail, so fragile, so ready to be done with this life. That fucking tube is still down his throat and I can still see anger in his eyes. Again, I take his hand, tell him I love him, promise him we'll get through this, just as he promised me the same so many times. I'm not sure how much, or even if, my words are registering given that he remains sedated. I take out my phone and show him pictures of Tiny, tell him his cherished horse is doing great, remind him that the eye surgery that upset him so much was a success.

Next, I pull up a little video I made just the week before, when a rare snow, heavy for Central Texas, blanketed the area, transforming the ranch into a majestic canvas of white. Bob, still recovering from his first heart attack but thrilled at the magical sight outside, insisted on getting out the golf cart and helping me feed the horses despite the cold, joking I better be careful lest I go snow blind. Then, like a teenager, he took a detour on the way back to the house, doing donuts across the snowy field in front of the chapel.

The footage I recorded of his hijinks perfectly captures who we are together at our best. We are laughing uncontrollably, me, out of frame, screeching at him to slow down, him, in profile, laughing louder now, refusing, bright sunlight reflecting across the winter wonderland before us. This is what I show him. "Look, Pop. Remember when we did donuts?" I wonder now if the universe sent him one last snowfall, the stuff he grew up in and fled when he moved to the ranch.

While I do not go so far as to tell him it is okay to leave if he needs to, a sentiment I've whispered to other dying friends while holding their hands at the end, I am very careful not to beg him to stay. If he needs to go, he needs to go. I watched my friend Molly linger in her cancer-ravaged body days longer than she needed to, stirring each time another visitor came, as if it were her job to comfort us, not the other way around. I do not want to add to whatever stress Pop might be experiencing, to selfishly suggest I won't be able to go on without him.

As I hold his hand, the thoughts of Peter that woke me melt just like snow in Texas, gone nearly as suddenly as they came. The rapidity of their retreat is more than a little unusual. For as much healing as I have done, I have yet to get through a single day in which I am not haunted for long stretches by sickening recollections of him. Looming death really is life's zoom lens though, and the entirety of my energy switches seamlessly to this man I love, my heart's focal point, my father. The words he has repeated so many times I now repeat to myself.

You have to let that shit go.

You don't need to take shit from anyone.

Makuna Hatata.

Ellen arrives early to relieve me. I have decided not to cancel writing workshop at the ranch. This is not about my workaholic tendencies. Many attendees have been in the group for years. We share our darkest stories and our greatest triumphs. They all know and love Bob. They are part of my chosen family. I need them. Driving home, I cue up Mason Jennings singing *Be Here Now*, blast it, and cry some more.

Though I am spent to the point of near collapse, workshop revives me, as does a visit from Patrick, my business partner, who is in town for his daughter's graduation. Patrick takes me to eat, which is good, because never mind the Bugles of the night before, I am back to feeling no hunger at all. Then the new dishwasher arrives. Bob ordered it for me weeks before, a very expensive, very sleek model that I insisted was too big of a gift.

He disagreed. The original drop-off was a bust, the first dish-washer damaged, and the timing of this replacement cracks me up, as if Bob has had a hand in it showing up while he is in ICU, so that I will be forced to stay at home and rest a little.

In the evening, before heading back to see him, I do the horse-feeding rounds on my own. I don't take the golf cart. I stumble through the task on foot, Tiny getting in my space, nudging me to hurry. Usually his playful impatience amuses me. Not this evening. My own patience is thin. I am listening to REM, Michael Stipe reminding me that everybody hurts sometimes. I am crying. I am telling myself that Bob will likely be gone any moment, that I must focus on all that he has given me, and not on the grief I will surely know in his absence. I am so tired of grief.

To my surprise, Bob rallies after a couple of days. I do not watch while they extubate him but hold his hand during the process. They switch him to an oxygen mask which is too tight on his face and hurts him badly, and he, voice scratchy from the respirator tube, croaks out that he is infuriated. Finally they heed his request and switch him to a cannula. The days melt into nights and then back into days. Three of his sons, a daughter-in-law, and two grandkids journey down from Indiana, all of us knowing but not saying this visit is for the purpose of farewell. Instead, Bob improves. He is moved to a regular room. They let him put his dentures in and his glasses on and sit in a recliner. He remains incredibly frail, but the spark is back in him. I remember what he told me up in ICU. "I want to live," he said. "I want to live."

And so he does.

Ellen and I, zombielike, are both about ready to beg to be put into medically-induced comas for a few weeks. Her job is tougher than mine. She is air traffic controlling a small army of relatives. She holds power of attorney, and all big medical decisions ultimately fall to her. She also, unlike me, celebrates

Christmas, which is closing in on us, and though holiday pressure is relatively small compared to everything else consuming her, there is that, too. I am so grateful for her, so grateful how, over the past year, we have come to share her father—his love and his needs—with a kind of grace. She is generous in spirit, does not get jealous. I have barely seen my own seven sisters in the thirty-four years since leaving home. In her, I have a true sibling. Still, we are about to lose our collective shit if things don't simmer down.

Bob's sons go on the hunt for a rehab facility. The doctors tell Bob this is his next step and he doesn't argue, though if he and I had our druthers, he'd come right back to the ranch. In the end, doctors' orders and wishful thinking both come to bear. He will go to rehab but there is a wait for a bed, which means I get him back at home for a few days.

Pop's return to the ranch is jubilant. His sons and daughter-in-law fill the dining room. Dawn is here, too. Our patriarch gleefully holds court, knowing he can get away with anything in this moment. He starts in on a little joke, which he repeats about every half-hour. Looking at me with a twinkle, he says, "Merry Christmas!!" though that day is not really here yet. He knows how much I hate Christmas, the lengths I go to, to escape it. I laugh every time he wishes me a Merry Christmas, and I am not just humoring him. I still have no plans to celebrate the holiday, but I certainly am celebrating this day.

Finally, everyone clears out and it's just the two of us. I'm cleaning the kitchen, loading my shiny new dishwasher, and across the island counter Bob is sitting at the same table we have sat at hundreds of times. We are giddy if wiped out. He says, "I need you to sit down. We need to discuss something."

Though I am safe, though I am so happy, I sense a slight, nearly indiscernible blip of misgiving rise in me. Growing up, to be called to an audience with my father meant only one thing. I was, again, "in trouble," being summoned to hear him tick off the latest list of ways I had disappointed him, to be reminded what a piece of crap I was. All these years later, my father in the ground nearly ten years, me gone from his house nearly forty, and still the pain of his words remains.

I should know better than to worry. How many times has Bob sat across from me offering lists far different than my father's, reminding me that I am good, worthy of love, the apple of his eye? The night I told him Peter had dumped me, he just looked at me directly and said, "I'm sure glad you're not drinking," and "You look so pretty right now." In the hospital, when his voice came back, he said, "I love you, hon. You're my partner." He only ever delivers words of praise, consolation, gratitude and love.

I take my place at the table now, wondering what is on his mind. He looks at me earnestly and announces, "You work like a borrowed mule. You have to slow down. I want to hire someone to start cleaning the house for you."

I want to protest. I do protest. I point out that our friend Exene does come and help me sometimes. He pushes a little more, tells me if I don't start taking time to rest that I'm going to burn out. I choke up. He's right. Even before I moved to the ranch to undertake the huge task of transforming it, I lived a very busy life. My busyness just *is*. Swimming in my own fishbowl, I don't always see the water in which I exist or take note of how furiously I am paddling, except times when it is especially full of motion-paralyzing shit and in dire need of cleaning, at which point my body gives out and I find myself too ill to move, stuck in bed for days.

I stop protesting for a moment and take in Bob's message. I have worked so fucking hard my whole life. Worked constantly for my father's approval, which never came. Worked for the stellar grades that netted me the positive attention I craved, from loving teachers if not from my parents. I worked low-paying shit jobs out in the world starting at fourteen, almost always holding down two or three at a time. I busted my ass to raise my son. Even now I still work seven days most weeks, going non-stop from early morning until late at night, teaching, performing weddings off-site and on, running the ranch, doing volunteer work. I am neither bragging nor complaining about all of this work, just admitting he is right. I'm a goddamned borrowed mule.

I am uncomfortable, in a very nice sort of way, to have Pop point out that slowing down is an option, that he wants to help me toward this end. I am also amused to be told that I work too much by a man who kept grueling farmers' hours his whole life, and who would, if I would let him, be out mowing right this minute.

The conversation drifts and I tell him how good it is to be sitting at this table with him again, our sense of normalcy restored just a week after I thought he was leaving me for good. I tell him about the time when Henry was little and excitedly announced after school one day, "Mom! Did you know some people eat *at the table?*"

Now, I'm sure we had, at some point prior to this proclamation, eaten at the vintage yellow Formica kitchen table that was a centerpiece for my son's childhood. But I took his point. As a family of two, we often ate in the living room, or sometimes a bedroom while watching TV, no sense of need for a formal dining ritual. Something else lay behind my table avoidance, though, and I know it. I explain to Bob that when I was little, my siblings and I were forced to have Sunday dinner with our tyrant father, who ate separately from—and better than—us the rest of during the week. We all sat around a huge table he made from a sheet of plywood, nine kids, my mother and him, perched on plastic-covered benches he also made, the lot of us looking like some modern day, South Jersey rendition of the Last Supper. Those were nights of terror. We were not allowed to speak. If any one of us made a sound, spilled a drink, looked at someone sideways, my father's wrath fell upon us, his glare, his hollering, and then banishment from the room.

Bob takes this story in then gestures like a king toward the other tables around us. The ranch dining room is gigantic, full of a hodgepodge collection of five donated tables that easily seat twenty-five. "I guess that many tables will cure you of the feeling," he says, and smiles at his little joke about exposure therapy.

I smile, too. What really cures me of my childhood trauma is being exposed to his daily love, of having him here to listen, to sit at the table with me literally and figuratively. His re-parenting is working. He is showing me, every day, what secure attachment is, so that I might let go of the anxious attachment that defined me for so long. The seeds this old farmer is planting are taking root. With Bob as my witness, I swear that, while I still have what appears to be an insurmountable wall of grief before me, that healing is going to happen. Never again will I let another abusive man near me. Even when Bob leaves me, he will still ride on my shoulder like a cartoon angel, his voice in my ear helping me to make good choices long after he's gone, just as he has helped me with smart decisions, both emotional and practical, since his arrival.

Shopping for my truck, I took Bob's advice. He has an old 2005 Dodge pickup and urged me to find the same. Amazingly, I was able to do just that, tracking down one the same year, thrilled to rev that V-8 monster through the gate and show him my new ride. Whenever I am driving it, I think of him. Not just how he influenced my purchase, but what he slyly did to it once I got it home.

Walking up the driveway one afternoon, I glanced at the truck and noticed something dangling from the back. In an instant, even before my eyes made out the shape, I grinned, knowing just what I was seeing. In Bob's family, he and all of his kids each have a tiny pig medallion hanging from their bumpers, a farmer's family's coat of arms. Now I found my own pig on a chain. With this gesture, he officially claimed me as one of his own.

He is my father now. I have a father. He loves me.

I am fifty-three years old when this sinks in. For fifty-two years I never imagined such things possible. And yet, they are true at last.

I have a father.

He loves me.

I am going to be just fine.

BABY BIRD

A COUPLE OF DAYS BEFORE CHRISTMAS, A BED opens up and Bob checks into a physical rehab center. The facility is cacophonous and crowded, residents hobbling and rolling down the over-lit hallways with the aid of walkers and wheelchairs. Bob puts on a good face, telling Ellen he will be "the hardest working sumbitch in the place," so he can be released as soon as possible. In truth, he hates it here. I do, too. His roommate lies, disgruntled, scowling, and non-communicative, in his bed on the other side of a thin curtain, his TV blaring. I am eager to spend time with Pop but at least as eager to get away from this waiting room for death.

Twenty-four hours later, he's had more than enough. He packs his things, checks himself out, and calls for Ellen to drive him home to the ranch. This incites another round of giddiness. Good for him for thumbing his nose at rehab, where they failed to mention to him prior to check-in that he wouldn't be receiving therapy until after Christmas. We decide to arrange home therapy in the New Year, and resume our routines as best we can, though Bob is still too weak to go outside and work the way he prefers.

The holidays, Christmas and New Year's Eve, pass in relative peace. I am so grateful to have him home, so grateful that the December Depression that typically grips me has failed to arrive. Work is slow, a welcome lull before the arrival of a college swim team—thirty-nine swimmers and three coaches—on January 3rd. My friends, Garreth and Mary, are visiting from Nottingham with their kids. They love Bob and lavish him with attention, and, in a nod to their hometown, make him a little paper triangle hat, balance it on his head, and declare that he is Bobin Hood.

Swim team check-in day dawns and my friends relinquish their ranch rooms and head into Austin. As he always does when paying guests are scheduled to arrive, Bob moves the things he'll need for the week over to the Crazy Uncle in the Attic Room. His body is moving slower but his attitude remains upbeat. Ellen picks him up to take him for a doctor's visit, which is when they discover the Buick, his preferred ride, is dead. They take another vehicle—between us we have a small fleet—and upon returning from his appointment, Bob hooks up the Buick battery to a charger and leaves it running for a few hours.

Evening rolls around and we watch the clock, waiting for our guests' fast approaching arrival. The house is in order, the chickens are cooped, and all seems well. We are ready. Bob asks me to go turn off the car for him, because it is very cold outside and also, he admits, once again his heart is acting up. I dash out, switch off the ignition, and notice some lights won't go out. Puzzled, I try pushing and pulling buttons. Nothing. I run back inside to report this mystery and see Bob now has that look again, the one that says things are about to get very bad, very fast. He sets aside this notion as we discuss the car light situation. I Google for solutions, come up empty. I run outside and try again. Still no luck. I am frustrated. Bob is frustrated I won't allow him to investigate. At last I give in and agree he can have a look.

Before we go outside, I get serious with him. I tell him we need to go to the hospital again. He isn't happy about this, nor does he protest. He knows I'm right. Then I ask him, very directly, what I should say if they try to intubate him. During his last hospital stay, he said he never wants to be on a respirator again.

Animal fear fills his eyes. "I don't want that," he says decisively. Then he pauses. "But I do want to live."

He never gives me a solid yes or no, and I figure we can finish the conversation once we solve the car mystery. Very, very slowly, he makes his way outside, using his walker, a recent acquisition because his cane is no longer enough to steady him. He dubs the apparatus his Walker Texas Ranger to ease the discontent he feels needing to rely on it. In the driveway, he looks at the car and announces, "Fog lights," pointing to a hidden switch under the dash. I must have bumped it into the on position that morning when I was out ferrying Garreth around.

I turn to Bob and see he is now sitting on the seat of his walker. "I think we need an ambulance," I say. He doesn't argue. I wrap him in my big sweater, pull out my phone, and call 911.

As I am talking to a dispatcher, trying unsuccessfully to follow her instructions to take Pop's pulse, I see headlights up at the gate and know this is my friend Michael, who owns East Side Pies, a fantastic pizza place in Austin. He is catering the welcome dinner for the swimmers. He and his friend Hans hop out of their truck and I give them a quick rundown of the situation as a firetruck pulls in behind them, sirens flashing, followed immediately by an ambulance, also with sirens flashing, followed immediately by four huge white vans full of more than three-dozen hungry college students and their chaperones.

Yet again, I activate my dissociation skills, tamp down any emotion, and, via staccato commands, flailing hand gestures, and pained facial expressions, communicate to the seemingly telepathic Michael that I need help. Without hesitation, he jumps into action, first running to the gate to make sure it is closed so the horses don't escape, then running back to ferry towering stacks of pizzas inside the house and set up dinner for the kids, then back out to the driveway where he and Hans sit with Pop while the paramedics talk to him, so I can show my guests around inside.

I wonder what the big group makes of all of this. I joke with them that the firetruck with its lights flashing is mere hospitality, me providing a way for them to easily find the ranch in the dark. Fortunately, the chaperones and their charges are unperturbed by my divided attention, urging me to tend to Pop, assuring me they know how to eat pizza. Back into the cold darkness I race. I climb into the ambulance. Bob is disoriented. I reassure him as much as I can. I find myself facing off with another gruff emergency worker, who snaps at me when I ask a question. This time I just let it go, not interested in yet another futile argument with yet another self-important man.

A firefighter swings open the ambulance door and asks, "Are you his wife?" I laugh and tell him no. I promise Bob I will get to the hospital as fast as I can, and tell him Ellen will be waiting on the other end when he arrives. Then, in one of those strange acts that often occur in emergency situations, I think to retrieve my big hand-knit sweater from Pop's shoulders, remembering that on his last ambulance ride they cut off all of his clothes and threw them away. Off the ambulance goes into the night, and into the house I go to make sure my guests are situated before, yet again, I speed to the hospital.

I find Bob and Ellen in ER. This time, he is back in Heart Hospital. He is again intubated. Ellen is furious. She is telling the doctor he did not want this. I have to explain the unfinished talk we had, in which he waffled about the respirator. I sense Ellen is frustrated that I failed to tell her this when I called earlier. She's not angry at me. But we are both still so worn out, and every ER trip we take, we seem to find another curveball aimed directly at us. The doctor isn't terribly helpful and pushes back when we ask her to extubate him. Pop is again sedated, half-conscious, but his tongue darts in and out of his mouth. He hears us and wants to tell us something. I ask him directly, "Do you want the tube out?" In and out his tongue goes. I tell the doctor that is a *yes*. She says it's not good enough for her.

Here is where the Big Blur begins. Over the next four days all sense of clock time disappears, minutes smear into hours, days, centuries, seconds. I look back and see and hear crisp, sharp moments. I look back and see a kaleidoscopic swirl of nonstop action mixed in with morphine-induced stillness. That first night I eventually leave—it's actually very early morning—to try to get some sleep. Before I go, the doctor finally signs orders to extubate Pop and again I hold his hand through the procedure, this time watching, more transfixed than frightened, though the process is very messy and, I see in his face, very uncomfortable for Pop.

The next morning, I go in to tag out Ellen, it's her turn to sleep. Bob is propped up in his ICU bed, unconscious, head lolled to the side, chin tilted up, dentures out, mouth a slightly caved-in O-shape. I look at him like that, hold his hand, and say, "Baby bird!"

He does look like a hungry little bird. His clavicles stick out like tiny wings. He is off all oxygen, breathing labored breaths on his own, morphine easing any physical pain. Ellen and I talk quietly. We know, fairly certainly, this time there will be no surprise comeback. We shift from hope to Vigil Mode.

The next day they move him out of ICU into a regular room. Ellen and I continue to take turns sitting with him. Big Red comes by, too, just as he did when Dante was dying. He strokes Bob's hair, speaks softly to him, then sits and we alternate talking with stretches of silence. Big and I have been through hell and back together many times in the three decades we have known each other. I need do nothing to entertain him here. He is good, steady company.

I have told a small, select group that Bob is readying for his final exit. Rachel sends a message saying she thinks that he might be holding on because he knows my birthday is coming right up and he doesn't want to ruin it. And then, magically, as I finish reading her note, my friend Angel texts that she is in town visiting from Philly and would like to come give me a hug.

I eagerly accept, and she arrives twenty minutes later bearing a small stack of birthday gifts. I take these upstairs and tell still unconscious Bob that if he is holding on for my birthday, he can stop, because the party is right now.

On Saturday, January 6th, I arrive at the hospital to find Dawn sitting with Bob. They have been on many adventures together. Her love for Bob is magnified by her gratitude for how he stepped in to fill the hole in her heart after the recent loss of her own father. She is playing Willie Nelson on a little portable speaker. The red-headed stranger's voice fills the room, singing *Angel Flying Too Close to the Ground*. Vigil continues. We hold his hands. We stroke his head. We tell him again and again and again how much we love him.

Then Dawn leaves, and once again it's just me and Pop. I thank him over and over. I promise him I won't ever again let another shitty man weasel his way into my good graces. I sing him the song I sang to my son every night for years when he was little, *Everything's Alright*, from *Jesus Christ Superstar*.

A caseworker comes to talk about moving him to hospice. Only Ellen can make this decision, and she is not with us, so I convey what we discussed earlier. If keeping him here is not depriving someone else of a needed bed, we want to keep him here. We don't want to move him anymore. The caseworker is nice enough, but still I find myself irritated with her vague corporate speak, of how she says this is a surgical hospital, that hospice is better, that there's no telling how long Pop might linger. I point out he hasn't had food or water in days and surely some data must exist to indicate how long before such deprivation causes death. She says it could be weeks, which surprises me and plants the idea in my mind that it is going to take him some time to cross the finish line.

When I am alone with Pop, I cry, I stop crying, I cry. I can't think of anything new to say, so I continue with the thank you's, the promises that I'll take care of Ellen and she'll take care of me, and—unlike during his last stay—I do now tell him it's okay for him to go. To please let go. From time to time his mouth moves as if he is talking to someone. I cannot hear any words. I think he is working out a few last things before he lets go. I hope he is talking to his beloved mother, Peggy. He told me so many stories about Peggy and about his childhood dog, also named Peggy. I do not subscribe to the notion of some afterlife and yet, in these moments, I like to imagine him and human Peggy and canine Peggy reuniting. Maybe he imagines this, too. I hope so.

Sunday morning, I wake up after a relatively decent night's sleep and yet I have an odd sensation of being pinned to the bed, my body paralyzed. I am unable to rouse myself. It takes several very long minutes to fight my way to the surface of semi-consciousness, stumble to my feet, fix coffee. I think about calling the hospital to check on Pop, but decide first I will do my half-hour meditation. It is 8:30 am when I start. At 9 am, I call and ask for his nurse. She is very apologetic. "He died at 8:30," she says. "I couldn't get through to Ellen and I didn't have your phone number."

This statement is false. My phone number is written huge on the whiteboard at the foot of his bed, along with my name, also huge, along with the word DAUGHTER. I do not waste time yelling at her, only confirm his body is still in his room, ask her not to move him, to wait until I can come to say goodbye. I hang up and call Ellen, who picks up on the first ring, further demonstration that the nurse was not lying but... but what? This is when I first begin to do that thing I have sometimes made fun of others for doing. I assign strange occurrences to the dead. I smile at the thought that somehow, as he took his last breath, Pop blinded the nurse to my contact information, right in front of her face, and muffled Ellen's hearing to her call.

"He's gone," I tell Ellen. "I'll be there as fast as I can."

Now off I hurtle, one last speed-limit pushing trip to the hospital. I've made a short list of people to immediately inform of Pop's passing, and voice-text them as I drive. My old high school friend, John Byrne, rings in immediately upon receiving the news. Pop and he had formed a splendid mutual admiration society the moment they met, months earlier, when John and some other school friends came down to the ranch just before Bob's birthday. My kindergarten crush, John Logan, my junior prom date, Dave, and their wives, both named Janine, rounded out the merry band of visitors. Those were an extraordinary few days, made sweeter because the Johns had helped organize the party, years before, that led me to reconnect with Patrick, which in turn led me to wind up with the ranch, which in turn brought Pop into my life. I was thrilled for them to see the Butterfly Effect of their kindness, all those dots connecting.

How they doted on Bob, impressed at his hollow leg when, on our first night together we went to Antone's, the famous blues bar in Austin, and Bob threw back more than a couple of strong cocktails. John Byrne brought Bob a t-shirt emblazoned with BOB, underneath which was a list of virtues supposedly specific only to Bobs. He brought me a t-shirt, too, the words BEST. BOB. EVER. in bold across the front. Bob took immense pleasure in showing off his shirt. He bragged often about John Byrne, what a fine man he is, both of us laughing every time we retold the story of how John had leaned across the table one night and, of my constant, glowing social media reports about Bob, conspiratorially informed him, "She really undersold you."

Even from a distance John dedicated time to amusing Bob, once grabbing from my Facebook wall a photo of him mowing the lawn and photoshopping it to make it appear as if Bob were mowing on the moon, in front of the Great Pyramids, at Stonehenge, and other far-flung locations. The first time Bob was hospitalized, it was John who led the cheer-up charge, sending him Chuck Norris memes via my wall, inspiring others to follow suit, amassing hundreds of outrageous Chucky Baby tributes that caused Bob such sustained hard laughter, I joked he was going to hurt himself given his delicate state. "That John Byrne, he's something else," Pop said, so many times.

Despite my phone aversion, I am so relieved to see John's name, and answer right away. I ask him to stay on the line, co-pilot me, keep me present on the drive because I am not fit to be behind the wheel. My right leg is shaking so badly I think I might not be able to exert even pressure on the accelerator. John's voice steadies me. We talk about how fortunate I am that Bob magically appeared. We talk about how, if you open your mind and heart and expand the definition of True Love, then surely, in Bob, I had at last found true love indeed. We talk about other things, though later I will not be able to recall what. John just keeps talking and listening, calming me. I will forever be grateful for this loving act.

At the hospital, I pinball through the hallways howling, as staff pops out like Whac-A-Moles from doorways, stopping just short of tackling me, hugging me, consoling me, all of them meaning well but, to my mind, an unwanted gauntlet, an impediment keeping me from Pop. At last I reach his room and step inside. Ellen, sitting with him, stands to hug me. We hold each other a long time, crying. I look at Pop, my Baby Bird, lying so still, spark gone, pain finished. I kiss him, thank him, the same dance of gratitude, genuflection, helplessness, and sorrow I've been doing now intermittently across six weeks, three heart attacks, and as many hospital stays.

Then, a moment of levity as I note aloud to Ellen that I am rushing through these rituals because I am scheduled, less than one hour hence, to perform a wedding at a prison out near the ranch. We giggle then, at the inanity of this hastened goodbye, because some young couple feels a need to tie the knot under great duress. One more kiss. One more. One more *Thank You*. No, wait. Just one more. Tears. And then, that's it. I walk out the door knowing I will never see Pop again.

My phone explodes with messages as I race back along the same path taken just an hour earlier, hoping to reach the prison on time. The bride texts that she's running late. I sit in my truck endeavoring to ground myself. Henry calls. He has just woken to my text. "When I shook his hand," he says, of the one time he met Bob, "I thought, 'Here's a guy who's going to be around forever.'"

If the last hour is one of the most bizarre I've known, the next hour flexes its creative muscles and tries to do that last hour one better. Now opportunities to assign still more post-death mischief to Pop abound. The bride arrives, and we pass through the metal detector and approach the guard's desk. He stares at his computer screen and, in classic bureaucratic red-tape fashion, announces that the bride is mistaken, there is no wedding on the books,. The bride insists politely that he is wrong. I excuse myself to use the restroom, where I find a sign posted, instructing me that it is best to wash my hands for twenty seconds, an interval which I can accomplish by singing *Happy Birthday*. This would be an odd message to find anywhere, but in a prison bathroom? Just the sort of silly observation I loved to share with Bob.

I return to my station by the bride's side. The guard continues to stare at his screen. The bride turns to me and makes small talk to kill time. "So, how's your day going?" she asks innocently.

I fumble. I am a terrible liar. "I really wish you hadn't asked me that," I answer and proceed to tell her about Bob. This yields one of the most touching stranger-bonding opportunities I've ever had, and I have had some pretty heavy ones before. She says she's so sorry for my loss. I say I'm so sorry for her canceled wedding. They send her away without being married. We hug in the parking lot and promise we will never forget each other or this day. (Four days later, we will meet again, this time for a successful get-married mission.)

I tell myself Bob has had a supernatural hand in the not-to-be wedding, sending me to run this fool's errand as a means of keeping me from dwelling too long with his body, so that instead of fixating on his empty shell, I will instead focus on better memories of him alive. Not just alive, but the most alive person I ever knew. The 89-year-old doing golf cart donuts in the snow on the front lawn, while I screamed at him with laughter, begging him to slow down. The late-in-life good father who hugged me and told me so many times how strong I was, how I never disappointed him. My Pop, who never let a day go by without saying how very glad he was to be alive, reminding me often, "This is the best year of my life!"

I remember a night months earlier, in summer, right after his first hospital stay, the one to rehydrate him and treat his vertigo. I had temporarily taken up quarters in his room, sleeping on a little mattress on his floor, worried he might get up in the night and fall, wanting to be nearby to monitor him. On this evening, I settled in as best I could to try to sleep, tried to acclimate to his dislike of air conditioning, sweat pouring off of me, thinking this must be what India feels like. I heard him emerge from the bathroom and then the click of the lamp's pull string. "Good night, Pop," I said.

"Good night," he said.

"I'll see you in the morning," I said.

"YAY!" he said, and with that another gift from him, another awakening. A reminder to us both that he knew his days were limited, mine, too, and that I must never forget every day we wake up is a reason to celebrate. Even the really, really shitty days. *Be thankful. Enjoy what time you have.* Every day, all day, he demonstrated this, never complained about his swollen feet, his failing heart, and how his slowing body made everything take longer. He never minded. He picked up life's planks, moved them a little, rested, moved them a little more.

Leaving the prison, I find myself facing a field of hay as I wait to turn onto the road. Heavy, ragged gray clouds sag from the sky like an old woman's bosom wrapped in a ratty sweater. There, before me, I see a lone John Deere tractor. Another Pop prank, I'm sure. I would not have been surprised if that big yellow and green farm machine had reared up on its back wheels and waved.

And then another bizarre coincidence. Garreth and Mary, slated to fly back to England the day before, are still in Texas, delayed by a freak snowstorm on the East Coast. They are staying in a hotel five minutes from the prison. So many times before, when I had been down and wished to isolate, Garreth had been the one friend I could will myself to see. When he and Mary and the kids moved from Austin back to his childhood home in England, I fell apart, overcome at not having ready access to him, as I had for years. Now, on a day when I need him most, here he is.

We meet in the lobby, order coffee and lunch. I have no appetite, no surprise there, but I am determined to not let my stupid eating disorder take me down, at least not on this day. Mary and the kids emerge from the elevator. The kids hold out a doll they brought along on the trip, announce they have re-named him Bob, and hold him out for me to hug.

I am both cloaked in the weighty blanket of grief, my mind fuzzy as dirty cotton, and simultaneously wide open, a raw nerve, hyper alert to the oddest details. This recalls the hours just after I attended a birth, when the whole world appeared in high definition, spring's bright green leaves vibrating, saturated with colors not on any spectrum I knew. Heading into the loo, my nose fills with a scent to put Proust's madeleines to shame. I recognize it instantly. This airport hotel uses the same soap as The Monhegan House, a little place on an island a mile off the coast of Maine, one of my happiest places on earth, where I have stayed many times. A minor detail perhaps, pure coincidence indeed, but in this moment the smell fills me, evokes an odd elation, given the circumstances. I go ahead and give Bob credit for this, too.

I sink into a couch next to Garreth and reveal to him the craziest coincidence of all. Days before, when we met for breakfast, he told me about a strange occurrence he'd once had, when a woman with whom he'd been talking morphed before his eyes, becoming beautiful in an otherworldly way. Not to say she wasn't already beautiful, and not to wrongly present this as some Beer Goggles moment. Just that something switched from one instant to the next, and she was, in that next instant, someone she had not been the instant before. As he described this, I could sort of conceptualize it, but had no similar personal point of reference to help me relate.

Now I do.

On what turned out to be our last day together, as I sat with Bob for hours, just the two of us alone, there came a moment when his face, a face I had examined for endless hours over checkers and coffee, a face I loved so dearly, transformed before my eyes, became that of my biological father.

At first, I could not comprehend what I was seeing. I wanted to chalk this phenomenon up to optical illusion. I wondered if perhaps the resemblance merely came from Bob's dentures being out, as my father often kept his out. As I continued to stare, however, these excuses fell away. For a few precious moments, my new father *was* my old father. I was no longer holding Bob's hand. I was holding the hand of Dutchie, the man whose cruelty laid the groundwork that led me to so many disastrous relationships with so many wicked men, Peter the pinnacle of the lot.

In those moments, astonishment, grace, and gratitude washed over me, filled me, inhabited every one of my cells. This was the final gift Pop gave me. To have my angry, abusive father show up inside of my loving, gentle father, afforded me another magical opportunity. Pure compassion flooded me then, a glimpse of how things might have been, had my father not been so mentally ill, so abusive, so impenetrable. This alchemy allowed me a sense of, if not pure forgiveness, then sympathy for who my father had been, a man not in his right mind, a man who missed the opportunity to love and be loved by me.

Had Garreth not described his own similar incident, surely he would have merely nodded politely and perhaps thought to himself how peculiar, the tricks one's mind can play. But he knows. He understands. This has happened to him. And he is, glory be to an East Coast blizzard, sharing this understanding right by my side.

When at last I return to the ranch, the horses, grazing by the gate, look up as I emerge from Bob's Buick. So often they ignore me when their focus is eating. But they know. I can see it. Side-by-side they amble slowly down the driveway toward me, heads hung down as if in sorrow, those same weighty gray clouds sagging from the sky behind them.

Inside the house, I smile, realizing there is no time to crawl into a ball and wail. The clock, now back to ticking real-time minutes, indicates the swimmers will be home momentarily and I need to have dinner ready for them. Another much-needed diversion. Has Bob also pre-arranged for this horde of kids to still be here, to need me, to keep me occupied? How grateful I am for their company, their sympathy, the distraction of dozens of teenagers asking me what they can do to help, not knowing that, in just being here, in being hungry, in being happy, they are doing the most I could ask for.

The next morning the sun, absent for days, resumes its habit of ascent. Pop and I loved watching the sunrise, loved the light pouring into the naked dining room windows, unobstructed by curtains. I step outside and his prized horses are right there, that orange disc rising behind them, illuminating their profiles. I think, "Nothing at this ranch will not remind me of him." A thought that comforts me immeasurably.

In the following days, thousands of condolences pour in from around the world, his social media fan club joining me both in my grief and in the joy of remembering all Bob has given me. If I live to be eighty-nine, if I live to be one hundred and eighty-nine, I will never, ever wrap my head around how crazy it is that he showed up at all, and how his love healed me more than I ever dreamed I might be healed. My friend Carol, whom Bob adored, put it best in a beautiful email:

> *You came together at a low tide in both of your lives and synergistically provided support for each other by combining your power source to keep running and heal. He had a purpose again and it was you and the world of Tiny T. He brought a grounded and stable presence to your life without being threatening. You exposed your vulnerable parts and trusted each other. That is beyond fantasy. If I saw a movie with this plot I would roll my eyes in disbelief. But it wasn't a movie. It was real and I saw it.*

It *was* real. I saw it, too. I felt it to my very core. I will always feel it. I will look back on my Bob time a year from now, and another year later and, if I am very lucky, many years later still. I will reverse connect the dots. The dot of inviting him to the ranch. All those dots when he sat at that table and promised me it would be okay, especially the countless despair-filled moments as more and more lies Peter told me surfaced, as I uncovered his cheating, as I revealed to Pop the full truth of his cruelty and violence.

And all those other, brighter dots, the realization that, in fourteen short months, we managed to cram in a lifetime of father-daughter moments, and so many Father Firsts for me. First Joyful Father's Day. First chance to be consoled, not criticized, for my missteps, the way my own father had only ever criticized me. First time to arrive home after a dinner date and find him up late, eager, waiting for the details. First time to say *I love you* to a father and have those words returned with equal weight and warmth.

I even sometimes find comfort and consolation wondering if maybe the whole Peter mess was a dot that had to appear on my timeline, in order that, for once, I might know at long last the love of a compassionate father cradling my fragile broken heart, assuring me, as Bob always did and my own father never could, that he was right here, that he loved me no matter what, and that together we would get through anything life threw at us.

One night, a month or so after Bob's arrival, I went to his room, far across the house, to bid him goodnight. We barely knew each other then, as I was still hightailing it to Houston several days most weeks. I said to him, "I want to be clear—as long as you're here, you are not a guest, this is your home."

At that point, the plan had been for Bob to stay only through winter, to head back to Indiana in spring. He leaned forward in his reclining chair, looked into my eyes and offered the kindest, most touching words anyone has ever spoken to me. "I'd really like to die here," he said, hopeful, not ominous.

I said yes in an instant. Everything changed then. Another dot connected. As with all of the dots, I did not see it for what it was in the moment. But I see it now, big and bright as a Harvest Moon. Pop and I committed till death did we part. We didn't know it then, but we were about to fully engage in the greatest ride of our lives.

Spring sprung, and rather than return home for good, he flew back to Indiana, stuck around just long enough to retrieve his tools and some other possessions, and drove back to Texas assisted by one of his sons. They cruised down the long dirt driveway of the Tiny T Ranch in his Sunday-Go-To-Meeting, silver 2005 Buick sedan, after a days-long, one thousand and eighty-eight mile drive. Bob stepped out into the sunshine, grinning like he might burst.

He was home.

AFTERWORD

WE THREW POP A GOING AWAY CELE-
bration on February 18, 2018, in
the Molly Ivins Pavilion at the
Tiny T Ranch. Bob made an
astonishing number of real and
virtual friends during his short time in Texas and many turned
out to honor him. They brought trees and vines and flowers and
seeds and vegetables to plant. Big Bubba offered free golf cart
rides. Ellen and I each read pieces recounting his life as a Texan,
and our friend Anne Rodgers spoke, too. Anne, whom I knew
from my journalist days, had married at the ranch the spring
before, and as she and her husband Dave spent a week getting
the place ready, they formed a fast, deep bond with Pop.

I had a few tricks up my sleeve for the event. My friends
Southpaw and Maggie sang St. Vincent's song *New York*, not at
all standard memorial service fare. It includes lyrics about losing a hero and a friend—so true of how I felt about Pop. It also
includes the line, *"...you're the only motherfucker in the city who
can handle me."* Swap out *country* for *city* and how true those
words rang in my ears. How well Pop knew how to handle me in
all my messiness, at my highest, at my lowest. Always.

Interspersed among tributes spoken and sung, my friend
Robert Kraft, an incredible voice actor and crooner, lent his
deep, smooth voice to the dramatic recitation of a number of
Chuck Norris memes, like how Chucky Baby once counted to
infinity—twice. And how the oceans are made of the tears of
his victims.

We concluded the service as I like to end all memorials I lead. I invited the room to rise to their feet and give Pop a standing ovation. They gladly obliged. And then, together, we shouted the message he worked hardest to teach me about letting the past go, that wonderful *Lion King* malapropism: *"MAKUNA HATATA!"*

Following the service, Ellen, driven in the golf cart and holding the box of Pop's ashes in her lap, led the processional out to the barn. Rachel swung open the heavy gate. It was a gate that Pop had somehow managed to drag from who the hell knew where on the property over here, to the yellow rope fence he made with the Forevers. The same gate across which we spent so much time training Tiny to be haltered. We all stepped inside the horse yard and gathered around Ellen, while Rufus, her dog and Pop's grand-dog, ran excitedly around her. Tiny and Queenie grazed in the distance. Ellen opened the box and scattered half of the ashes in a circle in front of the barn, that place Pop and I had visited so many times on morning rounds, one of his most beloved spots of all. After re-boxing the rest of Pop's ashes to save for a second celebration in Indiana, Ellen stood before us and sang his favorite song, *Red River Valley*, acapella.

> *From this valley they say you are leaving.*
> *We will miss your bright eyes and sweet smile,*
> *For you take with you all of the sunshine*
> *That has brightened our pathway a while.*
> *So come sit by my side if you love me.*
> *Do not hasten to bid me adieu.*
> *But remember that Red River Valley,*
> *And the cowboy who loved you so true.*

So much laughter that day. So many tears, too. But we kept the emphasis on happiness because that really was what Pop would have wanted. As the afternoon wound down, my friend Arlene

Youngblood and her friend Daniel arrived, getting to the ranch as soon as they could after church. I'd first heard Arlene perform many years before, when her gospel choir opened for a wedding over which I presided at the hallowed ACL Moody Theater. After that, despite my non-theism and distaste for most organized religion, I'd sometimes go to the Wesley United Methodist Church in East Austin to listen to that choir, joking every time that surely Hell was going to freeze over the moment I entered the building.

During Pop's first—and as it turned out only—summer at the ranch, Arlene came to speak to a large group of Danish students staying with us, to teach them the history of Black Music in America. She and Bob hit it off great, of course. And also, not at all surprisingly, by the end of the afternoon he was tooling her around in the golf cart. Arlene is such an energetic, shining person, and she brought the power of her voice and her soul to the room as she sang, along with Daniel and his beautiful presence and voice, a hymn about Jesus. Then they led us all in several verses of *Amazing Grace*.

Folks lingered for a while longer over a potluck worthy of Pop's Midwestern roots. The hearty spread stretched across tables and lifestyles, from hippie offerings to casseroles to the strawberry pie Ellen made in his honor. A pair of pugs wound up in the golf cart. The laughter continued. Then folks drifted and, being the borrowed mule that I am, I dashed off to perform a wedding in the Hill Country. Ellen headed home for a nap, after which she went for Chinese food. I mention her dinner because, upon finishing, she cracked open her fortune cookie to find this message: *Chuck Norris only needs one chopstick to eat Chinese food*. Prankster Pop was clearly at it again.

I wept a little that day—*Amazing Grace* gets me every time—but for all the crying I'd done in front of Pop during our short time together, I hardly cried at the memorial. In fact, I barely cry at all anymore. Sometimes, I wonder if maybe I am so far in denial that I am disallowing myself to feel the grief of losing him. But each time I check in with my heart, consult it as if it were a Magic 8-Ball, look closely to get to the truth of my feelings, the answer comes up the same: I'm fine.

No, wait. I'm better than fine. I am peaceful. I am amazed we met at all. I am so grateful that we got to have what time we did together. And I am happy now. So happy. Which is the best tribute I can think of for the man who only ever wanted that for me, who worked so hard to get me there. To get me here. In this moment. Where I can see and feel and know: I am safe. I am loved.

Sure, I miss Bob's physical being. But this does not cause me sorrow. I continue to feel him all around me. I talk to him all the time. I carry a little of his ashes in an ornate, silver, heart-shaped locket Ellen gave me. Often, I reach up and touch this, absent-mindedly, as if twirling a lock of hair around my fingers. "Hey, Pop," I say.

Perhaps a day is coming when the reality of his absence will crash into me, and I will fall back into the hole he pulled me out of so many times. I don't see it. Pop and I had no unresolved issues between us, only love. How grateful I was, how grateful I am, that I managed, before he died, to get to that place I so worried I would not, the place where he got to see me steady on my feet, if not totally healed from the trauma of all I'd been through, then at least far more happy than not. Truly happy. Happy because, of course, it was his unconditional love that brought happiness back to my life.

ACKNOWLEDGEMENTS

'M PRETTY SURE THAT WITH EVERY BOOK I'VE WRITTEN, and there have been many, I reached a point of cursing the process and swearing I would never write another. Then I get amnesia, tell myself it really wasn't so bad, and take to the keyboard again. But I can say with certainty that of all the books I've written, *The Tao of Bob* easily was the one birthed under the greatest duress. I'm not typically one to start and stop when writing—I'm a fan of plowing through drafts. That process was impossible this time around. So deep was my grief, so great my trauma, there were many days I could barely brush my teeth let alone face the next blank page.

With each new bombshell that fell, more energy drained away. Then came Pop's heart attacks and hospital stays. And through it all, I still had to run a couple of businesses, change sheets, feed horses and chickens, tend to the dogs, and on and on and on. Time and again, courtesy of emotional devastation, long days and nights in ICU, and plain old never-ending To Do lists, I had to set down the manuscript. Writing in nearly real-time also presented challenges. My thoughts and feelings shifted rapidly at times. Even when I reached a point where I felt I was pretty much done writing, thanks to keen feedback late in the game from one of my early readers, I realized a major overhaul was in order. How that frustrated me. How grateful I am that I heeded his advice.

Throughout all of this, I had—and continue to have—such an abundance of love, support, and encouragement in my life. I was joking with my business partner that this acknowledgements section would be at least as long as the book itself, so many true, incredible friends do I have. Which brings me to a fear I always have when composing these thank you notes. How I worry that I will forget to mention someone by name, fail to commit to print my gratitude to one friend or another. Allow me, then, to say this: If I left you out, please accept the truth this was not intentional. Despite having a memory that is so accurate it often startles people (and sometimes wears me out), I'm finally old enough that the machine is slowing down.

With that said, I would like to offer my endless thanks first and foremost to Ellen Stader, for being a true sister, for bringing Pop into my life, and for so generously sharing him with me so that I could know for the first time in my life True Father Love. Nothing has healed me more. Thank you, Sister, I love you.

I am grateful beyond grateful to my early readers: Carol Buchanan, Angel Joy Heart, Jack Ryan, and Garreth Wilcock. It is so very hard for me to receive feedback, so conditioned have I been to hear even constructive suggestions as harsh criticism. To a one, these friends know me so well, and handled the task with such a balance of tenderness and directness, that I could really, truly hear them, heed their sage advice, and apply it. When Jack came to me, late in the process, and told me things I did not wish to hear, I very nearly stuck my fingers in my ears and hummed to drown him out. But he was right. I listened. Thank you Brother Jack.

My life here at the Tiny T Ranch never would have been possible without the unbelievable generosity and support of Sean and Jen Manns. I can never adequately thank you. But I'll keep trying. You changed my life. Thank you for believing in me. Thank you for infinite patience and dealing with my spreadsheet allergy.

To everyone in my writing workshops—What a team we are! How hilarious and ironic that when I sat to write this I found myself facing so many fears and concerns I had spent years trying to convince you all were nothing to worry about. Hahaha. Thank you for turning it around on me, reassuring me, and listening to me go on and on (and on and on and on and on) through the many revisions of this manuscript. I love you so much. You are my family. Thank you for being there always. Keep writing.

To my Ink Family at Southside Tattoo—how y'all have changed my body, my mind, my spirit, and my life. Thank you for the transformation. And by extension, thanks to Gerald for moving to the ranch and helping me run the place, especially when Bob was in the hospital and now that he is gone.

There are not enough words, or even the right kinds of words, to properly thank my beloved Ben Gordon for knowing just when to hold my heart tenderly and just when to push me forward. Who allows me to push back against him, hard, times I do not wish to hear or believe the truth in the words and love he offers me freely, unconditionally, and always, as he teaches me what true loyalty, trust, and vulnerability with a man feel like, teaches me how to leave the house again, to eat again, to believe again. Pop loved Ben fiercely. And Ben has generously and humbly stepped in to fill the mighty big shoes of Pop as Guardian of My Heart. Thank you, Ben. I love you.

John Byrne, thank you for teaching me about crawling through broken glass, for the Chuck Norris memes, the Tastykakes, the soft pretzels, the '80s music, and the DEVO hoodie—my armor and my Linus blanket through all those hospital stays. Thank you for the empathy and the promise of sweet apathy. Thank you for the lesson in healing rituals. Thank you for making Pop laugh every day.

To my South Jersey family, both blood and chosen, thank you so much for making room for me to come back to the place I feared the most. With special thanks to my sister Kitty for always listening. And to John and Janine Logan and Dave and Janine Graham for coming to visit the ranch. Thanks to Scott Gruff for hosting the party that got the whole ranch thing going, and to everyone who helped organize that party and showed up.

Thanks to my Austin family: Jill and Kenan, Kat and Richard,

Everett and Tracy, Simon and Victoria, Deva and Jason, Katherine Martinez, Southpaw and Maggie, Chad, Lau and Jonas, Rick McNulty, Michelle Gatto, Ann and Jay, and Stevage. Plus all the rest of you. Holy shit what a long list.

Thanks to Dawn Tawwater, Pop's other honorary daughter and our incredible neighbor and friend. Dawn you know how much Bobby loved you and all the adventures you took him on. So grateful for all the times we got to hang out together.

Thanks to Michael McCarthy for being a steady rock and patient listener and for being the one who finally got through to me about how necessary it was for me to break away from the abuse. And for showing up and sitting by my side whenever death comes to visit.

Thanks to Ross Harper for damn near close to thirty years of being my parenting partner, my greatest confidante, my West Texas connection, and my daily sponsor when Pop need a break but I still needed someone to cry to every day the Summer of 2017.

Thanks to Emily and Kayla for helping me see more clearly through my panes and my pain. You are my beloved honorary daughters. I love you always. Fucking Namaste.

Thanks to Garreth for all the cheerful challenges, quick wit, and UK and Rome tours, and for being on the receiving end of my bazillion-word emails. Thanks, too, to Mary and Otto and Zoë for letting me be Uncle Spike and for giving Pop that last wonderful breakfast extravaganza at the ranch. And thanks to Raz for London pub time.

Thanks to Paula and Jay for my Galveston sanctuary, crab cake dinners, and the Writer's Garret.

Thanks to Erin Mayes for designing this book, inside and out, and for being a steadfast friend. And to Erin's partner Steve Wilson and their boys—thanks all of y'all for all the great dinners, holiday and otherwise.

Thanks to Melissa and Damon and Phoenix for so much love

and support and providing me with a fantastic second home in Brooklyn.

Thanks to Anni and Exene for loving on the dogs whenever I travel. And extra thanks to Exene for helping me keep this big old house and barn in order.

Thanks to Wyatt McSpadden for the amazing photo of Pop and me on the cover of this book. And thanks to Carol Buchanan for the author photo, the deep friendship, light on the path, and the incredible pen palship.

Speaking of pen pals, thank you Corwin Duncan for all the words given and received. And thank you Honore Power, most especially for all those inspiring emails back when I was so stuck in denial. And Deva? TY! ILYSM! YALS! You write the very best letters of all. How grateful I am for the way you make me laugh and cry, sometimes at the same time.

Thanks to Steve Milan for the many shared meals and deep empathy. For helping me sort through so many things. I love our meetings so much.

Thanks to Stori Walker for decades of friendship and consolation calls. To you my dear, I say FLAP. Thanks to Cindy Scovel for all the long talks. Thanks to my therapists, Victoria Sullivan Hendricks and Leslie Larson, for helping me understand trauma and myself, and how best to navigate both.

Thanks to my Portland people, David and Ken, and my Astoria people Iris and Joe and Martin and Sam, for hosting me and giving me a home on the West Coast. Thanks to my St. Louis people, Sue Reid and Megan Gillooly. Thanks to my Indiana people, the Staders, for sharing your Pop with me.

Thanks to Michael Freid for keeping a cool head and helping me so much Pop's last night at the ranch. Thanks to Natalie Freeburg for quietly and with amazing efficiency taking care of all the nuts and bolts of Pop's memorial service so I could focus on the event. Thanks to Robert Kraft, Arlene Youngblood, Daniel, Maggie and

Paw, and Anne Rodgers for participating in the service.

Speaking of Anne—thank yo,u Anne, and your wonderful husband Dave. Y'all rocked Pop's world. Tell Sherwood I said hi.

Thanks to all of you who donated money to help me buy the chapel. And thanks to everyone who contributed furniture, art, and kitchen stuff to make this house a home. With special thanks to Carol Austin, Terry Hiner, Ann Woodall, Denise De La Garza, and again, Carol Buchanan. And extra special thanks to Gail Boston for donating the table at which Pop and I spent so many, many hours together.

Thanks to Audra at TWILL in Portland for picking out my clothes for me. And thanks Danny Smith for keeping my hair in order and all the love for all the years.

Thanks to the Vampires for being early adopters of the ranch and for continuing to come back every month. And thanks to all of you who've married here, held events here, and have helped me make this business fly. I literally could not live here without your support.

Thanks to Mike Stravato for being Mike Stravato. And thanks to Jordan Weeks for time and time again preparing Pop and me incredible meals we could not resist. Brother Jordan. I love you and you know Pop loved you, too.

Thanks to Charlie Perkins for always fixing the plumbing, for introducing me to the Garfield community, and for helping Pop and me so much. Thanks to Dr. Chris Huddleston and his assistant EZ for all the help with the horses, especially Tiny's surgery. And thanks to Rachel Steen for still more horse help, and Nell Carroll for introducing us to Rachel.

Thank you Angel Joy Heart for being my true angel, for teaching me unconditional love, and for always breathing with me and holding my tender kitten heart both gingerly and firmly. ILYSM!

Thanks to all of you who are part of my community virtually and in real life: The Red Flag Dinner Society, my Dick Monologues crew, The Shit Boat—with extra special thanks to Jena Kirkpatrick for getting that group going, AA and ACA, my amazing Facebook friends—with a special shout out to Cindy Michell for so much wisdom and being such an incredible listener. And thank you to everyone in the #MeToo movement for the reminder that in telling our stories, we can affect great change.

Thank you, Doris Ann Newton, for helping me count my beans and track my words. Doris Ann patiently copyedited this book, not the first time she's helped with that challenging task. Thanks, too, for hot tub time and plant wisdom and knowing just where to hang the art.

Thanks to my people at Once Over Coffee, most especially Nicole, for providing me with office space, good company, and all those salt bagels, toasted with butter.

Thanks to all of you who pre-ordered this book and, in doing so, bought me much-needed time to write it.

Thanks to my beloved son, Henry Mowgli, for being such a beautiful human, for being so compassionate, for making me laugh harder than anyone else, for being my perfect boy. I love you, Bunny, the most in the whole world.

And finally, my deepest gratitude goes to Bob Stader, my Pop, who with his surprise arrival in my life turned my world not upside down but right-side up. Papa I miss you every day. I promise you I'm practicing not working like a mule and remembering how you reminded me always to *let that shit go*. Not a moment goes by you aren't by my side. *Makuna Hatata!* I love you.

RESOURCES

THERE'S A COMPANY CALLED DESPAIR, INC. THAT MAKES HILARIOUS *demotivational* cards and posters that mock all those creepy corporate team-building slogans. For many years, I had hanging in my bathroom one of their cards. It featured a picture of a sinking ship and the words: MISTAKES: *It could be that the purpose of your life is only to serve as a warning to others.*

Now, I know the reality is that for as much loss, grief, and pain as I have suffered, I have also been on the receiving end of a gobsmacking abundance of love, joy, adventure, friendship, and yes, material possessions. But right now, I want to focus on the hard stuff. I do hope that in telling my story, in sharing honestly some of my gravest mistakes and worst choices, that maybe these will be useful cautionary tales for others. Or, if you, too, have been down a similar path, I hope my words bring you comfort and remind you that you are not alone and that there is help and hope.

In addition to the support of so many friends who got me through the hell of my abusive relationship and listened to me when suicidal ideation would not leave me be, I also found many resources in the form of books, articles, guided meditations, and wonderful therapists.

If you are in the throes of an abusive relationship or working to recover from the trauma of same, the very first thing I want to say to you is this: *Please don't kill yourself.* I understand, I really do, when you are totally zeroed in on the hopelessness that seizes you when someone abuses the shit out of you, that trying to believe things will get better seems utterly impossible. Even if you have to frame staying alive as something you are doing to spite your abuser, then run with that. Do whatever you need to do to stick around so that you can come out on the other side. No, you won't ever be the same. But you will be stronger for having survived. I fucking hated when people told me that at the front end. I couldn't grok it. But here I am. I'm still recovering, I have a lot more work to do, but I'm definitely stronger. I no longer take bullshit from anyone. You can get there, too.

I want to share with you a few resources here. First and foremost, if you are feeling suicidal, I urge you to visit **SuicidePreventionLifeLine.org**. The number is **1-800-273-8255**. If you prefer to text chat with a counselor, you can do that at the website.

If you are being abused physically and/or psychologically by your partner, you can get immediate help at **The National Domestic Violence Hotline—TheHotline.org** or **1-800-799-7233**.

EMDR and Natural Processing are both extremely helpful therapy practices that can help you manage PTSD and c-PTSD, which often go hand-in-hand with being in a violent relationship. Find a therapist who specializes in trauma. This is especially crucial if you are dealing with Narcissistic Abuse, as general therapists do not always have the capacity to spot narcissistic traits, given the charisma many narcissists use to trick others, even therapists, into believing they aren't narcissists.

There are all sorts of Twelve Step Meetings available to help you understand your own issues and why you got in and stayed in an abusive relationship. You might not consider yourself an addict, but you also might be surprised to find groups of people with experiences nearly identical to yours. While it is traditional to contribute one dollar per meeting, this is not required. All are welcome. I have found great solace, wisdom and peace in **Alcoholics Anonymous** and **Adult Children of Alcoholics** groups. **AA.org** is a good starting point to find a meeting. A book that helped me let go of my fears around groups enough to step into the rooms is Russell Brand's ***RECOVERY***. I highly recommend the audio version.

Early on in my first feeble steps to heal, I had the great fortune of being directed to Kim Saeed's amazing website: **LetMeReach.com**. The site is packed with insightful articles on what Narcissistic Abuse is, how it plays out, and how to heal from the trauma.

My meditation practice, though at times excruciating when my mind felt like exploding, has actually helped me always keep at least one foot on the ground. There's a wonderful app called **Insight Timer** with lots of guided meditation and help on starting your own practice. You can also visit my blog **MeditationKicksAss.com** for some thoughts on the practice. And you can get an e-copy of my meditation book, *Sit. Stay. Heal.* at Amazon.

Keep a journal. Record your feelings every day. Later, as you are getting better, you'll be able to look back and see just how crazy you felt, but understand that you weren't really crazy, you were stuck in a bubble of denial. The trauma of abuse plays games with your memory. Having an account to which you can refer is very useful. Also, the research of James Pennebaker provides solid evidence that writing your way through trauma has amazing healing effects.

Tell a friend. Find a confidante, a truly loving supporting person who can ride the ride with you without judgement. I am fortunate to have many such friends. It can feel shaming and terrifying to reveal what is truly going on in your abusive relationship. You must do this. It will save your life.

Visit my blog—**EmotionalRapeSurvivor.com** aka **The Red Flag Society**. There I document my ongoing healing journey with all its ugly warts as well as many moments of breakthrough and triumph. You'll also find a link there to many powerful resources.

Adopt a senior. For many of us who find ourselves repeatedly in abusive relationships, close scrutiny reveals that we are reenacting what is known as the **Original Wound**. This dates back to childhood trauma. I didn't move Bob to the ranch thinking he could re-parent me. I thought I was just getting an old roommate. How mind-blowing then, to find myself immersed in a beautiful day-to-day therapy of sorts, in which so many of the wrong messages I received as a child—that I was worthless and unlovable chief among them—countered and corrected by the love of my new father. Remember what my dentist always says: *It's never too late to have a happy childhood.* I used to think he was full of shit. He wasn't.

Feel free to email me your story: spikegillespie@gmail.com. I am here for you. You are not alone. Let's heal together.